Winnetka

Prentice

Hall

Inc.

Englewood

Cliffs

N. J.

by

Carleton W. Washburne, olsey 1889–

Superintendent
Winnetka Public Schools

1919-1943

and

Sidney P. Marland, Jr. percy

Superintendent
Winnetka Public Schools

1956-1963

WINNETKA

The
History
and
Significance
of
an
Educational
Experiment

*Winnetka: The History and Significance
of an Educational Experiment,*
by Carleton W. Washburne and
Sidney P. Marland, Jr.
© 1963 by Prentice-Hall, Inc.
Englewood Cliffs, N. J.

*Library of Congress Catalog
Card Number:* 63-19896

PRINTED IN THE UNITED STATES OF AMERICA

96075—B&P

Foreword

This book is meant to represent a profile of educational evolution over the period, 1919-1963. It takes the form of a case study of a school system, intending to serve not as a model but as an exhibit of what has been going on inside the schools and inside the teaching profession over nearly a half-century.

The book is really two books, written separately and independently by the two authors. Carleton Washburne was the architect of the educational design that came to be recognized throughout the world as The Winnetka Plan. Sidney Marland has been the leader in Winnetka's current period of reappraisal, innovation and reaffirmation. Both were superintendents of schools in this "light-house" community in periods of high educational ferment, in both the public arena and the teaching profession.

In its two parts, the book is meant to be much more than a "before and after" accounting. It is a piece of evidence to be viewed thoughtfully by teachers, administrators and school patrons who would profit by the trials, errors and successes of a school system.

Note: For a much more complete description of the Winnetka Public Schools as they had developed up to 1940, and the philosophy underlying their work, see A LIVING PHILOSOPHY OF EDUCATION, by Carleton Washburne, John Day Co., N. Y., 1940. For a scholarly and comprehensive history of the schools from about 1912 to about 1950, including a very full bibliography, see the doctoral dissertation of John Tewkesbury at Northwestern University.

Introduction

The story of a small public school system which for nearly half a century has been on the growing edge of education and has become widely known throughout the world is worth telling. It is the story of the way a community, Board of Education, teachers and administration have consistently worked together in an attempt to make the schools as good as possible for the individual children and for the potential contribution each can make to the well-being and progress of the community and society at large. During these many years of cooperative effort and high aspirations, the Winnetka schools have made notable contributions in the fields of curriculum, method, "programmed learning," applications of mental hygiene, educational research, school architecture, and school administration.

This story may well be helpful to those who are, or aspire to become, educational leaders—principals, directors of instruction, superintendents. Classroom teachers will find in it suggestions of the vitally important part they can play in developing good schools. School Board members may find in the record of the successive Boards of Winnetka stimulus and practical examples of what a Board can do for the improvement of education. And laymen—parents and other citizens—who are the source and the beneficiaries of all that the schools do, will, we hope, find much of interest in what two generations of the Winnetka citizens have done so effectively.

The span of this book is 44 years. There is little doubt that these years have been the most exciting, the most anxious, the most productive and the most controversial in the history of organized education. It is during these years that the ideal of "education for all" has been placed hot upon the anvil of reality, and been beaten and shaped, still without conclusion, and far from perfection. It is during these years that a swiftly upcurving social conscience in our culture has placed education foremost among the concerns of our people. And it is during this same period that our concerns for education have been shaken and sharpened by international anxieties, by prominent critics and champions, and by the awesome burgeoning of knowledge.

Winnetka is a community of less than 15,000; its number of pupils, about 2,300, and teachers, about 115-120, could be easily encompassed in one building, as we compare ourselves with some large city schools. We consist of three elementary schools at about 500 pupils each, and the junior high school containing about 750 pupils. But our size has been to our advantage, permitting us to come to grips with the specifics of children, teachers, and the learning process in a fairly compact and visible unit. While we are small compared to city schools, we are slightly larger in number than the average school system. Therefore, we feel that what we have done, and what we are doing in Winnetka, has relevance to education beyond our village. As we have made use of the creative work of many others outside Winnetka, we welcome those who would make use of ours.

In telling this story we have not attempted to be modest. For the achievements have not been *our* personal achievements as superintendents of schools.

They are the achievements of a community long dedicated to good schools, the succession of selfless and courageous Boards of Education, and a faculty of teachers able and willing to give 17 ounces to the pound in any worthy educational activity. We have been the willing instruments of these forces, and count ourselves fortunate to have had a part as stimulators, co-ordinators, and facilitators. As authors of this book, we count ourselves also as the reporters.

Carleton Washburne
Sidney P. Marland, Jr.

To Jessie Knox

Table of

Contents

xi

PART ONE

Carleton W. Washburne

CHAPTER ONE

Origins of the

Winnetka Experiment

in Education

In the formation of a river there are usually more sources than one can count. As tiny streams merge into larger ones, these in time become well-defined small rivers with names of their own. At the point of confluence of two or three of these a larger river is formed, with its own name which it bears thereafter regardless of the number of new tributaries it may receive during its course to the sea.

The development of the educational system of Winnetka may be likened to such a river. There were three smaller rivers, each becoming well-defined about 1912. Their confluence in the Winnetka educational system, misnamed "The Winnetka Plan," took place in May, 1919.

The Origin in Winnetka

The event, giving identity to one of the three streams of origin, occurred in the little suburban city of Winnetka, about 20 miles from Chicago. There a group of men gathered in the home of one of them in 1911 or 1912 to discuss ways and means of establishing a private school for their children. These were fairly prosperous business and professional men who worked in Chicago and had their homes in Winnetka, which was then a village of about 5,000 inhabitants, on the wooded shore of Lake Michigan. They, or their families before them, had come from the eastern states and in their boyhood they had, for the most part, attended private schools in the East. Now they wanted to organize a similar private school for their own children, close to home.

But one of them, Edwin Fetcher, rose in the meeting and said, "Why don't we make the public schools of our village so good that we will be proud to send our children to them and will need no private school?" The chairman of the meeting ruled him "out of order"; the meeting had been called to establish a private school. Fetcher was a successful manufacturer of ornamental iron, a first-rate amateur cellist, a man of wide culture and influence. He was not easily suppressed and others added their voices to his.

It was therefore decided to call another meeting with mothers as well as fathers present. That meeting, after much discussion, came to a conclusion of historical importance to Winnetka and to education.

The action on Edwin Fetcher's proposal was this: "If you, Fetcher, will run successfully for election as president of our Board of Education, and are able to make the schools so good that we will be proud to send our children to them, we will abandon, for this time at least, the plan to establish a private school."

To this, Fetcher replied: "I can't do it alone. If a number of you will stand for election for the Board during the next years and work with me, I am willing to do my best."[1]

Others agreed to being nominated and all agreed to put on a vigorous compaign each year to bring about their election.

The incumbent members of the Board of Education were good,

---

[1] Of course, no one remembers the exact words Fetcher or the others said. I have given a paraphrase from what I remember Fetcher and others telling me forty years ago.

conscientious citizens of the local community. But for the most part they were uninspired, had little vision of what education could be, and were content to operate the schools honestly and economically, without any real superintendent; one of the old teachers, who was also a principal, nominally carried the title of superintendent, but the schools were operated by the Board itself. As the terms of office of the members of the Board successively expired, the men and women of the historic meeting were elected to replace them. These men and women were well known and respected and their friends knew how to organize a successful campaign for their election. Only one member of the old Board was reelected, and that was by universal consent—Charlotte McKenzie, a woman of dynamic energy, good sense, broad vision and a keen interest in public affairs and education.

After the first election, Fetcher had a majority of the Board with him. He and they took two steps. First, they employed William Wirt, then Superintendent of Schools in Gary, Indiana, and widely known for his educational vision and efficiency, to spend some time in Winnetka analyzing the situation and recommending ways to improve the schools. Second, they searched for a man whom they could employ as superintendent of schools in Winnetka to carry out the recommendations.

They selected, in 1914, E. N. Rhodes, then principal of an elementary school in Oak Park, a much larger suburb of Chicago. Under his administration a number of improvements were made: manual arts were introduced; home economics was added to the program; a school library was established; a special class for retarded children was organized; an excellent music program was put into effect; and there was a strong program in art. An unusually able director of playgrounds and physical education (Harry P. Clarke) had been employed even before Rhodes came.

It was also under Rhodes' administration that an attractive new elementary school called "Hubbard Woods" was constructed, and plans were begun for a junior high school on a large tract of land on the edge of the city.

At this point it should be stated that the Board of Education in Winnetka had (and still has) responsibility for education through grade eight. After that the Winnetka children attend the New Trier Township High School, along with the children from several adjacent suburbs. That high school, while situated at the south end of Winnetka, is under an entirely separate Board of Education, elected by the township as a whole, including Glencoe, Winnetka, Kenilworth, and Wilmette, in that geographical order from north to south along Lake Michigan, and, more recently, Northfield to the west. The new "junior high school of Winnetka" was to be (and became) a lower secondary school, embracing the sixth, seventh and eighth grades. This and the elementary schools of Winnetka were and are entirely independent of the New Trier Township High School, which admits all students who complete the eight years in Winnetka and the other suburbs.[2]

While many excellent things occurred during Rhodes' superintendency, one surmises that they were initiated by the Board. Rhodes apparently failed to gain the confidence of the Board of Education and the people of Winnetka. The Board, as we shall see, began in 1918 to look for a new superintendent.

Burk and the San Francisco State Normal School

The second stream that flowed into the Winnetka educational system had its identifiable origin in the San Francisco State Normal School. In those days, teachers for the elementary schools all over the United States had, typically, two years of training after completing their high school education. From the age of about 18 to the age of 20, they received intensive training in the history, philosophy, psychology, and techniques of elementary school teaching and did practice teaching. The institutions which gave this training were called Normal Schools and were usually supported and administered directly by the states. Some were organized and supported by the counties or by large cities.

The President of the San Francisco State Normal School was Dr. Frederic Burk. He was a man of high scholarship, even higher ideals, terrific energy, and great originality. His Normal School was widely known for its innovations in the education of teachers and the high quality of the teachers it trained.

About 1912 a member of Burk's faculty, Mary Ward, quietly carried

---

[2] This separation of the administration of the elementary schools and junior high school from that of the high school occurs in a number of suburbs of Chicago and certain other parts of Illinois for historical reasons and because, under Illinois law, more taxes can be levied for the schools when the two administrations are separate.

out an informal experiment. Under the program of that school, students began limited practice teaching almost as soon as they entered, rather than waiting, as in most normal schools, until their last semester. In the elementary school attached to the Normal School, two students were assigned as teachers to each class of 20 children for a third of the day, and taught usually only one or two subjects. Each supervisor of the subject being taught supervised four such classrooms. She (or he) therefore had responsibility for just eight students at a time, for 13 weeks. She planned their work with them day by day, watched them at work with the children, took over a class from time to time to demonstrate methods, and met after class with the students to criticize their work constructively, plan the next day's work, and assign readings for study.

Mary Ward was a supervisor of arithmetic. One day, after class, some of her students pointed out that the work planned for the children did not fit all of them; some were not yet ready for it, for others it was too easy. Miss Ward suggested that they prepare materials specially for the slower ones and other materials for the faster ones, and let each work at his own level. This was successful, but it soon became evident that the children did not fall into three neat categories—slow, average, and fast. The slower children had different degrees of retardation, the faster ones different rates of acceleration, and the "average" spread from almost retarded to almost accelerated.

Before long, the students were preparing work for each individual child. If it was well enough prepared, what one child could use today another could use next month—or later. By the end of the year the children had spread out very widely, no two having accomplished the same amount of work. The slowest one had successsfully completed a year's work; the fastest one, two years of work.

Miss Ward made a graph on the blackboard showing each child's accomplishment (*see* next page).

Calling in Dr. Burk, she told him what she had done and explained the graph. Always alert for new ideas, he caught fire. He called a special meeting of the faculty and asked Miss Ward to describe her experiment and its results. The key was the preparation of "self-instruction materials"—assignments and explanations written so simply and clearly that the child could to a large extent teach himself. Of course, the student teacher would be there to help where needed, but the materials were written as if no other help were available.

Burk proposed that every supervisor begin immediately with his or her students the preparation of "self-instruction bulletins" in his subject and for the classes he supervised. At first these "bulletins" were used with existing textbooks—assigning lessons, amplifying and clarifying explanations, and adding supplementary exercises. The "self-instruction bulletins" were prepared, mimeographed, tried on the children and revised where use showed them to be inadequate. In time many of them became complete in themselves and were printed for other schools as well.

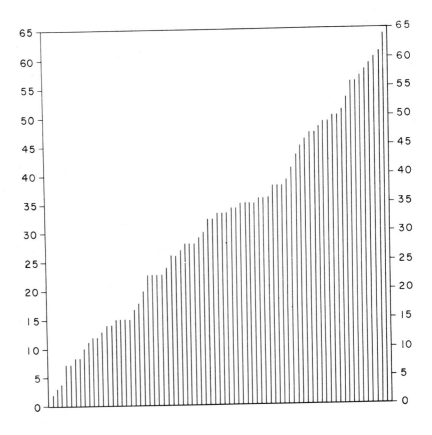

Figure 1

Days Required by Each Child to Complete
High-Second Grade Arithmetic

From that point on, instruction in the elementary school attached to that Normal School was on an individual basis, each child proceeding at his own natural rate, neither retarded by slower children nor hurried by faster ones.

Burk wrote a monograph on what they were doing, and why. Let me quote from it some passages of Burk's indictment of the traditional class system:

> The class system has been modeled upon the military system. It is constructed upon the assumption that a group of minds can be marshaled and controlled in growth in exactly the same manner that a military officer marshals and directs the bodily movements of a company of soldiers. In solid unbreakable phalanx the class is supposed to move through the grades, keeping in locked step. This locked step is set by the "average" pupil—an algebraic myth born of inanimate figures and an addled pedagogy.

> * * *

> V. *The class system does permanent violence to all types of pupils.*

> (1) It does injury to the rapid and quick-thinking pupils, because these must shackle their stride to keep pace with the rate of the mythical average. They do so, usually at the price of interest in their work. Their energy is directed into illegitimate activities with the result that in the intermediate grades a large portion of them fall into the class of uninterested, inattentive, rebellious, and unmanageable pupils.

> (2) The class system does a greater injury to the large number who make progress slower than the rate of the mythical average pupil. Necessarily they are carried off their feet by the momentum of the mass. They struggle along, with greater or less pretense, but eventually they are discovered and put back into the next lower class. . . . By setting the pace of a mathematical average, education for nearly one half the class is made impossible. *They are foredoomed to failure before they begin.* . . . This policy is, of course, as inhuman as it is stupid.

> * * *

> Could any system be more stupid in its assumptions, more impossible in its conditions, and more juggernautic in its operation? Every one of its premises is palpably false; every one of its requirements is impossible and every one of its effects is inefficient and brutal. Nevertheless this system has endured and has been endured for centuries.[3]

This monograph was widely distributed and read throughout the United States. It was followed by articles and other monographs. Swarms of visitors came to visit the school. There was nationwide interest in

---

[3] *Remedy for Lock-step Schooling.* Originally published by the Department of Education, State of California, and reprinted by the Winnetka Educational Press, 1935.

this effort to fit the school to the individual child instead of forcing the child into a rigid mold.

The Third Stream—My Early Experience

It was again in 1912—December of that year—that I was employed as "principal" of a two-room rural school in Los Angeles County in California (La Puente District). The school had eight grades in the two rooms: the first, second and third grades (about 50 children) taught by a young woman recently graduated from a normal school, and the other room, containing 35 children ranging through the fourth, fifth, sixth, seventh, and eighth grades, taught by the "principal." The principal who preceded me had lost control of the children, some of them large, overgrown boys who came to school to avoid farm work. The children literally drove the principal (a woman) out of the school and chased her down the road, throwing sticks and stones at her.

The local School Board (two farmers and a farm laborer) were desperate to find a new principal; it was December and most good teachers were already employed. Through the principal of the nearest union high school (El Monte, California), they asked, among other possible sources, a teachers' agency to try to find a "principal" for them.

I had graduated from Stanford University the preceding June. But I had not prepared to teach. I had started my university work to prepare for medicine; my father, grandfather, and great grandfather had all been medical doctors. But after completing three years of pre-medical and medical training I decided that I did not want to spend my life working with sick people. So I dropped my medical training and graduated in the department of physiology.

This prepared me for no vocation—unless I had wanted to take three or four more years of training in physiology and become a professsor of the subject, and I had no such wish. Consequently I had great difficulty in finding employment.

One day, in my search for work, I saw a sign: "Teachers Agency." I went in and registered. Soon afterwards I was called back and told about the two-room rural school in La Puente District which needed a principal.

I don't know why it had never before occurred to me to become a teacher. My mother had been deeply interested in education, had written and lectured on child study, and had lectured in a kindergarten training college. We lived in Chicago in my childhood and she was a close friend of Colonel Francis W. Parker of the Normal School in Chicago, the man whom John Dewey long afterwards called "the father of progressive education." She was also a friend of Dewey himself, then in the early stages of his educational experimentation and thinking. All my life I had heard new ideas in education discussed around the dinner table and fireside.

And I had always been fond of children. From my high school days on I had organized informal little clubs of boys and girls for a weekly storytelling hour or an hour of talk about science, or for long Saturday hikes, or for going out in the evening and studying the stars.

Strange that only the accidental passing of a "Teachers Agency" sign when I needed work brought me gradually to see education as my life's profession.

I interviewed the members of the rural School Board, walking from farm to farm, and was employed as teacher-principal. Back in 1912 the state laws in California permitted any university graduate to teach in an elementary school; so my complete lack of pedagogical training was not an obstacle to my employment.

This lack of training led me naturally into pitfalls I could have avoided, and I made plenty of mistakes. But my fondness for children, combined with the educational ideals on which I had been nourished from infancy, kept me from failure.

Anyway, my very lack of formal training in teaching and my isolation in a rural area gave me great freedom to experiment. I had to invent my own methods of teaching and handling children, and learn by experience those methods which were ineffectual and those which would succeed.

One of the first things I discovered was that all children classified as "sixth grade," for example, were not of equal ability or advancement. In arithmetic there were those who lacked the foundations they should have laid in the fourth grade, others for whom even the sixth grade work was too easy to be challenging. The situation was similar in all subjects and in all five grades.

So, not knowing any better, I planned each child's work to fit his apparent readiness. Usually there were several children, scattered through various classes, who seemed to be ready for the same assignment in arithmetic—who, for example, did not really know the simple facts of multiplication, or who could not read books of the same level of difficulty. I therefore organized the children into small informal groups, without regard to age or grade. In each group the children worked together and helped each other. The groupings changed from subject to subject, and week to week.

But I found I needed, often, seven or eight such groups, and the noise of so many groups doing different things, the children talking freely with each other, was distracting. Fortunately there was an extra room in the building and a tiny "library" which was also my office. So one group worked in the "library" and two or three groups in the extra room, and still another might be in the yard working on a garden. Meanwhile, I went from group to group and gave help and guidance and further assignments.

For music, I took all the children together and taught them to sing, at least lustily, many good songs. For art, too, they were all together and my young wife came in and taught them how to draw and paint.

And they were together for story hours—I always enjoyed telling stories to children and had a wide repertoire. Some of the stories we dramatized and later enacted for the parents.

The entire five grades participated in discussions of school organization and discipline. I was sure that self-government was superior to autocracy in school as in life.

We had a good year, and the children, for the first time in the lives of most of them, enjoyed school. And they learned a goodly amount.

While I was invited to continue a second year, a small town in central California (Tulare) offered me a somewhat less meager salary to take charge of a "special class." The superintendent of schools in Tulare had persuaded his Board of Education to establish, for one year only, a special class for children who did not fit into any of the regular classes. One child was deaf; another had a cleft palate and hare lip, and, aside from repulsive appearance, could not talk so that anyone could understand him; another was almost feeble-minded; several were just slow learners; and some of the big boys were simply too full of life and energy to submit to school discipline. There were 17 children ranging from eight years of age to fifteen.

The superintendent gave me *carte blanche*, with only one injunction: At the end of the year each child was to fit into some class in the school, or, for the oldest ones, be ready for high school.

Naturally, my work had to be individualized. I made some use of small groups where feasible, but often each child had his own particular assignments. I tried to plan the work so that no child would be expected to do anything that was too difficult for him to accomplish successfully with reasonable effort, and that no child would find his work so easy that his abilities were not challenged. I tried, too, of course, to show the children the reasons for learning each thing and to arouse their interest.

The boy with hare-lip and split palate I took by train to San Francisco where I persuaded an eminent surgeon to operate and close the gaps, without charge. Local merchants in Tulare, when I approached them, willingly contributed the cost of the boy's train fare and mine. The slow children had their first experience in being successful in their work and made unexpected progress. For the older boys, combined with others from regular classes, I organized a football team. It was so successful that it won games against all schools within travelling distance, and the energies of my boys had a wholesome outlet. They knew, too, that failure to work well at their studies would result in not playing on the team. They were ready for high school by the end of the year.

Two periods a day I was relieved of my class and taught arithmetic to a regular seventh grade and eighth grade. There again I discovered how far apart the children were in their knowledge and ability, and for a while I gave each child the work that fitted him. But the superintendent was afraid of such lack of orthodoxy, especially under a very young man like myself who did not have strict discipline. So I had to give the same assignments to all and give such special help as I could to the slower ones. This contrast with what I had done in my rural school and was doing with my special class made me acutely aware of the inefficiency and harmfulnesss—even cruelty—of trying to force widely differing children into a common mold.

Before the year had ended, and with it my job, the superintendent did one thing for which I have been grateful all my life—he gave me the little monograph that Dr. Frederic Burk had just published, *Remedy for Lock-step Schooling.*

It was balm to my soul. Here was a man who saw what I saw, who was on fire about the stupidity of ignoring the differences among children, and who, with vastly more knowledge and experience than I, was pointing out a road by which schools could be fitted to children.

I wrote Burk a long letter, telling him of my experiences and asking where I could find a position in which I would be free to carry out the ideas he and I had in common. A month later he sent me a postal card acknowledging my letter and saying I might hear further from him later.

Two Streams Merge

That summer (1914) I was directing a municipal playground in Oakland, California, across the bay from San Francisco. One day I got a telephone call from Dr. Burk, asking me to see him. It was the first of a series of conferences with him, conferences which to me were so stimulating that they were actually exciting. Burk's freshnesss of vision, his rapier-like wit, his devastating power of criticism, his keen sense of humor, his idealism and his practical knowledge and good sense, made me eager to work with him. At the end of the summer he employed me to organize and conduct the work in elementary science at the San Francisco State Normal School.

For the next five years I worked under the aegis of Frederic Burk. First he had me serve a three-month apprenticeship with Mary Ward, supervising the teaching of arithmetic, learning the technique of preparing and using self-instruction material, learning to know the children and the students. Thenceforward science was my realm.

While developing the program for training our students at the San Francisco State Normal School to teach science in the elementary school my own earlier training and interest were useful. In high school I had studied the biological and physical sciences for four years, and my university work had been predominantly in science. It was natural, therefore, for me to approach problems by the scientific method. Given the problem of developing a program in science for future teachers of the elementary schools, I set about investigating, through research, what knowledge such teachers would need.

Because this approach to problems through scientific research later became a vitally important part of the work in Winnetka, it is, perhaps, worthwhile to describe the research on which the new program in science for the San Francisco State Normal School students was developed.

What, I asked, are the common phenomena of everyday life requiring a knowledge of science if they are to be understood? And what are the questions children of the ages nine to fourteen are most eager to have answered?

To answer my first question I began by observing as many common experiences as possible—things fall when you drop them; a balloon rises; a kite flies; clouds form; rain descends from clouds; in a storm there are flashes of lightning, followed by thunder; a towel absorbs moisture; an automobile skids when it goes around a corner; brakes slow it; gasoline exploding drives it forward; soda neutralizes the acid in sour milk; soap removes dirt; and so on. Then I got my students and colleagues to make similar collections, writing each item on a separate small card. When I had thousands of such cards I used the Christmas holidays to sort and classify them under the scientific principles that would explain them.

To answer my second question I went into the classrooms of our elementary school, accompanied by a student. I invited the children to ask me any question they would like to have answered—any question at all that occurred to them. First the questions came slowly, then they came in torrents. My student wrote the questions on separate cards while I answered them.

The questions were sometimes not in the field of science, but the great majority were. Children soon began saving up questions for my next visit. But while the questions were numerous enough, the number of children was too small for generalization on my part. So next I had my senior students who were doing practice teaching in the city schools follow the same plan. Often they could not answer the questions; but then they promised to bring back the answers later and meanwhile they consulted me or books or both.

When I had many hundreds of these questions I classified them as I had classified the common phenomena. The principles needed to explain them were the same. This gave me the base on which to establish the curriculum in science for the children and on which to base the science training of the teachers.

It was also the base of my doctoral dissertation at the University of California in Berkeley. And from it grew my first two books.[4]

[4] Washburne, Carleton W. and Heluiz Chandler Washburne, *The Story of the Earth*, The Century Company, New York, 1916 (later revised and greatly enlarged as *The Story of Earth and Sky*, by Carleton and Heluiz Washburne, in collaboration with Frederick Reed, The Century Company, New York, 1933); and Washburne, Carleton W., *Common Science*, World Book Co., Yonkers-on-Hudson, N.Y., 1920.

Burk, who approved of this work and counselled me, had nevertheless other uses for me. He gave me responsibility for giving intelligence
tests to all the children in the elementary school—the Stanford Revision
of the Binet-Simon test had recently been published—and had me
organize and give the courses in psychology (and in school law!). Later
he put me in charge of developing tests of children's achievement.

It was in connection with this last that I conceived, with Burk's
strong approval, the idea of diagnostic tests which would identify the
specific weaknesses of the child and indicate the work he should do to
remedy them—an idea that was not fully developed until I was in
Winnetka.

The Final Confluence of the Streams

It must have been about 1917 when Gertrude Lieber of the School
Board in Winnetka first read one of Burk's monographs—I think it was
the one in which he described the first two years of the experiment in
individualizing instruction, *Monograph C*. She was much impressed
and showed it to a fellow member of the Board of Education, Edward
Yeomans, one of the original group who had supported Fetcher and
gone on to the Board with him.

Yeomans was a successful manufacturer of pumps in business life.
But he was also an amateur musician, a man with a strong interest in
handicrafts, and a man of culture and vision. Later he wrote a gem of
a little book on education, called *Shackled Youth* (Atlantic Monthly
Press); he wrote beautifully. He corresponded with Burk after reading
the monograph. It is a loss to posterity that this correspondence was
never collected and published—Burk vigorous, critical, peppery, even
acid; Yeomans graceful, literary, charming; both men idealists and
farseeing.

When in 1918 the Board of Education in Winnetka wanted to get
a new superintendent, Yeomans naturally sought Burk's advice—he and
Fetcher and Mrs. Lieber and the rest of the Board wanted a superintendent who would direct the schools in the spirit of the San Francisco
State Normal School.

Burk came to my office one day and said, "How would like to have
charge of the public schools in a small town near Chicago where they
want to try out some of our ideas?"

I fairly leapt to my feet as I said, "It's exactly what I want!"

He looked over his spectacles at me, under his bushy eyebrows, and just grunted, "Hm!" and left the office.

When he said no more during the following days and even weeks I began to worry. I was employed on an annual basis and could be dropped at the end of any year. And I had a wife and two children to support. Was Burk merely trying me out to see whether I really wanted to work with *him*, and would he drop me if he saw I was so eager for another job? And was there such a job?

After a month, I could wait no longer. I went to his office. "Was that a real job?" I asked, "or were you merely trying me out to see whether I wanted to stay here?"

"Oh, it's real," he replied. "A manufacturer of pumps, named Yeomans, in a little suburb of Chicago has been writing to me from time to time and has asked me to recommend someone as superintendent of their schools. You're a very young man. Winnetka is a very small town. If you fail it won't make a big splash. I guess I'll recommend you!"

My desire for the position grew out of the following fact: The many visitors to the Normal School would express their admiration for what we were doing, but then they would say, "Yes, this is fine here, but it could not be done in a public school. You have only 20 children to a class, all of normal intelligence or better; you have two student teachers in each class, and supervisors for every four classes. No wonder you can individualize instruction! We have 35 or 40 children in a class, un-selected, and only one teacher. Your system would not work under our conditions."

I wanted to show that the system was entirely practicable in a public school system; I had had my first experiences in public schools and, without the techniques and skill I had learned from Burk and his associates, had been able to adapt the work to the children's ability. I was sure that I could demonstrate the practicability and desirability of fitting schoolwork to individual children in a public school situation.

That summer the Winnetka Board of Education invited me to come for a week of interviews, not only with them but with leading Winnetka citizens. They had decided to keep Rhodes a little longer so that he could draw a pension, but the next spring they telegraphed me offering me the position.

In May, 1919, at the age of 29, I began work as Superintendent of

Photo 1: The "original cast" of the drama that started in Winnetka upon Carleton Washburne's arrival. The faculty in 1922. Dr. Washburne is in the center. A number of these teachers, all now retired, remain informally related to the Winnetka schools as friendly observers and counselors.

the Winnetka Public Schools. I remained for 24 years until the Army called me in 1943 to accept a commission as major and take training in military government at Charlottesville, Virginia. From there I was assigned to Italy, where, as a lieutenant colonel, I became Director of the Education Subcommission of the Allied Commission in Italy.

It was, therefore, in 1919 that what came to be known as the Winnetka educational system had its origin. The source was three streams—the educational desires of Winnetka, Burk's work in San Francisco, and my own early experiences followed by the rigorous training under Burk. Thereafter all three influences merged into one continuous stream which is still flowing. No other stream has followed the same contours, but countless fields have been watered by it.

CHAPTER TWO

Individualizing

Arithmetic

Being younger and less experienced than most of the 40 or so teachers I found in Winnetka, I knew that I had much to learn from them. So from the start I met with them in small groups, every two weeks—teachers of the first grade on alternate Tuesday afternoons after school; teachers of the second grade on alternate Wednesdays; and so on through the first six grades. Mondays and Fridays I reserved for work with the teachers of the seventh and eighth grades—the embryo junior high school—teachers who, like most secondary school teachers, each taught one or two subjects to a series of classes. At group meetings, teachers were encouraged to discuss their problems. They did so with zest.

Cooperative Planning

In these meetings—which continued for 24 years—the Winnetka educational system developed, research was done, self-instruction text-books were written and revised, diagnostic tests were devised, a philosophy emerged. In them a solidarity, a unity of purpose and of mutual respect evolved; there were never dissident factions. Democracy, and what was later called "group process," were fully effective. No one person, neither I nor anyone else, could claim credit for what was done. We, as groups and as faculty, always testing our ideas on living children, adapting ideas from many sources in both Europe and America, using the research of others and our own research to find scientific answers to our problems, tried to make the public schools so good that any parent would be proud and happy to send his children to them. We wanted to stimulate and help every child to develop his own personal and social potentialities in accordance with his individual design of growth.

Basic Program

At the beginning I asked the teachers in each group what their objectives were—what they hoped to teach their children during the year and what problems they were finding. Very soon arithmetic became a major subject of inquiry; above the first grade, arithmetic caused more failures among the children than did any other subject, in spite of more time being given to it than to any other study.

What knowledge of arithmetic and what skill did each successive grade seek to give to the children? The answers at first were general—addition, multiplication, fractions, and so on. "But specifically what do you expect every child to know at the end of the year?" I would ask. The teachers tried to specify—and they always specified more than every child could possibly master.

"But can *every* child know all that, well, by the end of the year?"

"No, but this is what we should try to teach them. We must keep our standards high."

"But is a standard which a child cannot reach, even with every effort, a useful standard? Have we a right to tell a child he must do what he cannot do and that failure to do it will be punished by low marks or by repeating the grade the next year? Have we a right to deceive parents into thinking we will teach their children things we know many of the children cannot learn at this stage of their development?"

Through such questions, pursued with the rigor I had learned from Burk, the teachers gradually became more clear thinking and realistic. In time they agreed with Burk's maxim: "A YEAR'S WORK IN A SUBJECT IS WHAT THE *slowest, normal, diligent* CHILD CAN ACCOMPLISH IN A YEAR." Children below normal intelligence should not be pushed beyond their ability—let them successfully complete as much of the year's work as comes within their ability. Children above normal intelligence should not be held back, but encouraged to do as much more than a year's work as they can. Children who were not diligent would be penalized by slower progress, but their interest, and consequent effort, should be stimulated by the teacher.

Agreement was reached on this principle, discovered by the teachers themselves through rigorous analysis of their objectives and their experience. But how could the teachers handle classes of 35 or more children if each child was proceeding at his individual rate?

Self-Instruction Materials

At this point I told them of the self-instruction materials at the Sun Francisco State Normal School. They became enthusiastic about developing such material. They asked if they could stay on a week after school closed and write material together for the following autumn and if I would have it mimeographed for them during the summer.

Rather than take a week off their vacation for this I persuaded the Board of Education to let me close the schools two days early—on a Wednesday—letting the teachers work Thursday, Friday, and Saturday of that week and only Monday and Tuesday of the first week of vacation.

During those five days the teachers worked in groups—teachers of the first grade in one group, those of the second grade in another, through all the grades. Each group used one of the classrooms, and I circulated among them, helping, criticizing, encouraging. They had already, in their earlier group meetings, decided just what was to be taught. They had their textbooks, and they did a prodigious amount of work.

My new young secretary, Jessie Knox, who, until 1962, continued as secretary to the successive superintendents of schools, spent that

Photo 2: For many years self-instruction, by whatever name, has been basic to Winnetka's design. Here second-grade children work on reading speed and comprehension.

summer typing and mimeographing the materials the teachers had prepared—Winnetka's first self-instruction textbooks. These, or the revision
of them a year later, were the model on which the first published "work
books" were made by a commercial publisher.

We started out the next fall with arithmetic individualized, each
child able to proceed at his individual rate, no two, except by accident,
doing exactly the same work each day. If a slow child did not finish a
year's work that year, he got no low mark, he did not repeat, he simply
began the next autumn where he left off. Most children, however, finished at least a year's work, and many got well along with the work of
the following year.

The individualized program in arithmetic will be described in considerable detail in what follows, since it illustrates well all the fundamental principles of individualization of mastery of any skill, at any level.

Self-Correction

Self-instruction textbooks, however, did not solve the problem of
individualizing teaching in large classes. The children accomplished so
much work that the daily correction of it imposed too heavy a burden
on the teacher. Almost immediately, therefore, we introduced the means
of self-correction. After each group of arithmetic exercises we inserted
a sheet of answers. When a child had completed the group he turned
to the answer page and corrected his own work. If he had made errors
he was directed to re-read the explanation and then try a second, very
similar group of exercises, labeled "B," the first set being labeled "A."
Again he corrected his own work, and if he still had errors, he did assignment "C" and corrected it from the answer sheet. No child was sup-
posed to continue to the next step until he had completed an "A,"
"B," or "C" assignment without error.

While working, or while correcting his work, he was free to ask other
children for help or to raise his hand for the teacher to come to him.
The teacher was continuously circulating among the children, helping
and encouraging them. The room was a beehive of activity.

Step-by-Step Procedure (Programming)

To make the work as simple and self-instructive as possible, not only were the explanations made very clear and illustrated with model problems worked out for the child, but the process under study was itself broken into small steps, each containing just one new element of difficulty. We did an intensive job of what is now called "programming" instruction. For example, let us consider the first steps in simple multiplication taken *after* a child had mastered all the basic multiplication facts (2 x 3, 4 x 8, 3 x 6, etc.). The process was broken down into three steps as follows:

Step 1—No zeros, no carrying, e.g. $\begin{array}{r} 41 \\ \times 2 \\ \hline \end{array}$

Step 2—Zero, at end of multiplicand, e.g. $\begin{array}{r} 20 \\ \times 4 \\ \hline \end{array}$

Step 3—Carrying introduced, e.g. $\begin{array}{r} 13 \\ \times 5 \\ \hline \end{array}$

Each of these steps had A, B, and C exercises.

Diagnostic Tests

But, any teacher will ask, why did not children cheat? Sometimes at first, or when they came new from another school, they did. We let them—and the other children smiled knowing what was coming. For at the end of a series of steps there was a diagnostic test. This was made up of one example of each step and usually an example combining all steps. It was made in five forms, all of the same difficulty and all constructed in the same way. Three of these forms were in the child's book, with an answer sheet for self-correction, like this:

1. If Bill wanted to make 3 notebooks, each with 26 sheets, how many sheets of paper would he need?
2. Susan was making cookies for a large party. The recipe made 32 cookies. If she made the recipe 3 times, how many cookies would she have?
3. Carolyn said she could save 20 cents a week to buy a new record. In 4 weeks how much could she save?

The answer sheet looked like this:

1. 26 sheets
    ×3
    78 sheets—*Step 3*

2. 32 cookies
    ×3
    96 cookies—*Step 1*

3. 20 cents
    ×4
    80 cents—*Step 2*

If the child missed an example, the answer sheet showed him on what step he was weak and he went back to the explanation, then did an exercise in that step in a supplementary correction book, and tried the second form of the test. If necessary, after further study and such help as he needed from teacher or fellow pupil, he gave himself the third form.

When he had completed one form of the practice test without error, he asked the teacher for a "real test"—the fourth form of the test. For this he had no answer sheet and must have no help. Since very few in the class, usually only one or two, would be taking the same real test at the same time, it was easy for the teacher to see that he was unaided. She had an answer sheet, keyed with references to the appropriate steps for examples missed, and if the child made an error she simply marked the test with the number of the step or steps on which he needed further practice. This practice work, and a self-corrected practice test had to be shown to her before she gave the child the fifth form—the second form of the real test.

Children very quickly learned that any cheating of themselves simply resulted in more work, that a day of reckoning was close at hand. If, however, a child thought he could do a practice test before doing the preliminary exercises, he was quite free to do so; all we wanted was mastery of the process and a child was at liberty to achieve this in the quickest way possible. But we never accepted a test with *any* errors; the child must pass it 100 per cent before going on to new assignments.

At intervals, the child had to take a review test. This consisted of examples covering all preceding work and the answers were keyed to the process in which the child showed weakness. The review test was also in five forms—three self-corrective practice tests and two real tests to be corrected by the teacher.

Record Keeping

The teacher, child, and parent kept track of the child's progress with a "Goal Book." This contained a list of the tests for two years of work in each subject, arranged in vertical columns, from bottom to top, with a space after each for the date on which it was passed without error (*see* next page).

When a child passed a test he took his goal card to the teacher who entered the date. The rising column of dates showed his progress. Every six weeks the teacher drew a red line across the top of the highest date in the column, thereby showing the rate of progress. There were no report cards with marks "excellent," "good," "poor," etc.—every child was 100 per cent in all he had done. But some had done much more than others.

Since each child kept his own goal card at his desk, the teacher had a record of her own in her "Goal Record Book." Here a page was given to each subject. For arithmetic, for example, the names of all the children were in the left-hand column alphabetically. At the head of all the rest of the columns were the names of the tests in that subject, ranged in order from left to right. So when a child passed a test the teacher not only entered the date on the child's goal card, but in her own goal record book.

When the principal or I visited the classroom, we often inspected the teacher's goal record book. At a glance we could tell which children were making unusually slow progress by the short row of dates after their names. Variation we expected—and desired—since children varied. But extreme slowness called for attention. The teacher might know and explain the reason and what she was doing about it. If, however, she herself was puzzled and had been unable to diagnose the cause or find a remedy, we tried to help. Later, unusually difficult problems of this sort were referred to the Education Clinic for analysis and remedy—but of that, more later.

At first glance, all this machinery seems elaborate and time-consuming. Actually, the teachers had much less paper work and correction of children's daily work than do most teachers. The preparation of the materials was of course very time-consuming at first; but we all

ARITHMETIC

Test	Date
Liquid measure	
Review Test II	
Easy simple multiplication—speed review	
Easy subtraction—speed review	
Easy addition—speed review	
Easy short division—speed	
Subtraction facts—speed review	
Easy simple multiplication—speed	
Easy simple multiplication	
Easy multiplication facts—speed review	
Easy division facts—speed	
Division facts—Steps 7 to 11	
Division facts—Steps 1 to 6	
Dollars and cents	
Review Test 1	
Addition facts—speed review	
Easy subtraction—speed	
Easy subtraction—Steps 4 to 6	
Easy subtraction—Steps 1 to 3	
Subtraction facts—speed	
Inches, feet and yards	
Easy multiplication facts—speed	
Easy addition—speed	
Easy addition	
Addition facts—speed	

worked at it, all the teachers from the three elementary schools dividing the work among themselves at their fortnightly group meetings. Once the materials for teaching and testing were prepared, later work consisted of revision and improvement over the years.

Number Facts (Use of a "Teaching Machine")

In the preparation of self-instruction materials in arithmetic, we have so far discussed the successive arithmetic processes. But the elements used in the processes are the basic facts of addition, subtraction, multiplication, and division. Inaccuracy or hesitancy on these basic facts —6 + 7, 12 − 5, 3 × 9, 18 ÷ 6, etc.—necessarily makes any work in the process using them inaccurate and slow. Our aim was, therefore, to see that every child, before beginning a processs, should know with quick, almost automatic, precision the basic facts.

To give this mastery we devised little cards, like this:

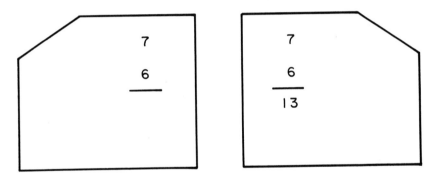

Two sides of one card

Figure 2

The clipped corner assured that all cards were right side up—clipped corner to the top and left. With these the child played games. The most efficient one of these was solitaire: The child took a small stack of cards. He looked at the face, perhaps 7 + 6. He said to himself the answer—without counting or hesitating, then instantly turned the card over to see if he was right. If he had said "15," and saw that it should have been "13," he placed the card in a pile on his left. But if he had said "13," he placed it in a pile on his right. He continued thus to the end of his pack. Then he took the cards in the pile on the left—the ones on which he had missed—shuffled them and proceeded as before. He kept doing this until all cards were on the right. A comparable set of cards has recently been called a "teaching machine."

This technique gives instant correction of errors. It avoids wasting time practicing on facts already known. It gives repetition in proportion to the difficulty the child has in learning the facts. And it is rather fun. (I have used the same system in learning vocabulary and verb forms when studying foreign languages and found it both interesting and highly efficient.)

Another game is played with a partner. Each child gets half the pack. One child exposes the front of a card to his partner. If the partner gives the right answer, he gets the card and it is his turn to expose one. But if he misses, the child who exposed the card tells the answer, shows it to the partner, keeps the card and exposes the next one. When either child uses up his original pack he shuffles those won and continues as before. In time one child wins the game by exhausting all of his partner's cards.

Ingenious teachers and the children themselves invented various other games, and the facts were learned.

Speed Tests

To be sure of speed in recall, we also devised "speed tests," where all the facts of any one operation were printed (or mimeographed) on a sheet. The teacher had the children sit with pencils poised for a signal, then time was called at the beginning and end of three minutes. A minimum number of answers had to be written, without error, for the child to pass this test, which was given from time to time each year.

Relating Program to Child's Maturity

But *when* should a child begin to study the facts of addition and when those of subtraction? When, indeed, should each process in arithmetic be introduced? To these questions we early began to turn our attention.

We searched the teaching literature and found no evidence that anyone had a scientific answer. We investigated the practices of other schools, through letters to various parts of the United States, and found that practice differed widely. So we began some simple studies with the children in our own schools. There appeared to be no doubt that some aspects of arithmetic could be readily learned and *retained* at an early age while others required considerable maturity. Further, it seemed evident that mental age as shown on intelligence tests (we had soon begun to give intelligence tests to all our children) was a more important factor than actual chronological age, or the class in which a child was sitting.

The Committee of Seven

At that time (about 1921, if I remember correctly) I was made Chairman of the Executive Committee of the Northern Illinois Conference on Supervision, an organization of the superintendents, principals, and supervisors that met annually for a two-day conference on problems of common interest. That association provided in its constitution for a Committee of Seven to make studies of school curricula and to report back to the Conference each year. Prior to my advent in Winnetka, there had been a number of such studies, based on the discussions, experience and reading of the committee members, but not on direct research. My predecessor, Rhodes, had been a chairman of the old Committee of Seven. But for two or three years no Committee of Seven had been appointed.

Here I saw my opportunity. It was my responsibility under the constitution to appoint a Committee of Seven. So I appointed Harry N. Gillet, principal of the University of Chicago elementary school; Raymond Osborn, associate principal and later principal of the Francis W. Parker school in Chicago; J. R. Harper, Orville T. Bright, Howard Storm, and William Hamilton, all superintendents of schools in northern Illinois; and myself. The committee made me their chairman.

To this committee I proposed my problem: *At what mental age can children most effectively learn each aspect of arithmetic?* We immediately began research on this problem. We continued our research for 15 years, reporting our progress and results annually to the Northern Illinois Conference on Supervision and in articles in professional publications.

Gillet, Harper and I served on the Committee for its entire 15 years, and Storm and Osborn for most of this time. For shorter periods Turner Chandler and O. E. Peterson served. The statistical work of the Committee and all details and correspondence were handled by the Director of Research in the Winnetka Public Schools, Mabel Vogel (later Mabel Vogel Morphett) most of the time, Vivian Weedon and William Voas *ad interim.*

Our method was essentially as follows: We prepared units of teaching material and tests for each phase of elementary school arithmetic, using to a large extent the materials the teachers in Winnetka had prepared, because these were self-instructive, organized in successive steps, and tested diagnostically. At first we worked in our own schools, trying the materials on children of varying mental ages, and giving retention tests after a period (usually six weeks or more) in which no further teaching or review of the item under investigation was done.

As we began to get significant results, we recognized that we were studying a relatively small population in a limited geographical area. So we sought the cooperation of other cities over the United States. The variation in school programs was advantageous to us—for example, some schools taught long division as low as the third grade, others not introducing this until the fourth or even fifth grade. These schools could therefore try our materials at different levels without disrupting their normal sequence. And, of course, in any class the range of mental age is about four years. So actually each unit of work was tried with children ranging through six years of mental age.

In time we had the cooperation of 500 American cities. As far as I am aware it was the most extensive, longest continued scientific investigation in the history of education.[1]

The results of the studies and the details of their technique have been fully published in professional literature and are well summarized in the 38th Yearbook of the National Society for the Study of Education.[2]

Only a few major findings will therefore be repeated here. These are:

---

[1] An exception may be the work of Piaget, in terms of continuity, but not, I believe, in terms of the number of cities and children involved.

[2] *Child Development and the Curriculum,* 38th Yearbook of the National Society for the Study of Education, Part I, Chapter XVI, Public School Publishing Co., 1939 (now University of Chicago Press, Chicago, Ill.).

1. There is a point in the mental development of children before
   which learning of any specific aspect of arithmetic is relatively
   inefficient and after which there is relatively little gain by postponing the learning. Characteristically, each topic follows what
   statisticians know as an S curve. It looks like this:

Figure 3

The vertical scale represents effectiveness of learning, the horizontal scale mental ages. As can be seen, effective learning
increases more and more rapidly as one attempts it at successively higher mental ages, but there comes a "point of flexion"
where the curve bends the other way, and from that point on
there is less and less gain in effective learning through increased
mental age.

   We drew the graph two ways. In one the vertical scale represented average scores on retention tests; in the other it represented the percentage of children who had attained scores of 90
per cent or higher on the retention test. The two curves were
very similar and pointed to identical conclusions. But for practical purposes the second was more useful. Using this, the
Committee proposed that no topic should be undertaken until
a child had reached the mental age at which most children
achieved successful learning. "Successful learning" meant that
after a six-week period for forgetting they still could pass a test
with scores of 90 to 100 per cent correct.

2. A process usually considered as a unit to be taught in one
   school term often contains aspects which belong at widely different mental ages. For example, the multiplication facts with

products under 20 can be effectively learned at a mental age of eight years, but multiplication facts with products above 20 (except 5 × 5 which comes earlier) are not effectively learned and *retained* until three years later—a mental age of 11. Similarly, long division with divisors of two digits can be learned readily at a mental age of 11 if all multiplication facts are fully mastered and if there are only two digits in the divisor and if it does not require "trial division," *e.g.* 992 ÷ 32; but a mental age of at least 12 years 9 months is necessary for efficient learning of the more difficult aspects of long division.

The following table shows the appropriate mental age at which, according to the Committee of Seven findings, each aspect of arithmetic can be effectively taught:

	Mental Age
Addition and subtraction facts, 10 and under	7
Measurement of lines in even inches	7
Reading clock to even hours, distinguishing morning and afternoon, recognizing meaning of A.M. and P.M.	7
All subtraction facts and simple subtraction (*e.g.* 48 − 19)	8
Multiplication facts, products 20 and under (also 5 × 5)	8
Easy square measure	8
Reading clock to quarter hour	8
Relation of minutes, hours, days, weeks	8
Elapsed days in same month	8
Column addition to 3 digits wide, 3 high	9
Simple multiplication (*e.g.*, 4 × 23). No partial products over 20	9
Division facts, dividend 20 and under	9
Short division, no partial dividend over 20	9
Meaning of simple fractions (*e.g.*, ½, ⅓, ¾, etc.) "Half" can be learned much earlier	9
Addition and subtraction of very simple fractions with same denominator	9

	Mental Age
Simple linear measure, with conversions	9
Simple square measure	9
Column addition, 4 digits high, 3 wide	10
Simple decimals and their addition and subtraction	10
Addition and subtraction of commonly used fractions and mixed numbers with common denominators	10
Reading and making simple bar graphs not involving fractional estimates	10
Linear measure—measuring and drawing lines to ¼ inch; estimating common length, units of measure for distance between cities, height of building, etc. (not closely related to mental age), measurement of perimeters	10
Addition, subtraction and multiplication of feet and inches not involving change of unit (*e.g.* 4 feet 8 inches minus 2 feet 5 inches; 4 × 2 feet 1 inch)	10
Table of time complete, from seconds to years and leap years. Reading clock to exact minute and writing time (*e.g.*, 10:22 A.M.)	10
Calculation using time units	10
Multiplication facts complete	11
Simple multiplication (*e.g.*, 8 × 4267)	11
Compound multiplication (*e.g.*, 267 × 4928)	11
Short division (*e.g.*, 208 ÷ 9)	11
Long division with 2-place divisor and 1-place quotient	11
Decimals—common fraction equivalents (*e.g.*, ⅜ = .375)	11
Decimals—division by integers; multiplication by decimals	11
Square measure, relation of square inches to square feet, etc. (little relation to mental age)	11
Long division (possible to complete here, but better results a year later)	12
Fractions of groups of objects (*e.g.*, 3 is ⅓ of 9)	12

	Mental Age
Multiplication and division of fractions	12
Percentage, Cases I and II, where divisor is whole number	12
Measurements—accurate to ⅛ inch; inches in fraction of a yard; scale measurement of maps	12
Time—multiplication of hours and minutes with change of denomination; elapsed time in hours, days, weeks, etc.	12
Long division, complete, all difficulties	13
Decimals, multiplication and division complete	13
Percentage Case II complete	13
Measurements, calculation involving change of unit	13
Fractions complete. Manipulation of denominator numbers involving changing denominators complete	14

It will be noted that the mental age for each topic is considerably higher than the age at which schools usually teach it. The Committee's findings indicate that there is much lost effort on the part of teacher and pupil in the common practice; children "learn" the topic only to forget it and have to relearn, and discouragement and dislike often result. By *waiting* for the desirable maturity, learning is relatively easy and much more adequately retained.

3. "Foundations" are at least as important a determining factor as mental age. A child who does not have command of the facts of addition cannot, regardless of mental age, be expected to learn effectively to add columns; one not knowing subtraction, multiplication and division facts cannot effectively learn the simplest types of long division. The Committee of Seven always arranged to have children tested not only for mental age but for knowledge of those facts or processes prerequisite to the topic they were to learn.

4. "Meaning" is a vital factor—that is, the child must have a real understanding of the concrete meaning of the numbers he is

dealing with and the process he is learning. The Committee discovered this late in its research, so it was only tested in connection with fractions. In this field, a "meaning of fractions" test was a part of the "foundations test." Probably the reason that 6×3 can be readily learned at a mental age of eight while 6×9 requires three more years of maturity is that 18 is a number that has meaning to the average eight-year-old while 54 is meaningless until the child has had much more experience. Future research may show that the Committee of Seven findings will be altered by experiences that make the learning more meaningful.

*   *   *

The work of the Committee of Seven affected textbooks and programs all over the United States and Canada. The effect, however, fell far short of the Committee's findings. Textbooks followed, to a considerable extent (and still do), the order of arithmetic topics to be introduced and the mental age of the *average* child in each successive grade who might be expected to learn a topic. But all children in a grade are not of one "average" mental age; as mentioned earlier, in any grade there is a spread of four years in mental age. The Committee's findings showed clearly that it was the *individual child's* mental age, knowledge of foundations, and understanding of meaning that are essential to effective learning, not the "average" of a class. Tradition and inertia (and lack of knowledge as to how to individualize instruction) have made practice lag far behind scientific findings in this (as in all fields).

The work of the Committee of Seven has, of course, been criticized. The most valid criticism is one that the Committee itself recognized and repeatedly published: We do not know how far the results have been affected by (*a*) the empirical and more or less arbitrary length of time assigned by the Committee for the study of each topic (it was the length of time we had found necessary in Winnetka); (*b*) the length of time (six weeks), purely arbitrarily given, for forgetting; (*c*) the arbitrary standard of mastery—why 90% to 100% scores rather than 80% or 85%? and, most important (*d*) the *method* employed in teaching. The method used, and the materials, were those used in the first decade in Winnetka (1920-1930), and Winnetka itself, as we shall see later, greatly improved on the methods and materials of arithmetic instruction in later years.

Unfortunately no one has repeated the work of the Committee of Seven using different methods, materials, and standards for the whole range of topics. Professor Leo Brueckner of the University of Minnesota, among others, has repeated certain aspects of the Committee of Seven research and his results have tended to verify the Committee's findings. Until an equally careful and extensive investigation shows how and where the Committee's findings can be effectively modified, they still form our only guide as to the effective stage of development at which each child can learn each aspect of arithmetic.

Now, in the early 1960's, there is a tendency in the United States, and even in Winnetka, to try to push instruction in arithmetic lower in the child's development than was indicated by the Committee of Seven. It began in the near-hysteria following the success of Sputnik. Americans were shocked to find that the Russians were able to put a satellite into orbit sooner than we, and drew a completely unjustified conclusion that this was because of a greater emphasis on science and mathematics in the early grades of the elementary school in the USSR, rather than the emphasis a totalitarian government was able to place on the training, incentives and facilities offered to a relatively small number of highly selected specialists.

The Committee of Seven itself showed that many children *could* learn the various processes of arithmetic at a mental age lower than the optimum. It also pointed out that change in method, and especially prior meaningful experiences, *might* change the designated optima. But no scientific evidence has, to date, as far as I am aware, tested this hypothesis. Is there not danger that in the current tendency to push instruction downward in the curriculum, to try to force children to learn mathematical processes before they have reached the maturity and had the experience necessary for *meaningful* learning, we may do two serious harms? First, we may discourage children and give them a dislike for mathematics, if they find that they do not have success proportionate to effort. Second, we may encourage children merely to learn to manipulate numbers, to learn the tricks of arithmetic so that they can pass tests, instead of seeing mathematics as a wholly rational and meaningful process.

Do we have any evidence whatsoever that children's understanding of and interest in mathematics is hampered by waiting for the learning of any particular process until they have the maturity and experience necessary for effective and lasting learning—or even waiting somewhat beyond this stage? Yet we do have much clinical evidence as well as some experimental indication that attempts to learn too soon do damage.

Certainly the more mature and gifted children should proceed at a much more rapid rate and go much farther than the less talented. Certainly they should be challenged—all children should be challenged—to develop their full potential and use their full ability. This was—and is—a major purpose of individual progress in Winnetka.

That this purpose has not yet been adequately achieved may be at least partly due to the tendency of parents, teachers and school authorities, even when the principles and facilities for individual progress are present, to retain a vestige of the old notion of "grades," of thinking of a class as a whole and expecting from each child what may be expected from the average child of the grade, of trying to keep the class together. Such carryover from tradition always reduces the effectiveness of the application of sound thinking and research. But it does not justify departing from the results of research without further research, nor the abandoning of sound principles.

Revision of the Winnetka Program

In Winnetka we continually revised our arithmetic program in accordance with the results emerging from our Committee of Seven research, and of course we revised our goal cards correspondingly.

During the first few years we had concentrated on the mechanics of arithmetic, and it was with these that the Committee of Seven largely dealt. People criticized Winnetka for the isolation of arithmetic from other subjects, but we, rightly I think, said that the accomplishment of a skill always required isolated practice, as a musician must always do technical exercises, not devote his time entirely to playing whole compositions with an orchestra. We gradually recognized, however, that we were understressing the meaning to the children of what they were doing, its personal and social value and application. Our textbooks (we had a whole series published) [3] were almost exclusively explanations, drills and problems.

---

[3] Carleton Washburne and Associates, *Washburne Individual Arithmetics*, World Book Company, Yonkers-on-Hudson, N.Y., 1925 to 1930.

About 1932, therefore, we began a general reorganization of our teaching method in arithmetic. We did not discard any of the original principles: self-instruction, self-correction, complete diagnostic tests, review tests, and the A, B, C practice exercises. But our introduction now always showed to the child the value of what he was about to learn.

First of all, the teacher *sought in the various other activities* of the children for mathematical implications. The "group and creative activities" (to be described later in this book) were full of such examples. Children could not build without using certain *quantities* of materials and using measurements; they could not buy without calculating the money needed and the money available. They could not take excursions without calculating distances and time—and so on endlessly.

With the class as a whole, regardless of the progress of individual members, the teacher pointed out these mathematical implications. She (or he—we were increasing the number of men on our faculty) would say, for example: "Let's see how much this picnic will cost," and write the items on the blackboard. She would then add the columns, with the help of any children who had progressed far enough for this, saying, perhaps, "Notice the decimal point—the little dot I put between dollars and cents. Notice that I write them exactly under each other. You haven't studied decimals yet, but you will, and this will be important so you can know in your answer how many dollars are needed and how many cents."

If some members of the class were approaching the study of long division, she might say, "Now if the picnic will cost $7.35 and there are 28 children in the class, how can we find out how much each one should pay? We have a way of doing it that was not discovered until after America was discovered. It is called 'long division.' I will show you how it is done." She then might work the problem for them on the blackboard, and say, "Later, when you can subtract and multiply, and when you can divide easy numbers, you will come to long division and learn how to do this kind of problem."

Teachers were careful not to spend enough time on this sort of preliminary instruction (we called it "adumbration") to interrupt or warp the activity in which the children were engaged, or to twist the activity to yield an excuse for teaching arithmetic. It was kept incidental. If, in a later class, some children had already learned the process thus illustrated, they helped the teacher work the problem on the blackboard, and it served them both as a practical application of their knowledge and a review, while it served the others as a stimulus and a reason for proceeding with their individual work.

We did not rely exclusively on this informal adumbration as a means of showing the value and use of each process. When a child came to the point of beginning the process, our new teaching material directed him to carry out certain specific activities—we called them "*ad hoc* projects"—which would show the necessity and use of the process. For example, "Take a pile of drawing paper that the teacher will give you. Count the sheets. Count the children in the room. See if you can find out how many sheets to give each child so all will have the same number." After the child has struggled with this problem, the text tells him that there is a simple way of solving it—and thousands like it. For each part of the explanation that follows, with worked out examples, there is a comparable practical problem. The numbers all refer to real things *within the child's experience,* and the purpose is kept sharply before him.

The practice exercises thereafter consisted, at first, not in mere numbers to manipulate, but in realistic situations within the child's own experience, calling for the manipulation of the numbers. Only after a number of such problems did the child do exercises with detached numbers, and even then the numbers were such as could readily be fitted into realistic problems.

We had to eliminate many types of exercises we had previously used. For example, in the multiplication facts, $6 \times 0, 7 \times 1$, etc. had to be omitted; no real problem calls for such senseless "multiplication." Later, in multiplication of numbers of two or more digits, a problem could well contain 1's and 0's—7×30, or 8×31, for instance. That was the time to introduce the idea that in one case there are no units to multiply, so a 0 goes into the unit column of the answer, or, in the other case, that eight 1's means simply eight units, so 8 is written in the units column of the answer. In fractions we eliminated all that were not in common use, concentrating on the simple practical ones like halves, thirds, fourths, eighths, tenths, etc. Unusual ones, like sevenths or elevenths only occur in life commonly as forms of division already known to the children, and do not have to be added, subtracted, multiplied and divided. Let the reader try to think of any life situation likely to occur in a child's experience, where he would have to add $\frac{3}{5} + \frac{2}{7} + \frac{5}{8}$, or subtract ⅛ from ⅚. And under what practical conditions would anyone want to divide ⅖ by ¾?

By keeping all the arithmetic work in the realm of the child's experience, we gave him a sense of its reality and usefulness; we gave arithmetic *meaning*. And by never expecting a child to study a process until he had reached the necessary level of maturity we gave him the confidence of success proportional to effort.

Arithmetic no longer caused large numbers of school failures and no longer occupied a disproportional part of the children's and teacher's time.

CHAPTER THREE

Reading

While we were working on the arithmetic program we were also, of course, working on the other subjects—we had to teach all the elementary subjects.

Reading was the subject in which the largest number of children failed in the first grade all over the United States, and poor reading in higher grades was a common cause of failure in other subjects—including arithmetic when children could not read their textbooks or problems. Reading was, therefore, one of the first subjects to which we directed attention.

The teaching of reading falls into two rather distinct categories: (a) the first introduction of reading, getting meaning from the simplest kind of printed material, and (*b*) the later improvement of reading facility, of ability to read well aloud, of ability to read more and more advanced literature, and the ability to read intensively for information.

In discussing this subject I shall not try to treat our work chronologically, but rather its nature and application as it was gradually evolved. Let us take, first, reading in the beginning stage.

Mental Age for Beginning

At what mental age should a child begin to learn to read? If he begins too soon from the standpoint of his own maturity, he will find it difficult and become discouraged. Indeed, the forcing of reading at too early a stage is probably by far the most common source of later difficulties. When one is discouraged, one dislikes the subject which causes discouragement. The less one likes to read, the more one will avoid reading when possible. The more one avoids reading the less progress he will make in it and the more discouraged he will become. But, on the contrary, if one learns to read easily, one is delighted with the new acquisition, wants to read more, grows in reading ability, and reads more and more, progressing as he does so.

We found that no one had yet made a scientific study of the stage of maturity necessary for ready acquisition of early reading skill. Our work being individualized in Winnetka, our schools became an excellent laboratory for the study of this problem.

We therefore measured the progress of all our children in the first two grades and compared it with their mental ages. The result was the same kind of S curve that we later found for arithmetic processes. Up to a certain point, the longer one postponed the beginning of reading the more one gained in effectiveness of learning; after that point, postponement still increased effectiveness, but to a less and less degree. We found that this point of flexion in the curve was the mental age of 6½ years. Our results were published and received wide attention.

Other investigators have since made similar studies and the results have always been approximately the same. The *mental* age of six and a half years is now the commonly accepted age in the United States for beginning formal instruction in reading. Unfortunately, most schools deal with *averages*, and think in terms of chronological age rather than mental age; by definition the *average* child who is 6½ years old chronologically has a mental age of 6½ years. But a large proportion of children in any class are not "average." Therefore in many schools children below 6½ years mentally are still being forced to try to read, and conversely, but probably harmlessly, reading is unnecessarily delayed for the more mentally mature children.

Testing Intelligence

In Winnetka we gave every child an individual intelligence test before he began the work of the first grade. This would seem to be a costly procedure, but we rather easily resolved that problem. When we had a school psychologist we had him train our kindergarten teachers in the giving of individual intelligence tests (Stanford-Binet or Kuhlman Anderson) to children of approximately 5½ to 6½ years of age. They had a natural rapport with children of this age and had, of course, taken some courses in psychology before becoming teachers. They proved apt in their learning of the testing technique, and after giving a number of tests successfully under observation, they were entrusted with the responsibility of testing children ready to enter the first grade. We closed kindergarten in the spring a week earlier than the rest of the school and during that week each kindergarten teacher tested, by appointment, each of her own pupils who was likely to enter the first grade in the autumn.

A child who showed both in the test and in his general immaturity that it would probably be more than a year before he would be ready to begin reading was usually kept in the kindergarten for another year, after a conference with the parents.

We tried—not always successfully—to disabuse parents of the idea that there was something to be ashamed of in this. They knew, we said, that some babies got their first tooth at five months of age, some at six or seven months, some not until nine months. They did not urge a dentist to lance the gums and try to force the tooth to come sooner. And eventually one child chewed as well as the other. Some children learned to talk and to walk much later than others; but if once let nature take its course, they eventually talked and walked fully as well as their more precocious fellows. Just so in reading—if we gave the child *time* to mature, and a rich variety of *experience*, he would normally learn to read very satisfactorily. If, on the other hand, we tried to make him read before he was ready, we could do irreparable harm by giving him a mental set against reading, a discouragement and dislike that could impede him ever after. And we could give concrete examples of these facts from our own records.

In kindergarten and for the children in the first grade who were not yet ready for reading, we had a rich program of experiences—care of pets, excursions, stories, picture books, dramatic play, music, rhythms, work with colors and clay, gardening, construction with large blocks and orange crates, and so on.

Today American schools generally have a "reading readiness program" of such experiences which give background and meaning to the reading that follows.

Method for Beginning

We used, from the start, the method of teaching beginners to read that is widespread in American schools and has been shown by many investigations to be most effective—first an experience; then the writing of that experience by the teacher on the blackboard or on a chart, in very short, simple sentences dictated by the children; then learning to recognize the sentences or phrases of the story. Gradually the children are taught to recognize the individual words as wholes. These we call "sight words."

As the children master a number of sight words, stories are built of these. In Winnetka (as people did in many other places) we prepared and had published primers, built of the commonest sight words, only one or two new words appearing on a page, and all being many times repeated. In selecting "sight words" we relied on studies that had been made elsewhere.

Phonics

The next step was to help children to work out, by sound, new, less usual words. This process is known as "phonics," and the sound units (an, in, as, ing, etc.) are called "phonograms." A group of words containing the same phonogram is listed and the common element is pointed out: m-an, c-an, r-an, p-an, f-an, etc. The children learn the phonograms and the different initial consonants. As they develop skill in this they can read words which are not in their sight-word list.

Meanwhile they are reading a great deal of very simple material, becoming accustomed to getting interesting meaning from the colorfully illustrated printed pages of their books. Most children, when they have the necessary maturity and background, find all this fun; they love reading and progress rapidly.

In connection with the work in phonics we found that no one had made a scientific study of which phonograms were most useful. So our first grade teachers analyzed many beginners' reading books and tabulated all the phonograms in the words. The ones we found to be most frequently used, and therefore useful, were the ones we thereafter taught. This study was published and was, as far as I know, the first piece of research in that field.

A by-product of our study of phonograms was the discovery that one of our first grade teachers had a remarkable knack and zest for this kind of study. She was a former student of mine at the San Francisco State Normal School and we had selected her to come to Winnetka as a teacher. More and more we used her in research, sending her to the University of Chicago evenings, Saturdays and summers to take courses in research and statistics. It was she (Mabel Vogel Morphett) who was secretary for the Committee of Seven and became Director of Research in Winnetka.

Group Work

We did not try to individualize fully the work of beginning reading but worked with small groups. These young children needed the direct help of the teacher. So she would work with five or six children, of about equal readiness, while the other children carried on activities that needed less supervision—drawing, block building, clay modelling, looking at picture books, feeding pets, etc. Only after children gained enough independence to read primers did they work individually on their reading.

Later Reading

The second stage in reading, after children had learned to read simple material by themselves, consisted of reading books appropriate to their ability—many books. From this stage on, we used no textbooks in reading, no anthologies. Each child read 20 to 30 or more books a year. We developed a library in each school, and from this each teacher kept changing and renewing a small library in the corner of his or her classroom. The teacher also withdrew 30 books at a time from the public library to replenish the library in the classroom. And children were encouraged, first by class visits, to use the public library independently. The children's librarian in the public library was glad to help them learn to use the catalogue and select books.

The Right Book for the Right Child

But this extensive reading occurred only to the degree that the children found it interesting. A child who selected a book because of its title or pictures and found it too difficult, and therefore uninteresting, looked for another without finishing the first; if that, and successive ones were inappropriate to his reading skill, he lost interest in reading, became discouraged, and in time came to be "a reading problem."

It soon was apparent that an essential factor of the reading program was the fitting of the books to the individual child. That started us on a long, extensive piece of research, which culminated in the preparation of uniform report slips (*see* next page).

The child filled out the blanks on the front, except "reading age," and wrote a comment on the book on the back. He handed this to his teacher each time he read a book in order to be credited with the book on his goal card. The teacher filled in the "reading age" of the child on the basis of a standardized reading test (The Stanford Achievement Test, Paragraph Meaning section) which was given to all children at the beginning of every year. These slips were collected from all three elementary schools and the junior high school, and were sorted and analyzed.

There were not enough of these reports on any one book, however, to give us definitive information about the stage of maturity at which children found it most interesting. We needed more children, many more. And, if our study was to be of use elsewhere, we needed children from many different schools in different kinds of communities.

The uniform report slips (pieces of paper about 3 × 5 inches) on which each child reported on each book he read looked like this:

	Reading Score
Complete title of book	
Full name of author	
Publisher	
Name of child	Age	Boy or girl
School	Class	Teacher

☐ One of the best books I ever read   ☐ Too easy

☐ A good book; I like it   ☐ Just about right

☐ Not so very interesting   ☐ A little hard

☐ I don't like it   ☐ Too hard

Write on the other side of this slip what you like best about this book, or why you like it.

Figure 4

Large Research Project

We saw that to collect large numbers of reports and analyze them we needed money. So, through the American Library Association, we applied to the Carnegie Corporation for a grant and got it. Then we enlisted the cooperation of 500 cities. All agreed to give their children the standardized reading test and to have the children report on books they read of their own accord. In this way we collected more than 100,000 reports.

For analyzing the reports we employed a small research staff to do this in our research office under the direction of Mabel Vogel Morphett (or Vivian Weedon *ad interim*). We found that for 1,000 different books we had a large enough number of different reports to give us significant results. On these books we had reports from 37,000 children under 800 different teachers. On several thousand other books, reports were too few on any one to be significant.

For each of the 1,000 books we prepared graphs. The most valuable of the graphs were those that showed interest in the book compared with the "reading age" of the children reading it. "Reading age" is the age of the average child making a given score on the standardized reading test. If a book was rated by a child as "one of the best books I ever read," we gave it a score, for that child, of 100. If he rated

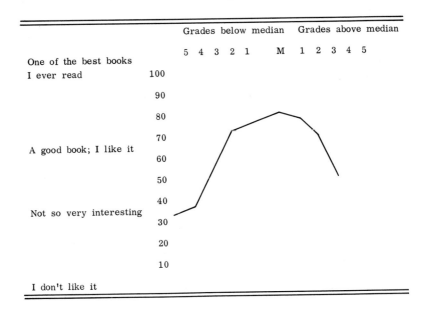

Figure 5

it "a good book—I like it," we gave it a score of 67; "not so very interesting," was 33; "I don't like it," 0. These numerical ratings made it possible to average the ratings given by many children.

For each book we found the average rating given to it by children at each successive reading age. Thus a certain book might be rated, on the average, 35 by children of reading age 8 years 6 months, 56 by children of 9 years, 78 by children of 10 years, 70 by children of 11 years of reading age, and so on. The resulting graph characteristically looked like the one depicted on page 52.

The graph almost always showed a marked rise up to a certain point, then a levelling-off, followed by a slight decline. It meant, obviously, that until a child reached a certain reading age, a particular book was relatively uninteresting, while at the right reading age, other things being equal, the book reached maximum interest value. After that it remained almost equally interesting for a year or two, and then became somewhat less so.

Selection of Books

We then asked the American Library Association to appoint a committee of expert children's librarians to rate the 1,000 books from the standpoint of their literary merit—a subjective evaluation. Each, independently, rated each book:

1. of unquestionable literary merit
2. valuable for the list, although not of high literary quality
3. not recommended—because of low literary value
4. not recommended—because of subject content

The librarians differed considerably in some of their judgments. *Huckleberry Finn*, for example, received all four ratings by one or another. But where the librarians were pretty well agreed that a book was without merit, we omitted it from our published list. (There were about 200 of these and we mimeographed separately the list of them, with their analysis, for people interested from a scientific standpoint.)

The remaining list of 800 books, deemed acceptable or excellent by most of the librarians, was published as a book, *The Winnetka*

Graded Book List,[1] for use in libraries and schools. Full data for each book were given in the following form; this example is for the English translation of the Italian classic, *Pinocchio*, obviously very popular with American children as it is with the children of Italy:

* *Pinocchio.* Collodi. Ginn. 64c.
    "This book was about a wooden boy. Once he told a lie and his nose grew so long he could not move." [2]

	No.	% Liking	Value	Age	Rdg. Grd.	4-5-6	50%	Cities	Index
Boys:	193	93	77	10.1	5.2	74%	4-5	31	1178
Girls:	221	89	89	10.0	5.4	75%	5		

The table is interpreted as follows: the asterisk at the beginning means that our committee of children's librarians considered it to be of outstanding merit. We had reports from 193 boys and 221 girls. Ninety-three per cent of the boys and 89% of the girls liked it. The average rating by boys was 77, by girls 89 (remember that 100 is "One of the best books I ever read"; 67 "A good book; I like it." Seventy-seven is therefore very high—next to the highest [95] of all books of this reading level). The median age (chronological) of boys who read and liked the book (*i.e.*, whose ratings were 67 or 100 for it) was 10.1; that of girls, 10.0. The median reading ability of the boys who liked it was that of the fifth grade (grade 5.2); the same was true of the girls (grade 5.4). Seventy-four per cent of the boys and 75% of the girls who liked it had reading ability within one year of the median (*i.e.*, of grades 4, 5, or 6). The middle 50% of the boys who enjoyed the book had reading ability equal to the average for the fourth and fifth grades in school; the middle 50% of girls had the reading ability of the average child in the fifth grade. Reports on this book came from 31 cities. The popularity index of the book, 1178, is the product of the number of children who reported liking it and number of cities from which the report came. Only four other books, in all grades, had a higher popularity index: *Tom Sawyer, 2272; *Little Women, 1873 (both seventh grade); *Heidi, 1848

---

1 Washburne, Carleton and Mabel Vogel, *The Winnetka Graded Book List*, American Library Association, Chicago, 1926. Reprinted as *What Children Like to Read*, Rand McNally and Company, Chicago, 1927.
    2 The annotations were quoted from children's comments.

(sixth grade); and *Black Beauty*, 1450 (fifth grade, like *Pinocchio*). The commentary on the book is a direct quotation of one of the children's reports, selected as most likely to appeal to other children.

The first edition (5,000 copies) of *The Winnetka Graded Book List* was sold out within three months. Then arrangements were made with a commercial publisher (Rand McNally and Company) to re-publish it under the title, *What Children Like to Read*.

Developing a Formula

Our research was not yet completed. New books for children were being continuously published. Many of them were excellent. It would have been impractical to repeat our whole study every few years, and always it would fail to include new books which had not yet attained wide availability and popularity. We needed a formula by which any book could be classified as to the reading age at which it could be easily read and enjoyed by children.

We began this part of the research by a rigorous analysis of the 800 books in *The Winnetka Graded Book List*. In what measurable ways did a book classified as "Fifth Grade," *i.e.*, reading age about 10 years, differ from one classified as "Fourth Grade" (reading age about 9 years) and from one classified "Sixth Grade" (reading age 11 years)? And so on through all levels.

We tested out about 100 hypotheses. A number of elements correlated fairly well with the reading levels of the books. Using statistical methods (Professor Karl Holzinger of the University of Chicago acting as our consultant for this), we gradually selected three factors which had the highest relation to our criterion—the reading age assigned to the books—and the least relation to each other. These were combined in what is known as a "regression equation" to yield our formula. The three factors were:

1. Out of 1,000 sample words, taken from one line on each page, scattered evenly through the book, how many were among the 1,500 most common in the English language? (We used Thorn-dike's studies [3] of the commonest words for this.)

---

[3] Thorndike, Edward L., *The Teachers Word Book*, Teachers College, Columbia University.

2. Out of the same 1,000 words, how many were different? (This was the most significant of the three measures.)
3. Out of 75 sample sentences, scattered evenly through the book, how many were not "simple," *i.e.*, had coordinate or subordinate clauses?

Each of these measures was multiplied by a fixed decimal number (statistically determined). The resulting products when added gave the reading age for the book. The accuracy of prediction was within one half year up or down, close enough for all practical purposes.

We checked the accuracy of the formula on books for which we already knew the reading age level. We also took new books, graded by the formula; and induced Winnetka children to read them and report on them. For this we deliberately chose children of a range of several years of reading age to report on the same book. The result was that the book proved most enjoyable to the children of the reading age indicated by the formula.

Satisfied that we now had a valid measure of the difficulty of children's books, we again asked help from the American Library Association, which secured us a second grant from the Carnegie Corporation. Again we asked the American Library Association to appoint a committee of children's librarians, this time to recommend the 1,500 best available books for children. What, we asked, would be the best 500 books for a small library for children? The *next 500* that should be added if possible? And the *next 500* if the library (in school or in a public library) could be expanded to 1,500 volumes?

The librarians then wrote brief annotations on each of these books, and we analyzed each book with our formula, classifying it according to the school grade in which the reading age would place it.

The resulting book was called *The Right Book for the Right Child* (John Day Co., 1932). Four years later we published a second edition, in the meantime having refined our formula to meet certain criticisms by statisticians (notably Shuttleworth). In 1940 a third edition was published, to include new books published after 1936 and to eliminate books no longer available.

These publications influenced the selection and grading of books in many libraries and schools.

The chart used in analyzing the books was also published, first by the Winnetka Educational Press, more recently (and today) by the Betts Reading Clinic.[4]

This chart, still obtainable at very low cost, contains a list of the 1,500 commonest words in the English language, spaces for all tabulations, directions for use, and the formula. It is still used by those who wish to obtain an accurate and objective measure of the reading difficulty of a children's book.

A number of other formulae have been prepared by various investigators, but the Winnetka formula has continued to be among the most valid.

Wide Reading

In Winnetka we found that by encouraging children to read books *at their own reading level*, we not only got great interest in reading, but marked progress. Repeatedly, over the years, we measured our children's reading ability with standardized tests and compared it with that of children in the United States as a whole as shown by national norms. Invariably the Winnetka children were, on the average, one to two years more advanced in their reading skill.

In many American schools there is stress on different kinds of reading: reading for general understanding, as in fiction; reading intensively for facts and concepts; "skimming," or reading very rapidly with no attention to detail, to get the gist of a book; reading for enlargement of vocabulary, and so on. In Winnetka we found such specialization to be, as a rule, quite unnecessary. In studying school subjects—especially the social studies, and even in arithmetic—children inevitably got continuous practice in intensive reading for detail. By the reading of many books, they automatically increased their vocabulary. Standardized tests on all types of reading showed that our program, without specialization, was obtaining results equal to or better than those obtained in schools where the study of reading was dissected into many parts.

Oral reading, however, did require attention, especially in the lower grades. There we had the children form little groups at about the same level of reading age. These groups were scattered about the room and in each the children took turns in reading to the others from a book

---

[4] Betts, Emmet, *Winnetka Chart for Determining Grade Placement of Children's Books*, Betts Reading Clinic, 257 W. Montgomery Ave., Haverford, Pa.

at their level. The teacher passed from group to group, helping, correcting and encouraging the children. The room was a buzz of children's voices, but not disorderly. Children got far more practice in oral reading than is possible when children, one at a time, read to the entire class.

Children needing extra help in oral reading came, one by one, to the teacher's desk during periods for silent reading, and read aloud to her individually.

Children Who Need Special Help

While these ways of individualizing the instruction in reading were, on the whole, very effective, there were, and are, always a few "reading problems," children who for one reason or another fail to progress satisfactorily. Each case of this kind has to be separately analyzed and treated. Sometimes the cause is physical—the child may have a visual defect, for example, not discovered in the routine physical examination. One of the first things to do with a child who is having serious difficulty with reading is to have his eyes examined carefully by an oculist. Or a child may not hear well; hearing should be carefully checked. A very common third cause is emotional; somehow parents or earlier teachers have unwittingly given him an emotional resistance to reading.

In Winnetka, such factors were analyzed for each child who had marked difficulty with reading. The number of such children was small, but for each an appropriate remedy had to be found and applied. Our Educational Clinic (to be described later) was our resource in meeting these problems.

Postponement of Formal Learning

Before describing the individualization of other subjects, it will be well to pause here to describe an interesting and significant experiment related primarily to arithmetic and reading. It was initiated by a mother.

Katharine Dummer Fisher was the mother of six children, four of them in school, two others approaching school age. She had been for several years the president of the Winnetka Parent-Teacher Association.

Her own early education had been in the Francis W. Parker School in Chicago and she had many advanced educational ideas. Repeatedly, as her first four children entered school, she had said to us, "We should not begin formal teaching so early. Six-year-old children do not yet have the maturity and experience needed for learning arithmetic and reading. Let them grow up more, live more, have more foundation in the realities of life before teaching them *symbols* that represent words or numbers."

Her plea appealed to me, but for several years I saw no practical way of experimenting with her idea. Parents are eager to have their children learn to read and write and calculate almost the moment they enter the first grade. Would they tolerate a wait of a year or two before their children started to learn the traditional subjects?

Then, in the spring of 1932, when Mrs. Fisher's fifth child was about to enter the first grade, she came to me with a definite proposal to meet my objections:

"Carleton," she said, "if I can get 30 families to agree to the experiment, will you organize one class made up of their six-year-olds, and postpone all systematic teaching of reading, writing and arithmetic until the middle of the second year in school?"

After some discussion, I agreed, subject to the approval of the Board of Education. She then called a meeting in her home, inviting the parents of the kindergarten in the school atended by her young son. I attended the meeting and made it clear that the experiment was at their risk. I said I did not fear the ultimate result, but that no such experiment had ever been tried under scientifically controlled condition, so I had no proof that it would succeed. Mrs. Fisher, however, had such faith in its success, spoke so eloquently, and was so much respected, that 30 pairs of parents agreed to enroll their children in the experimental class if we would organize it.

We then set up plans for scientific controls. Each child in the proposed class would be matched by two children in other classes in the three elementary schools. There would be altogether eight beginning classes in the autumn so there were more than 200 children among whom to find the sixty "controls." The "controls" for each child in the experimental class would match him in intelligence, as shown by individual intelligence tests, in age, and in the socio-economic status of the parents. The "controls" would follow our usual program and begin individual work as soon as they had reached the appropriate mental age. The children in the experimental class would do no systematic work in reading, writing or arithmetic, no matter what their mental age, until they had been in school a year and a half.

The plan was presented to the Board of Education, Mrs. Fisher attending the meeting and urging its acceptance. Since the parents concerned had all agreed and the superintendent recommended the experiment, the Board gave its consent.

For the next year and a half the experimental group was given an unusually rich program of group and creative activities and experiences. They had many excursions. They had experiences with construction—large blocks and empty orange crates—dramatic play, work with colors, clay and block building. They sang and danced. They raised pets. They played games and had story telling—both by the teacher and by each other. The teacher, Emily Forbrich, was very resourceful and gave heart and soul to the experiment.

There was *incidental* exposure to reading, writing and arithmetic. Many picture books were available, and when a child asked what a word or sentence in these books said, the teacher told him. When the children wanted to write a letter to a mother who had entertained them, they dictated it to the teacher who wrote it on the blackboard; this was sometimes voluntarily and painstakingly copied by a child. Games, blocks, etc., often involved numbers, and the teacher used these numbers freely and the children often did likewise. But no child was ever asked to try to read, write, or combine numbers and there was no systematic instruction.

At the end of a year and a half, a standardized test was given to the children in the experimental group and to all their controls. Naturally, the controls were far ahead. Only one or two of the experimental children could read even a simple primer or knew more than a few of the simplest facts of addition and subtraction. On the average the experimental children were a full year behind their controls.

Thereafter the program of the experimental class was just like that of any class. They had periods of systematic individual work, according to their own readiness, and periods for group and creative activities. They received neither more nor less time for individual work or group activities than the other classes.

At the end of the second year they were, on the average, only half a year behind their controls. At the end of the third year they were fully equal to the controls. At the end of the fourth year they were half a year ahead. By the time they entered Junior High School they were a full year ahead of the controls in reading, arithmetic and likewise on a standardized test in social studies, and to the best of our knowledge, they never lost this lead. In short, by "losing" a year and a half at the beginning, they regained that and another year as well. They learned in five and a half years what their controls learned in eight.

Mrs. Fisher's faith was justified.

Why this gain through postponement? The answer lay partly in the results of another type of control:

During the third year of the experiment, a psychologist was borrowed from the National College of Education. She was to visit five classes daily for a week, each class at a different hour each day. We told her that some kind of experiment had been conducted in one of these classes. She was to make note of each child who showed a special zest in his academic work, or who showed unusual initiative in such work, and to do the same in regard to group and creative activities. Since she could not know the children by name, each child wore a large number on his chest that week, put there ostensibly for a game introduced for the purpose. She did not know which children had been in the experiment. Since the children were accustomed to many visitors, they paid no special attention to this one.

The psychologist found that in the group and creative activities there was no significant difference between the experimental children and their controls. But in the individual work in reading, writing, spelling, arithmetic, etc., the experimental children showed much more enthusiasm for their work and much more initiative.

Four years later, when all the children were in the Junior High School and the experimental children were mixed indiscriminately with their controls and all others, we asked the "home room" or "advisory group" teachers, those who knew their groups of children most intimately, to rate every child in regard to the same factors previously used by the psychologist—zest and initiative in academic work and zest and initiative in group and creative activities. From these ratings, Mabel Morphett, Director of Research, sorted out those that applied to the experimental children and their controls, and made a comparison. The results were strikingly like those of the psychologist four years earlier: in group and creative activities the experimental children were indistinguishable from their controls, but in academic work they showed markedly more zeal and more initiative.

It must be borne in mind that the teachers who did the rating rated *all* their children and did not know that they were doing so in relation to an experiment carried out years before. And they did not even know which children had taken part in that experiment.

Our deduction from these data was this: The experimental children had spent their first year and a half having an unusually rich program of experiences. Then, with their added maturity and the foundation of experience, they began work in the "tool" subjects ordinarily undertaken a year and a half sooner. They found such work very easy, and quickly achieved mastery. This gave them confidence, a feeling of accomplishment, and eagerness to go on. The proverb "nothing succeeds like success" was applicable. Consequently, their whole attitude toward learning the skills was a positive one. This attitude, and the firm foundation, and the sense of the meaningfulness in what they were learning, persisted throughout their school lives. Results of the experiment tend to support the following conclusions:

1. A foundation of experience gives meaning to symbols.
2. Maturity gives greater success proportionate to effort.
3. Success gives confidence and a desire to go forward along the lines that have led to success.
4. This combination of factors leads to understanding, interest, and consequent effective learning.

One may ask why there was no significant difference between the experimental children and their controls in regard to non-academic group and creative activities. Our interpretation of this fact is that *all* the children, experimental and control, had from the beginning had a full and varied program of this kind and always thoroughly enjoyed it. The fact that the experimental children had, for a year and a half, more of it than the others evidently did not either increase or decrease the enthusiasm and initiative most children have in such activities.

This experiment did not have a direct effect on the Winnetka program or that of other schools. Logically, on the basis of the results, we should have postponed all systematic individual work in the tool subjects until the middle of the second year in school. But the pressure of parents' ambition to have their children begin to read and write and calculate early is very strong, and parents are not easily convinced by scientific studies. Indirectly, however, the experiment had a real effect. Much less pressure was put on early learning. Parents of slow children were encouraged not to push them.

CHAPTER FOUR

The Language Arts

The "language arts" have several interrelated aspects. Basically they involve the expression of thought in language, oral and written, for the purpose of either communication or the satisfaction of uttering one's own thoughts and feelings. For such expression it is necessary to develop technical skills.

The skills of oral expression are normally developed almost unconsciously before the child enters school, and the school's function is to give stimulus and opportunity to express oneself orally and to refine the already learned techniques—pronunciation, enunciation, use of voice, and grammatical conventions.

The refinement of oral expression was not

part of the systematic instruction in Winnetka. It was incidental to oral reports and stories and especially to creative dramatics and dramatic art, where the need for improvement in speech was obvious. It was individualized only in the sense that the correction and improvement of his speech was necessary to an individual child. The major effort was to provide ample opportunity and stimulus for oral expression; and this fell naturally into the aspects of education that we called group and creative activities, to be described in a later chapter.

Written expression, on the other hand, requires organized instruction from the start, and systematic practice. In our society a certain minimal amount of skill in written expression is a common essential. Everyone needs to be able to express his thoughts in easily legible written language, without serious violation of accepted conventions of spelling, punctuation, capitalization and grammar. It is with the development of skill in the mechanics of written expression that this chapter deals. It was this which we attempted to individualize in Winnetka from the beginning.

In discussing the individualization and development of the mechanics of written expression, we need not go into so much detail as was necessary in regard to arithmetic and reading. The basic principles were the same.

Penmanship

It was after my wife and I, accompanied by Mabel Vogel and Florence Brett, two Winnetka teachers, had spent four months in 1921–22 visiting experimental schools in England and Europe that the Winnetka faculty decided to introduce the new system of handwriting, called "manuscript writing," which was becoming widely used in England. Basing our work on that of Marjorie Wise of England, we prepared self-instructive exercises in this, and tests for both legibility and speed. It was exceedingly easy to individualize practice in this skill.

As far as the children were concerned, the new system was decidedly successful—writing was much more legible, more frequently good-looking, and no slower than the traditional "cursive" writing. The beginning of reading and writing was easier, because both used essentially the same alphabet. But parents gradually became impatient:

"When will our children learn to *write* instead of print?" they would ask.

Had we known how long and difficult it was going to be to win parents' approval of the new system I doubt if we would have introduced it. That it was an improvement we were sure. But did it make enough difference to justify the struggle? We finally had to make a compromise.

We agreed that when a child reached the fifth grade, if his manuscript writing had reached a satisfactory stage, we would, at his parents' request, teach him to join his letters and use a cursive script. We had prepared a writing scale consisting of facsimiles of children's manuscript writing from very poor to excellent. It was by comparison with this scale (patterned after the well-known Ayres scale for cursive writing) that we judged the progress of each child's quality while he wrote a paragraph, timed for speed.

One of our teachers (Julia Krenwinkel) then prepared a self-instructive textbook, *From Manuscript to Cursive*. With this as a guide, using an alphabet based on that for manuscript writing but with the letters joined, children quickly made the transition to cursive writing.

Not all parents insisted on their children making the transition and many children continued to use manuscript writing on into high school and the university.

Since, in spite of our compromise, objections were still raised, we carried out a piece of research comparing the speed of writing in manuscript versus that in cursive. There had been several such studies, but their results were inconclusive, largely because those tested in manuscript did not use it habitually. By this time there were Winnetka children who had used manuscript all through the elementary school and junior high school, and were continuing to use it in the senior high school. These we tested, at every level, comparing their speed with national standards.

We found that in the earlier grades (first through fourth or fifth) the manuscript writing was somewhat slower and more painstaking, though much more legible and attractive. By the fifth or sixth grade it was usually as fast as most children's cursive. Thereafter it was at least as fast, sometimes faster, as compared with the rate of writing of children who used cursive in other schools.

When a group of parents petitioned the Board of Education to discontinue the system of manuscript writing, the results of our investigation and a display of samples of the children's work convinced the Board that we were right, and manuscript writing with the option to make a transition to cursive is taught in Winnetka to this day.

Spelling

In English the extreme irregularities of spelling, resulting from the agglomeration of Anglo-Saxon, Latin and old French and from various developments of sounds, make spelling a difficult subject for many children. One sound, like the *u* in "prune," may be spelled *u* (truth), *ou* (route), *o* (to), *oo* (too), *wo* (two), *ue* (true), *eu* (pneumonia), *ew* (brew), *ough* (through), etc. A combination like *ough* may be pronounced with the obscure open sound (enough), with the long sound of *o* (though), or the short *o* (thought), or like *ow* as in "plough," etc. Letters may be silent (p)sychology, list(t)en, ca(l)m, kil(n), de(b)t. These are only a few samples of the hundreds and hundreds of irregularities in English spelling.

Spelling is, therefore, largely a matter of thousands of relatively independent memories. Many children learn it rather easily, unconsciously remembering how words look on the printed page (writing in the "manuscript" style helps to bring out the similarity between what one writes and what one reads). But for some children no system ever devised succeeds in making them anywhere nearly perfect in their spelling. This is still true after more than half a century of research by many investigators.

In Winnetka the system we devised was never wholly satisfactory, but it saved a great deal of time for the children who learned to spell easily, and it improved the spelling of those who found spelling difficult. And it was individualized. Briefly, it consisted of the following steps:

First, we combined the best available lists of the words other investigators had found to be the ones most commonly used by children of the elementary schools. Second, we tested these words on many children and found which ones were most often spelled correctly by children in the third grade, which of the remainder were usually correctly spelled by children in the fourth grade—and so on up the scale.

This gave us a graded list of words, listed in the order of difficulty.

From this list it was possible, later, to make a graded scale with samples of words from each level, and to make seven or eight equivalent forms of the scale so that every year a child's general level of spelling ability could be measured.

Before we made the scale, however, we had a spelling textbook published [1] with the complete list of commonest words arranged according to the grade level at which most children spelled them correctly. At the beginning of the term the teacher spent ten minutes a day dictating all the words assigned to her grade to the entire class, twice through to catch accidental cases of correct spelling. The children did no studying for this preliminary test. Then in each child's spelling textbook the teacher checked all the words which that child had misspelled. Those checked words constituted each child's individual spelling list for the semester.

Children were then divided into pairs. After a child had studied a small group of checked words (perhaps ten) in his list, he asked his partner to dictate them to him, and together they corrected his work. Then they reversed, the first child now dictating his partner's words. Toward the end of the semester, each child dictated to his partner all the words he had studied during the semester. These papers were corrected by the teacher. Words that were correctly spelled were marked "OK" in red ink, in a blank column that was provided in the spelling textbook. The words still misspelled became the first words to study on the next semester's list. Until a child had two successive red "OK's" after a word, it remained in his list for study.

At first, the results were very gratifying. The general level of spelling ability rose from below the national standard to about 20% above it. But after a few years, a strange thing happened: To refute many criticisms from parents, we gave a standardized test in spelling to compare the performance of Winnetka children with that of others over the United States. To our dismay, our children's spelling ability had dropped to that of children in general, or even lower.

What had happened was that both teachers and children had become utterly bored with the system. Mechanically, it was good. Psychologically, when the newness wore off, it was very dull.

Then individual teachers asked if they might devise their own sys-

---

[1] Washburne, Carleton, *Individual Speller*, World Book Co., Yonkers-on-Hudson, New York, 1921.

tems. We agreed, then tested results. Regardless of what system they used, spelling improved—while the system was fresh and new.

It was then that we made our scales and said: "We will measure the general spelling ability of all children at the beginning and end of each semester. We will then tabulate the *growth* in spelling ability of each child in each class. In terms of average *growth* of the children during the semester in each class we will list the classes in rank order, from best to poorest. Each teacher will be told the rank of his class, and thereby be able to see how effective his own teaching has been."

This worked. Teachers used many parts of the old system—the graded lists of words, the idea of allowing children to work on individual lists, etc.—but they used their ingenuity to find ways of varying procedures, of getting lively interest in words on the part of the children, in devising games. Those who were most successful one semester usually did less well the next one, for they tended to stereotype the successful method. Those who did poorly one semester did much better the next one, for they found new and interesting ways to improve their records.

No method, however efficient it may be by scientific measures, remains effective if it becomes stereotyped, loses variety, does not call forth interest and zest on the part of children.

English Composition

The subject of written English (or any other language) divides itself naturally into at least three parts: creative expression, communication (which may or may not involve creative expression), and the mechanics of writing. While the ideal composition involves all three aspects, there is a necessity for separating them at times in the learning process.

Creative expression should be as free from mechanical hindrances as possible, and is necessarily individual. It begins as early as the first grade (and orally, much earlier). When children tell little stories and the teacher writes to their dictation in the first grade we get the beginning of written creative expression. But before the child can himself write creatively he must know at least enough of the mechanics of writing to form words and sentences. Creativeness is temporarily subordinate.

This is likewise true of communication—letters, reports on what one has done or read or plans to do, and so on. But it is in writing for communication (and the sharing of creative writing is a kind of communication) that the niceties of form become important. Incorrect spelling, illegible writing, the failure to follow conventions of capitalization and punctuation interfere with the clarity of communication and offend the reader as would bad manners.

In either case, the purpose (creation or communication) should be the goal, clearly evident to the child, giving motive to the arduous acquisition of skill in the mechanics of writing.

In Winnetka we tried to keep this principle in mind. We also recognized, very early, that the acquisition of the mechanics was much easier for some children than for others, that it required varying amounts of practice, and that it needed testing.

The methods of teaching penmanship and spelling, both mechanical aspects of writing, have already been described. It was necessary, also, to prepare self-instructive materials and diagnostic tests for learning to punctuate and to capitalize: the uses of the period, the comma, the question mark, when one begins a word with a capital letter, at the beginning of a sentence or a quotation, for the names of persons and places, titles of books, etc.

The preparation of these materials followed approximately the same procedures as that for arithmetic—"programming": an analysis of the elements to be taught; experimentation as to the level at which they could be most efficiently taught; the writing of simple, self-instructive explanations followed by practice exercises (few for those who needed few, more for those who needed more); means for self-correction; and complete diagnostic tests.

Such materials were prepared, tried on the children, revised in the light of experience, then rewritten. This process has continued to the present day.

Although children were continually writing both for creative expression and for communication, we tried to keep the *practice* in the mechanics separate. Of course, the written composition had to *use* the mechanics, and formed the motive for learning them. But when a child, full of sensitive pride and eager for approval, brought a story or poem to the teacher, the teacher gave first attention to what he was trying to say, not to how he had written it. His creative effort got appropriate commendation, however bad his penmanship, spelling or punctuation might be. Those weaknesses were being corrected elsewhere.

When, however, what the child wrote was, in essence, especially good, the teacher might say: "This is a beautiful story, but its clothes are very ragged. Wouldn't you like to try now to dress it up? Look it over and see if you can find how many words you did not remember how to spell, or what punctuation would make it easier to understand. Then I will look it over again and help you to correct it. And when it is all corrected you may copy it in your *best* handwriting, so that it will look as beautiful as it is."

Or, if it was a letter or an article for a school publication, or a report on some activity, the teacher might say: "I think I understand this, and what you are trying to say is good. But the way you have written it makes it hard for other people to read. And as you know, there are ways that people agree are the right ways to spell a word, right ways to capitalize and right ways to punctuate. Before sending this, let's make it *right* in all ways."

With many variations on this theme, the teacher tried to help each child to apply the mechanics he was learning, to use them in his composition, to see the need for learning them. But *never* should she let the mechanics suppress creative effort, or discourage a child from writing freely.

As an encouragement to composition, the lower classes maintained a classroom "journal"—an artistically covered collection of the most interesting and well-written compositions. The children themselves browsed through this, and their parents (parents visited the schools informally and frequently) always enjoyed looking through it for their children's work. In the upper grades there was a mimeographed periodical and in the junior high school the children printed both a news weekly and a more literary periodical, both illustrated.

Grammar

Grammar, as such, was postponed, in due course, to the sixth grade and the junior high school. In the earlier grades, of course, gross errors were corrected, but simply by saying, "This is not the way people say what you are trying to say—the right way is like this," followed by the correct grammatical form.

When children began a systematic study of grammar we first used the customary logical presentation. We found that many children disliked it and consequently learned poorly. So we reversed our method. In preparing self-instructive teaching material we selected (from the research of others) the most common grammatical errors in English speech and writing. We graded these in terms of the number and difficulty of the grammatical rules which were needed to explain the error, from "The men was going," to "between you and I." The former required knowledge of subject and verb, singular and plural, and agreement of subject and verb. The latter required knowledge of prepositions (they are not always easy to identify), knowledge of pronouns, recognition of the object of a pronoun, and this recognition even when the pronoun is separated from its preposition by a conjunction.

At the beginning of each exercise, we presented both the common error with which it was going to deal and the correct form:

He done it.
He did it.

"Why is the first form wrong and the second form right?" we asked. Then followed the explanation and the practice exercises.

No grammar was taught that did not have this sort of direct usefulness, a use that children approaching adolescence and naturally desirous of conformity could see for themselves.

Some of our teachers were alarmed by the omission of many grammatical terms and rules commonly taught elsewhere. Our children, when they left junior high school, went to a senior high school under another administration, it will be remembered, and three-fourths of the children attending it came from more conventional, although very good, schools. The teachers of English and the teachers of Latin and modern languages would expect all the children to have been taught English grammar before they entered the senior high school, and our children would be at a disadvantage.

Those of us who were convinced of the rightness of our approach said, "Let's wait and see." We watched, in some suspense, the results of our children's first year in the senior high school, after the first of our classes which had learned grammar the new way had left us. The senior high school cooperated by letting us have the grades of all children, from all schools, in English and foreign languages. The results fully vindicated our faith—the Winnetka children, on the whole, did decidedly *better* work than the children with conventional training. We followed successive classes in the same way, year after year, and almost without exception the children taught grammar *functionally*, in Winnetka, were superior to the rest in both English and other languages in the senior high school.

The reason is clear: The other children had half-learned a multitude of rules. They forgot much and had to be given extensive reviews. They were uncertain of themselves, and many had developed the feeling that grammar was difficult or even disagreeable. The Winnetka children, on the other hand, knew well what they knew. Their feet were on solid ground and they had confidence. Most of them had thoroughly enjoyed their study of grammar and brought to their later work an eagerness to learn. Such rules and terms as were new to them they picked up from the reviews being given to the other children, and they built them on the solid foundation they already had.

We published our grammar book, *Functional Grammar*.[2] Some years later, during the Second World War, the United States Armed Forces Institute was examining all school textbooks for those which could be used in the armed forces for self-improvement by the enlisted men. From among all books on grammar, the Winnetka book was chosen. I was invited to Washington to rewrite the exercises in terms of the experiences of our armed forces; we had deliberately written them in terms of the experiences of junior high school children. I could not afford the time, so I sent the principal author of the textbook (Agnes Spangler), one of our junior high school teachers.

She learned army ways of talking and army experiences and rewrote the exercises, following, however, exactly the same pattern of presentation as we had used in Winnetka. The book was published [3] (enlivened with clever cartoon-like illustrations) and became one of the most popular of all the Armed Forces Institute publications. More than half a million copies were sold to the armed forces.

So strong are tradition and inertia, however, that no commercial

---

[2] Spangler, Agnes and Carleton Washburne, *Functional Grammar*, Winnetka Educational Press, Winnetka, Ill., 1940.

[3] Spangler, Agnes, *English Grammar* (A Self-Teaching Course Based on *Functional Grammar*, edited by Carleton Washburne), published for United States Armed Forces Institute, Madison, Wis., The Macmillan Company, N.Y., 1943.

publisher has yet been willing to publish *Functional Grammar* as a school textbook.

Conclusion

Arithmetic, reading, and the language arts (penmanship, spelling, written English, and grammar), these are the "tool subjects," skills in which all children need to acquire a high degree of mastery in our present society. These were the subjects which we sought to teach on and individual basis, the only basis possible for reasonable mastery by all children. The techniques—self-instruction, self-correction, diagnostic testing, and individual rates of progress—came to be known as "The Winnetka Plan." But, as will be seen in what follows, the individualizing of instruction in these subjects was only one aspect of the work in Winnetka. We wanted not only to give each child the tools, the academic skills, he needed, but also knowledge, understanding, appreciation, desirable attitudes and interests. We wanted to help him develop his personal and social potentialities. To attain these objectives, different kinds of procedures, facilities and activities were necessary. It is with these activities that we deal in the chapters that follow.

CHAPTER FIVE

The Social Studies

In the earlier years in Winnetka we attempted to individualize the social studies as we were doing with subjects requiring skill, such as arithmetic and reading, although social studies dealt not so much with skill as with knowledge and understanding.

What knowledge in this field was essential for everyone? Many investigators had analyzed the common needs in arithmetic and spelling. The amount of skill needed in reading was less definite, but it was easy to know the minimum amount that all literate people must have. But what is the minimum amount of knowledge of history and geography necessary for intelligent living in the world today? If we could identify this we would have a base for teaching and testing and could make sure that each child, at his own rate, attained that knowledge.

How does one use history and geography in life? What facts, names and places are of so much importance to *everyone* that a person will be handicapped without them?

We had much discussion in our group meetings. We tried many hypotheses and discarded one after another as it failed to identify specifically the facts that everyone needed to know. Finally we found a tenable theory.

Allusions

Every intelligent person in our society reads newspapers, magazines, books. News items, articles and stories assume a certain basic knowledge of history and geography on the part of readers. When an article mentions Rome, for example, there is no explanation of what "Rome" means. The writer does not say, "Rome, a city in Italy on the Tiber River, once the capital of the western civilized world"; if he did he would be assuming that the reader knew what "Italy" meant and where the Tiber was. If he doubted the reader's knowledge of "Italy" he would have to explain it in terms of Europe and the Mediterranean Sea, and assume that the reader knew those terms. And so on. It is evident that some basic framework of knowledge of both history and geography is assumed by all writers and is necessary for all readers. What is that framework?

Our method of finding the answer was as arduous as it was direct and simple. We examined a wide sampling of periodical literature and noted every reference to a person, place or event that was *not* explained, where the writer assumed that the reader was acquainted with it. We selected periodicals rather than books because the number and variety of books was endless. We selected types of periodicals—newspapers from the most serious to the most sensational, magazines from widely read serious and literary magazines to the most popular. To avoid seasonal or temporary emphasis, we selected issues evenly for each month of the year, and distributed our study evenly among those published in each of the past 20 years, before, during and after the First World War.

The Winnetka teachers divided themselves into teams, each examining certain periodicals for certain years, using the public libraries for the bound volumes of the periodicals. Each person, place or event to which unexplained allusion was made, was recorded on a separate slip, with its source.

When this part of the investigation was completed we found ourselves snowed under with thousands and thousands and *thousands* of slips of paper, each with its "allusion." We had done all this work voluntarily, evenings and weekends, on top of all our other work. The sight of these quantities of data awaiting sorting and interpretation appalled us. We asked for a research grant—and got it (from The Commonwealth Fund, a Rockefeller subsidiary).

With this money we employed a full-time research assistant and a secretary for a year. By the end of the year the data were sorted and tabulated. The research findings were published in the 22nd Yearbook, Part II, of the National Society for the Study of Education.[1]

Unfortunately, the pressure of other work and the time limit for publication prevented the analyzing and classifying of the data. We presented them in strict order of frequency of ocurrence. This resulted in some amusing distortions:

Rudyard Kipling just outranked Christians (including Christianity)
But Christ (including Jesus) just outranked Napoleon Bonaparte
William J. Bryan just outranked Shakespeare
Princeton University outranked Julius Caesar
Charles Dickens outranked Denmark

To assume from such a tabulation that, from a teaching standpoint, these were reliable measures of the relative importance of the topics was absurd. As a consequence, this study had, as far as I am aware, no influence outside of Winnetka.

In Winnetka, however, we proceeded to work over and classify the data. The findings were exceedingly useful. For example, in ancient history the order of the highest ranking "allusions" was: Greece; Christians (including Christianity); Christ (including Jesus); Julius Caesar; Palestine; Mediterranean; Athens.

In English literature before the nineteenth century, the highest rank

---

[1] Washburne, Carleton W., *A Basic Fact Course in History and Geography*, in the 22nd Yearbook of the National Society for the Study of Education, Part II; Public School Publishing Company, 1923 (now University of Chicago Press, Chicago, Ill.).

went to Shakespeare, while for the nineteenth century, the order was Robert Browning, Charles Dickens, Thomas Carlyle, etc.

In the geography of Europe the top ranking allusions were, in order, to England, France, London, Germany, Paris, Italy, etc.

With this kind of information now available, we planned our social studies curriculum. We decided to devote the time of the fourth, fifth and sixth grades to a history of Western Civilization, more or less chronological, with all the pertinent geographical and sociological factors included. We continued in the junior high school with a similar treatment of what, in time, became the United States, with special emphasis, in the eighth grade, on government and civic education.

For the fourth, fifth and sixth grades we had to write our own books—American schools usually devoted only one year to "Old World backgrounds," and gave American history two overlapping treatments. Louise Mohr, who had been my assistant and successor at the San Francisco State Normal School, had been brought to Winnetka to develop our program in science, but was taken off from this work to write our social studies textbooks. For the Junior High School we used the Social Science Series prepared by Harold Rugg and Associates, since it fitted our plans admirably.

Miss Mohr spent years of scholarly research in writing our material and produced a series of small, interesting and authentic books.[2] In these she was guided, as to facts to be surely included, by our study of allusions. Perhaps unknowingly, therefore, those schools which used her books did profit by our study.

While in our tests and map work we kept for years to the principle of individual progress and mastery, and used the study of "allusions," we did not fully individualize the social studies as a whole. One reason was that we wanted the life of the people of other times and places to be as real as possible to the children. This involved class trips to museums and libraries, much class discussion and dramatization, and a wealth of visual materials—slide projections, motion pictures, mounted illustrations from

---

[2] Mohr, Louise M., *Social Study Series: History and Geography* (ed. by Carleton Washburne and Willard W. Beatty), Rand McNally and Company, Chicago, 1928 to 1940. The series included: *Days Before Houses, Egyptians of Long Ago, Babylonia and Assyria, Palestine and Syria, Greeks and Persians of Long Ago, In the Days of the Romans.* Other volumes on *Why We Believe As We Do, The Middle Ages, Building a New Civilization in Europe, I and II, The Renaissance,* and *Exploration and Discovery* were published by The Winnetka Educational Press, Winnetka, Ill.

such periodicals as The National Geographic, posters and charts made by the children individually or, more often, in groups, and so forth.

Furthermore, at that time we were organizing our "group and creative activities" program (soon to be described) and we found that the social studies gave us the best base for this work. For that purpose, as well as the above, it was essential that the class as a whole be working on a common topic. The *reading* the children did on the topic was adapted to their individual levels of ability to a large extent, and for a long time they were individually tested on the essential facts.

After some years, however, we discovered that the program in social studies, flanked by the group and creative activities, gave our children such a fund of basic knowledge that the detailed facts did not require individual tests. On standardized tests we found that our children were much better informed than American children in general.

We then recognized that whereas skill subjects, like arithmetic, reading, spelling, and language, required intensive practice, subjects that involved not skill but knowledge and understanding, like social studies and elementary science, were readily learned incidentally in a rich program of activities, visual aids, reading and discussion. That some learned more than others was inevitable and harmless—the amount of knowledge and understanding that can be used by individuals is highly variable and immeasurable. We felt our children were getting not only the bare essentials necessary for everyone, but much, much more.

CHAPTER SIX

Science

The science program in Winnetka was never individualized in the elementary grades, and only partially so in the junior high school. Research as to the commonly needed knowledge in science had been done previously—it was my doctoral dissertation at the University of California. Logically, we should have attempted individualization of instruction in the common essentials of knowledge of science as we at first did in the social studies. That we did not do so was probably due to circumstances.

There was, already in 1919, a highly qualified special teacher of science, Mary Payne, who was giving the children in all three schools excellent experience in nature study and other aspects of elementary science. All our time and energy were being devoted to sub-jects which were causing failures and frustrations, and there was no pressure to change the quite satisfying science program. When Miss Payne left we sent for my former assistant in science instruction at the San Francisco State Normal School, Louise Mohr, primarily to take over and develop what Miss Payne had been doing. But the need for Miss Mohr's help in developing the social studies program, as described in the preceding chapter, was more urgent and she was diverted into that field. Then we brought in Frederick Reed as specialist and advisor in elementary science and in group and creative activities. But after a year or so we needed him as principal of one of our elementary schools.

By that time our experience with the social studies was leading us to the conclusion that for content subjects like science and social studies, the individualizing techniques that were essential to the mastery of skills were not really necessary—the common essentials were learned inci-dentally in a rich activities program with a wide variety of experiences. Thereafter our efforts were to provide the experiences and stimulate the interest in science rather than to give systematic instruction in scientific facts and principles.

The science curriculum in the early grades, through third, consisted in giving children experience with nature: field trips, growing plants, caring for pets from fish to rabbits and setting hens, stories, pictures, and other visual aids, and simple experiments. These were all informal, and without pre-planned sequence. They tended to develop out of children's questions and teachers' special interests, and experiences children were having out of school. The advisors in group and creative activities, especially Frances Presler and Florice Tanner, helped and encouraged the teachers in this work and provided them with audio-visual aids and museum items.

In fourth grade, as a first step in science, the children took up basic elements of geology and astronomy, using as a base a book written by my wife and me with Frederick Reed, founded on my earlier research as to the questions most commonly asked by children of that age level.[1] This book formed a systematic starting point for exploration and a

---

[1] Washburne, Carleton and Heluiz Chandler Washburne (in collaboration with Frederick Reed), *The Story of Earth and Sky*, Appleton-Century-Crofts, 1933 (at first an earlier version was used).

variety of experiences, collateral reading, trips to museums and to the planetarium, motion pictures and slides, and class discussions and reports.

In fifth grade, health and physiology were systematically introduced. They had, of course, been dealt with earlier as need or opportunity arose, but in fifth grade they became an organized course. It was in this grade, as part of this course, that we took up the essential biological facts of human reproduction. In the earlier grades the teachers had simply answered, frankly and without evasion, any questions children asked dealing with sex. But in grade five it was natural to include human reproduction along with and as a part of instruction regarding human physiology.

This subject was developed more fully in the junior high school. Here all children took two science courses, one in the physical sciences, the other in biology. Sex education became an obvious part of the biology course, and could be dealt with more fully and in its relation to all plant and animal life than was possible in the fifth grade; and the social and psychological aspects of sex could be discussed. Since boys and girls had physical education separately, it was administratively simple to schedule the biology classes to alternate with those in physical education, thereby bringing about a segregation of boys and girls without seeming to do so to give sex education. It was felt that children in early adolescence would talk and ask questions about sex with less inhibitions if in segregated classes. For a while the girls were taught by a woman, the boys by a man. But thereafter for many years a well-qualified woman, Elizabeth Meadows, usually taught boys as well as girls.

The sex education, as a normal part of the biology course, was handled in such an objective and scientific manner that the children accepted it in the same spirit, asked many questions and discussed freely.

During the first three or four years, some parents were shocked or distressed by the frankness of the instruction. A small minority tried to get the Board of Education to abolish this part of the biology course. But a far greater number expressed gratitude and appreciation, and before long all expression of opposition had ceased. The story of the early struggle and the ways in which opposition was ended is told rather fully in A *Living Philosophy of Education.*[2]

---

[2] Washburne, Carleton, A *Living Philosophy of Education*, John Day Co., 1940, pp. 84-92.

The above described program in science in the Winnetka schools remained intact in its major outlines for more than 30 years. Then when Sidney Marland became superintendent the entire science curriculum was revolutionized and vastly improved, as will be seen in Part Two. The sex education aspect, nevertheless, has continued as an integral part of the science curriculum.

To the best of my knowledge, the Winnetka Public Schools were the first public school system in the United States or elsewhere to include systematic sex education in either the elementary or the junior high school curriculum for all children.

CHAPTER SEVEN

Group and Creative

Activities

We now come to a second and essential part of the Winnetka program, the group and creative activities. Here adaptation to individual differences of children takes on a different meaning and requires different techniques. For the skill subjects of arithmetic, reading and the mechanics of the language arts there were certain minimal requirements where, sooner or later, children had to achieve uniformity. One does not want originality in spelling or in the basic conventions of punctuation or in the knowledge that $6 \times 9 = 54$ or in the essential meaning of a printed page. Therefore, for these aspects of learning, adaptation to individual differences involves, primarily, variation in *time* to fit each child—when he shall begin a unit of work, in accordance with his own maturity and experience, and how rapidly he shall accomplish it. There may also be differentiation as to the method of teaching.

On the other hand, in life there are many aspects of learning where wide differences in accomplishment and emphasis are harmless, desirable and even necessary. There is the need for variation in interests and activities; initiative, originality and creativeness are highly desirable in many fields. For such types of learning there are no standard measures. In the school program what is needed is the time, the facilities, and the encouragement for the development of the *different* potentialities of each child, and the practice of coordinating these different interests and abilities with those of his fellows.

The child who is gifted, who has capacities high above those of most others, intellectually, creatively or socially, must be encouraged, inspired and facilitated in developing these individual potentialities; and the child who is far below the "average" in any of these fields must be given the chance to achieve the minimum necessary for effective living and the encouragement and opportunity to develop highly the best of his more limited but real potentials with confidence and self-respect.

The group and creative activities in the Winnetka program served these needs. They belonged not to the category of set minimum needs common to all, with variation in time for their fulfillment, but to the second category. In them our concern was for what each child derived from the experience and adapted to his own interests, abilities and maturity, not, as in the case of the tool subject, the time required to achieve a set standard of mastery.

Because we discuss these two categories of the program separately it has often been assumed that there is sharp separation between them, a dichotomy between the individual work in the tool subjects and the group and creative activities. A *distinction* between (*a*) individual mastery of the commonly needed skills and (*b*) the opportunity to develop one's own personality in the group and creative activities does exist, as such distinctions exist in life; but there is continuous interplay and interdependence between the two major aspects of the program.

In this chapter we shall deal with the group and creative activities in Winnetka under the headings of projects, economic enterprises, art, music, electives and clubs, physical education and recreation, and democratic citizenship. Actually, *these are all interrelated with each other;*

and they give motive and meaning to the tool subjects and give them practical application.

Projects

In Winnetka, projects were group undertakings, sometimes by small groups but usually by a whole class in the elementary schools. They usually lasted from a month to four or five months, and were allotted one to two hours each day. What they were can be best explained by two or three concrete examples.

A Project in the First Grade

Our children in the first grade tried to become familiar with their surroundings. Let us say, for example, that a class had jointly dictated a letter of thanks to a mother for having donated a setting hen to the class. The teacher might say, "How will this letter get to her?" Children would answer, "You put a stamp on it and mail it." "Where do we mail it?" "There is a box on the corner where you put it," would be the reply. "But then," asks the teacher, "how does that get to her?" "The mailman brings it." "Does he take it out of the box, with all the other letters, and take each one to the person for whom it is meant?" Some think this is the case. "But there are letters in the box for many people in many different houses, some far away. How could one man get all these letters to the right person? Let's go see."

The class would then go to the mail box, deposit the letter, and watch, at the correct hour, the collection. They then follow the mail collector to the post office. They see letters postmarked and sorted, and they see each letter carrier take his own pile and start out to deliver the letters in one section of the town. They see the man who will deliver *their* letter and talk to him.

Back in school this is the subject of much discussion. The children dictate a story about it. Then, spontaneously, some child says, "Let's play post office." In no time they organize themselves into mail collectors, post office men and carriers. They "write" pretend letters and "mail" them. First the desks serve as collection boxes, post office, houses.

Soon, however, they want their post office to be more realistic. They go to the fruit store and collect orange crates. With these they build a "post office" in one end of their room.

The construction, and refinements of construction, engage them in more and more creative activity. For some days they are content to build, then to play in the "post office" and to collect and deliver "letters" from each other and to each other. Then, perhaps, the teacher suggests that they have such a good post office that the school could use it. They eagerly accept the idea. Small groups (to give each other courage) go to the other classes in the school, and say: "We have a post office in our room. If you have any letters to send to people in the school, we will collect them and take them where you want them to go." They say the same to the principal. Each afternoon before they go home they go to all classrooms and the office of the principal to collect the letters or messages. Next morning, with the help of the teacher, they sort these in their "post office," and different "carriers" then deliver the mail to all classes and the principal.

This whole "project" may last a month or two. When the teacher feels that it is no longer calling forth creative ideas and may soon lose its savor, she gives the class another and different experience which leads to a wholly new project. Or, she may build on the first by discussing what happens to letters for other cities, then take them to see a train bring and take mail. The question of trains will soon engross them. The one-time post office is dismantled and forms a train. There are conductor, engineer, and passengers—and a bright new project is underway.

A Project in Science—Fourth Grade

Let us glance at two other examples of projects. Here is a fourth grade project:

The children have been learning about the solar system and stars. They have been to the Planetarium in Chicago, going with the teacher in the school bus. They have had two "star gazing" parties in the evening—on one of these the teacher, using a flashlight with long narrow beam, has pointed out the constellations. They have seen pictures of them at school. On another evening one of the fathers who has a small telescope mounted in his garden has let the children look at the craters of our moon, at the moons of Jupiter, and, fortunately visible the same evening, the rings of Saturn.

In discussion of the differences among the stars one sees in the four seasons, they have, in class, learned about the zodiac and why the ancients thought the sun moved from one sign to another. This has led to two kinds of construction.

First, the children, with the help of the school custodian and a ladder, suspend a large yellow ball from the center of the ceiling, to represent the sun. Children, each representing a planet and wearing a sign naming it, push all seats to the walls and circle the sun, maintaining the order and rate of travel of each. That takes considerable calculation and the teacher has to help. The principal of the school, Frederick Reed, had a good deal of knowledge of astronomy and was called in from time to time to help when the teacher's knowledge was inadequate to the children's needs. One boy has the idea that the signs worn by the children to indicate the planets should show the relative sizes of the planets. Using the earth as the unit, circles of proportionate diameter are drawn on the signs. At first they want the sun to be in proportion, but they find that the circles for the planets would then be too small to make or to be seen, and abandon that idea.

"Well," says a girl, "we could make the distances right." "Can we?" asks the teacher. "Let's see."

When they find that to make distances proportionate to the size of the planets they have drawn they would have to go far, far beyond the classroom, they are not daunted. Using little clay balls, a baseball, a soccer ball, and balloons, they get the sizes proportionate, then they begin placing their balls at the right distances—in the classroom, out in the school yard, out in the village, and, for Neptune and Pluto, they take the school bus to the right distance out in the country.

Back in class, they resume their play of the revolution of the earth around the sun. This leads to a second kind of construction. They decide to paint a mural around the classroom representing the signs of the zodiac. On long strips of wrapping paper, which they attach to the wall above the blackboard, the children, in groups, standing on chairs, paint the signs. (We use calcimine paint for such things, since it costs very little and is easy to apply.) Now as a child, representing the earth, circles the sun, he sees the sun in the successive signs of the zodiac.

This project, from beginning to end, with ideas and embellishments too numerous to mention, with reading, pictures, and discussions, lasted most of the semester.[1]

---

[1] This project obviously took place before the days when space travel became a real prospect. Today it would inevitably include this possibility.

A Project in Social Studies—Sixth Grade

Now a glance into a sixth grade: In social studies the children had been studying the Middle Ages and the building of cathedrals. In their reading they found some medieval legends. One Christmas legend especially attracts them, "Why the Chimes Rang," and they decide to dramatize it. Elaborating freely on the legend, taking turns in playing the various parts, improvising their speeches and learning to coordinate them—no two "casts" do it exactly alike—they develop a play.

But then they want scenery. Before long we see the windows edged with cardboard cut into Gothic arches. Then colored tissue paper makes stained glass windows. Other properties are added—and behold! The classroom is transformed into the interior of a cathedral in which the drama is re-enacted.

It is almost Christmas, so the children think the rest of the school would like to see the performance in the school assembly. The cathedral in the classroom is dismantled and the "stained glass windows" are mounted on the stage in the assembly room, with electric lights placed behind them. A beautiful "stained glass" rose window is added and mounted high in the back center of the stage. Other properties are constructed.

Throughout the school the children have been learning various Christmas songs, and certain of these, of medieval origin, have been learned by all, in preparation for the presentation the sixth grade is going to give.

The last day of school before the Christmas holidays, the entire school of four hundred children comes together for the Christmas exercises. The sixth grade presents the play, and all the audience sing the appropriate songs at the right moments.

These three samples—the post office in the first grade, the star-study in the fourth, the sixth grade play—are only three of literally hundreds that might be selected from the projects of various classes and years.

Dramatic Expression

As illustrated in the first and sixth grade projects, drama plays an important part in the group and creative activities. There are three successive phases of dramatic expression—dramatic play, creative dramatics, and dramatic art. Dramatic play, as in the first grade example of playing post office, has no organized structure, no plot, no idea of performance for an audience; it is a natural form of expression of all young children: playing house, playing school, playing train, and so on endlessly. It is play living. This is the appropriate dramatic expression in kindergarten and the first two or three grades.

Creative dramatics may begin at about the third or fourth grade level, around the age of nine, and continue indefinitely. It usually originates, as in the sixth grade example given above, with a story or an experience and a deliberate plan to dramatize it. It grows, with continuous variations and suggestions by the children, as it goes along. It is not written out and parts are improvised by each participant, not memorized. But with guidance by the teacher it assumes form and unity. If it seems to be turning out well, plans are made for presenting it to an audience in another class, an assembly, or a parents' meeting. Children take turns in playing the different parts, each giving his own interpretation in words and actions that feel appropriate to him. These are later criticized or approved by the rest. For the culminating performance, the class chooses the actors for the various parts according to their judgment as to who plays each part most convincingly. The children themselves plan and work out costumes and scenery. The teacher suggests, as needed, improvements and ways of getting across to the audience— voice, diction, position of actors when speaking, and so on.

Dramatic art belongs at the junior high school level and higher. Here a real play is used or the children write one. Parts may be memorized. The performance to an audience is a goal from the beginning. Skill in the technique of acting, including voice and diction, staging and properties, is developed. Attention is given to scenery, lighting, costuming, make-up, publicity and business management, to assure a successful performance.

These three forms and their educational purposes are much more fully discussed and illustrated in chapter 15 of A *Living Philosophy of Education*. In the present summary we merely want to suggest the very important place dramatic expression has in the group and creative activities.

Common Elements in All Projects

No two classes ever repeated, exactly, the projects of preceding ones. Children, accustomed to this kind of activity, burst into spontaneous suggestions as to the way the project shall develop. But in all projects there were certain common elements.

First, there was a base of knowledge and experience, from trips, visual aids (such as slides, mounted pictures, films, etc.), from reading or being read to, and from discussion.

Second, there were no subject-matter boundaries. The experiential base, however, was usually the social studies, science or literature.

Third, there was no attempt during the hours devoted to the project to *teach* any specific skill or to have the children learn any specified facts. Incidental learning, a very great deal of it, inevitably took place, but it was purely incidental and never the primary purpose.

Fourth, there was much creative acivity—it was the creative ideas and work of the individuals in the class that brought about the entire development of the project.

Fifth, there was cooperation. The children learned to coordinate their ideas with those of their fellows and they learned to cooperate with each other toward a common end.

Sixth, all aspects of the schoolwork were freely used—reading, of course, arithmetic frequently, composition from time to time, art very often, music, rhythms, and obviously social studies, science and literature. None of these were forced into the project, but any or all might play an important part.

Finally, seventh, this work was in a sense individualized. Each child contributed *his* special talents, interests and ideas, different from those of any other. No child was asked to do anything beyond his capacity. No child was impeded by less mature or less able ones. The project might be called coordinated and cooperative individualization.

How Is There Time for Projects?

How did the school find time for all these big projects? The answer is simple. In the first place, individual work in the skill subjects, each child working at his own pace on work adapted to his maturity, was much less time-consuming than traditional classwork. In the second place, the stimulus, motive, and practical reality given incidentally by the projects, gave interest and meaning to the skill subjects and this always means increased rate and effectiveness of learning.

So in planning the daily division of time for classes, a double period (about an hour and a half) was set aside for projects. There still was plenty of time for all other schoolwork and activities.

Origin of Winnetka "Projects"

During the first few years in Winnetka we had no such projects. We were concentrating on the time-consuming, failure-producing skill subjects. From the beginning we recognized that once we could keep these subjects from monopolizing the school day, we could find time for more creative work and more social experiences. And as we got our self-instructive materials prepared and improved and the work individualized, we found that we had time to spare. But how that time was to be used was left to the individual teacher. Some teachers, trained and experienced in traditional methods, were at a loss as to how to make good use of this time; some had constructive ideas. But one, Frances Presler, a teacher of a third grade, who had taught in the Francis W. Parker school in Chicago, proved to be a veritable genius in developing really creative and social experiences.

Consequently, we took her out of her classroom and freed her to help all teachers. It was she, more than anyone else, who was responsible for our developing a philosophy, a program, and a technique for the kind of projects we have been discussing.

Projects and Other Activities in Junior High School

Up to this point we have spoken only of projects in the first six grades. What about the Junior High School?

Fundamentally, the activities on this level did not differ from those of the lower grades—the purpose and philosophy were much the same and the techniques did not differ radically. But the nature of the projects and the school organization and program took on a quite new semblance.

The Junior High School in Winnetka

Before describing the form activities took in the Junior High School, I must go back a moment to the first years of my administration in Winnetka. When I arrived in 1919, there were three elementary schools. Two of them had kindergartens and the first six grades. The third (and oldest and most central) had kindergarten and eight grades. Children from the other two schools finished their last two grades in this central one, Horace Mann. The work of the seventh and eighth grades was departmentalized like a high school, children moving from teacher to teacher for the different subjects.

Already the Board of Education was preparing to build a junior high school. A very desirable and ample plot of ground had been bought on the western border of the town, which was rapidly growing; the population almost doubled between 1920 and 1930 (from 6,694 to 12,166), a growth that was partly anticipated by the Board of Education. And architects had drawn the plans for the new school.

There were, however, many citizens who opposed moving the upper grades away from the old Horace Mann school, located in the center of the town. The new school site was three-quarters of a mile further west, on the edge of the community, where as yet there were few houses. These opponents opposed the very idea of a junior high school with laboratories, shops, library, and ample playgrounds. On the other hand, there were many who agreed with the Board of Education and saw the possibility for much more adequate education for their children on the ample grounds of the proposed new school and with a school building which was modern and built to provide suitable education for young adolescents. The issue had to be decided at the polls. This was in 1919-1920.

After an acrimonious campaign, there was a special election in which practically every citizen voted. The Board of Education won by a large majority.

But how was the money to be found for the new building? Money from taxes lagged about two years behind growth of population, and more children needed more teachers and more classrooms immediately. Furthermore, during the First World War, the Board had spent as little as possible on school buildings and maintenance and was now trying to catch up to needs. The consequence was that there was not enough money, nor enough borrowing power under state restrictions, to construct the new school.

Then Winnetka did a remarkable thing. The citizens, including many of the defeated opponents of the junior high school, carried on a campaign to get voluntary contributions to construct the new school. Contributions ranged from a couple of dollars to $10,000. One wealthy citizen, Louis Kuppenheimer, contributed $60,000 for a large assembly hall in memory of his daughter. The total was sufficient to erect an ample and handsome one-story building. It was named "The Skokie School," the quietly beautiful marshlands to the west of it having been called "Skokie" by the Indians.

To organize and head the new Skokie School and to be Assistant Superintendent of Schools, Willard W. Beatty was invited to come from San Francisco; he and I had been colleagues there under Burk. He gave the school its initial character. His successor, Rae Logan, four years later, continued the work and, with his staff, added many new features to the school during the next 20 years.

It was Logan who was largely responsible for the development of the economic enterprises which to a great extent took the place, at the junior high school level, of the projects of the elementary schools.

Economic Enterprises—
The "Skokie Livestock Corporation"

The economic enterprises grew gradually over the years. One of the first was the "Skokie Livestock Corporation." Some of the students decided to raise rabbits. At Easter, especially, there is a great demand for baby rabbits as pets. Discussing the idea with their teacher, the students realized that they would have to have money for lumber to build the rabbit house for shelter, to buy the breed animals, and to buy feed. Since they expected to make a profit, they recognized that those who did the work of cleaning the rabbit house and feeding the rabbits should be paid. All this required capital.

In their arithmetic class they had begun to study a little about corporation stocks. The arithmetic teacher seized on this new interest to help the children learn what stock companies are, how they are organized and managed and how they keep their books. The originators of the idea, with the arithmetic teacher as their advisor, organized a "corporation." It got its charter from the school instead of the state, and of course had no legal standing. The incorporators then sold stock in the enterprise to all students who wished to buy, at 10 cents per share. It was agreed that stock still held by those who went on to the Senior High School would be bought back, finances permitting, by the corporation.

The whole school of 500 children became actively interested, and the stock issue was oversubscribed. There were plenty of "laborers" glad to earn a little by care of the rabbits, and there was a board of directors. The social studies teacher later took advantage of some unrest of the workers who felt they were underpaid, and introduced the topic of labor unions. The children were eagerly interested, and soon there was a union, with collective bargaining between union and management.

So that the students might learn both sides of this universal struggle, it was suggested that there be a certain rotation, laborers becoming managers and vice versa.

The whole story is too long to tell. With variations, successes and failures and elaborations, the "Skokie Livestock Corporation" continued for many years as successive classes came into the Skokie School.

The School Newspaper

Another of the earliest enterprises was the weekly school newspaper. This was organized on the "municipal ownership" plan. The school was the "owner" and furnished the printing equipment. But for running expenses—ink, paper, linotype work, etc.—the newspaper had to be self-supporting.

In the print shop of the school the children, boys and girls, learned to set type. This they did for headlines and advertisements. But for the body of the composition they paid a commercial printer to put their articles in linotype. Then they made up the paper and printed it on the school press.

Such a paper involved many more workers than the students in the print shop. There were reporters, contributors of stories and poems, illustrators, solicitors of subscriptions and solicitors of advertising (local merchants, knowing the paper went into 500 homes, were glad to pay to insert advertisements). And, of course, there was the whole matter of accounting and finance.

While one teacher served as general advisor, many teachers helped—

the arithmetic teacher with the accounting, the art teacher with the illustrations, the social studies teacher with the social responsibilities of journalism, the English teacher with the composition of articles and stories, and so on. The children took trips to see how a regular newspaper was managed and published and came back with ideas for improving their publication.

The enterprise permeated the whole school and gave both motive and application to many studies.

With changes and developments from year to year, this enterprise has now continued for more than 30 years and is still a vital part of the school.

"Biology Bureau of Bees"

Some time after the organization of the newspaper, children in the biology class, studying bees, decided to raise bees and sell honey. The "Biology Bureau of Bees" was organized as a cooperative. Logan and his faculty wanted the children to experience the three types of economic organization—capitalistic (The Livestock Corporation); socialistic (the "municipal ownership" of the newspaper); and now cooperative.

In their social studies class the children studied the cooperative movement—the Rochedale experiment in England, the Scandinavian developments, and the growth of cooperatives in the United States. The biology teacher, however, was the responsible advisor for the enterprise. In his class the children studied bees more intensively than before and added practical apiculture. The members of the cooperative bought their first hive and placed it in the courtyard just outside the biology laboratory.

Like the other enterprises, this had many ramifications, including publicity for the sale of honey, financial management, articles for the school newspaper, experiments in the laboratory, wide reading, excursions to bee farms, to mention a few. The Biology Bureau of Bees lasted for many years, always developing different aspects as new classes took over the enterprise.

These three illustrations will suffice, but we might describe many more, such as the bank and credit union, the school store, the Skokie Fisheries (for raising and selling fish for aquaria), the Insurance Company (to insure children against loss from breaking dishes in the lunch room), the publicity organization for publicizing all enterprises and school activities, and so on and on. Some had relatively short lives, others sprang up in their places. Some have continued right to the present. Some have been of one type of economic organization, others of another. But all have certain features in common.

Common Elements

They always arose from a real need felt by the children and were organized and conducted by the children.

Each always had as advisor a teacher who accepted responsibility for counseling them.

They always cut across subject matter divisions and involved a variety of classes.

They always involved comparisons, through visits and reading, with corresponding adult enterprises.

And, the seven elements common to all projects in the elementary school (*see* page 94) were common likewise to the enterprises of the Junior High School.

Other Group and Creative Activities

Let us now turn, much more briefly, to other social experiences and opportunities for creative self-expression. In the examples that follow, as in the projects and economic enterprises, each child may acquire such experience and learning as are indicated by his individual needs. The common goals are broad and general, such as ability to adjust his individual desires and interests to those of his fellows so as not to interfere with their equal rights; the habit of cooperative effort toward common objectives; the development of a social conscience; the stimulation and freeing of his self-expresssion; the appreciation of beauty; and so on. None of these are measured to see whether each child attains them in the same degree. Life demands variety rather than uniformity in these fields.

Art: In art, time for which was provided at all levels, the teacher's concentration was on freeing the child to express himself in a variety of media—finger painting; painting with brushes; drawing with pencil, charcoal, and colored crayons; modeling with clay or plasticene; constructing with wood or wire or any other material. Inexpensive supplies in liberal quantity were made available. The work was never dictated.

Technique was subordinate to free expression. But when a child was trying to get a result, yet was hampered in his desire by lack of technique, the teacher answered his need by showing him how he could reach his own goal more effectively. A little child needs to know, for example, how to keep his colors clear, how to attach a paper to an easel, etc. Later, usually around the age of eight, children cease to be satisfied with a drawing that does not depict what they are trying to represent, and want help in doing so. Sooner or later, children judge the attractiveness of the work of others and can be helped to see why one picture or sculpture is more pleasing to many people than is another.

Some techniques were taught at each level of a child's development, but only those which the child clearly needed and wanted. We felt the teacher's responsibility is to give children the release of their creative powers, and the means—materials, time, technical help, and encouragement—to give expression to their creative urge.

This philosophy evolved gradually in Winnetka. The art teacher who was already there in 1919, Alta Gahan, had the beginning of it and was already achieving some beautiful and free work from children. She helped find a young assistant, Myrtle Ness (later Myrtle Ness Craddock) who, more than anyone else, during the next quarter century, helped all teachers, especially in the elementary schools, to see the principles just outlined and to apply them in freeing the children. The art work done by the children, freed and helped in this way, was extraordinarily good—spontaneous, uninhibited, and often beautiful.

Music: In music, too, the evolution in Winnetka began very early. Before 1919, Edward Yeomans on the Board of Education had sought the advice of Thomas Whitney Surette, the eminent music educator of Boston. Basing its choice on his recommendations, the Board selected Carolyn Kohlsaat to teach music and help teachers at all school levels. She was succeeded a few years later by Rose Damberg in the elementary schools and Lawrence Yingling in the Junior High School. To these three goes the credit for having made music in Winnetka a joy to the children and to all who hear them sing.

It is singing which is the natural foundation of music, and it is singing in which every child participates.

As in art, technique was subordinated to expresssion. Children began by singing by rote simple songs of high musical merit—such as the best of the folk songs of Europe. As they grow older, they learned to sing more difficult songs. Songs were selected in terms of high musical value, suitability to children's voices, and their level of difficulty. By the time children reached the Junior High School they sang such music as madrigals and Bach chorales.

From the third grade on, each child had music books (lent by the school library) for all songs and could see the scores before him as he sang. Whenever such an explanation would help them, but only then, the teacher pointed out the meaning of the musical notation. "Notice how much higher this note is written than the one before it—you must sing it higher." "Notice that this black note has two little flags on it, and the one before it has only one—that means it must be sung twice as fast." "See the little symbol between these two notes—that means you must rest a beat." And so on. With singing every day, year after year, it is extraordinary how much ability to read music is absorbed without drill.

A standardized test (Kwalwasser-Dykema) [2] showed that Winnetka Junior High School children had considerably more skill in reading music than the national average in spite of the fact that most American schools spent many painful hours learning solfeggio and technicalities. It is true that not every child learns to sing at sight from notes, but this is even more true in schools that concentrate on the techniques of reading music. And whereas in many schools music is not a subject enjoyed by most children and discipline is often a difficult problem during the music period, the children in Winnetka, almost without exception, loved the music period, and they had a great repertoire of beautiful songs which they thoroughly enjoyed singing.

Instrumental music is elective, but a large proportion of children learned to play instruments. Each school had its own band and its own orchestra. Many children took individual lessons from private teachers of piano, violin, etc., outside school. But in each school a small room was provided for lessons in instrumental music, and the Board of Education employed teachers of piano, strings, and wind instruments. These teachers were paid from the very modest fees charged to the children.

[2] Kwalwasser, Jacob and Peter W. Dykema, *Kwalwasser-Dykema Music Tests*, University of Iowa, Iowa City, Ia., 1929 (rev. 1949).

The teacher can obviously charge less per lesson when assured of a full program with a rent-free studio, than when he or she has to rent a studio or lose time going from house to house of the pupils. Instruments could be rented by the children from the school at a very low cost—just enough to cover cost of repairs and replacement over a period of the life of the instrument.

In playing an instrument, of course, a child had to learn the exact significance of the musical notation and had to have the usual amount of repetitive practice to master difficult techniques. But no child was required to learn to play an instrument and his learning was highly motivated since his right to play in the band or orchestra depended on his acquiring sufficient skill. Children who elected to play an instrument, therefore, thoroughly enjoyed the experience. In instrumental music, as in singing, emphasis was placed on music of high quality, yet simple enough to be within the children's range of ability.

Electives and Clubs

In the Junior High School there were a number of subjects which were elective—just as band and orchestra were electives throughout all the schools. All Junior High School students had to take at least one elective in some form of manual arts: woodworking, metal work, printing, automobile mechanics, etc. They also had to take one elective in music and one in art. They *could* take dramatics, typewriting, or additional work in manual arts, cooking, music, art, etc. And there were clubs of all kinds, formed voluntarily by groups of children to follow their special interests: a madrigal club, an astronomy club, a stamp collector's club, a writer's club, or any other kind, the variety changing from year to year. There was an allotted hour in the timetable for clubs to meet once a week, and during that hour the entire school was given over to club activities.

There were also opportunities for clubs in the elementary schools, but clubs at this lower level were not as universal as in the Junior High School.

Through these electives and clubs, children had an additional opportunity to develop their special interests and talents in cooperation with other children of similar interests.

Physical Education and Recreation

As far back as 1913, the Board of Education employed a highly competent and experienced director of physical education and recreation (Harry P. Clarke). He served for many years and gradually selected and trained his co-workers and those who succeeded him when he retired. By 1922 there was a director of physical education and recreation for each elementary school, and for the Junior High School there was one for boys and one for girls.

In turns, throughout the day, the various classes had periods for physical education and recreation. And the director was on duty both before and after school for the supervision of the voluntary activities and team games. Each school had a gymnasium for use when outdoor activities were prevented by rain or snow, or to use for rhythms and dancing.

The program included little or no formal gymnastics. Instead, there were field sports, folk dances, rhythms, modern dances, and team games. In the team games, all competition was between teams of approximately equal ability. Every child had his chance to play. In these competitions the ideals of sportsmanship and fair play were emphasized. The competitors were considered as partners who, by the very intensity of their competition, made the game interesting and called forth one's best efforts. The ideal of cooperation was developed both within the team and with one's opponents. Herein lies an important aspect of both character and citizenship.

Citizenship and Democracy

To some extent even before 1919, and to a rapidly increasing extent thereafter, the schools of Winnetka were organized on a democratic basis. The democracy within the faculty and administration of the schools has been indicated by the way in which the total program has been developed. There is also democracy in the classrooms themselves.

Each classroom in the elementary schools was to a considerable extent a self-governing unit. The children, with some guidance (but not dictation) by the teacher, worked out, from year to year, the standards of group behavior and the forms of group organization most suitable to them. They had legislative and executive authority, within the framework of the larger democracy of the school as a whole, the community and the state, and they elected their own officers and committees.

The children did not, however, have judicial authority to try and punish offenders. This would have been contrary to the principles of mental hygiene. A persistent offender was considered as a patient rather than a culprit. The knowledge and skill of the teacher, or, in more serious cases, of a pediatrician, psychologist, or psychiatrist, are needed to diagnose the causes of persistently undesirable behavior and to find ways of remedying the causes.

Children did have the right, however, to protect themselves from the antisocial behavior of a classmate by refusing to allow him to be a part of an activity where he was disruptive rather than cooperative. This borders on the judicial function and in a sense involves punishment, but it differs radically in its purpose and feeling. The purpose is not to make the child suffer but solely to protect the group. A child so eliminated by a group requires special help and attention from the teacher and is allowed to participate in group activities as soon as he is willing to try to do so in an acceptable manner.

In the Junior High School the same principles of self-government were applied, but the organization was different. No longer were the children with the same class and the same teacher all day. According to their individual time schedules they were grouped with different children almost every period, and had different teachers. Each child was, however, assigned to one "home room" or "advisory group." This room, until recent years, was composed about equally of children from each level of the Junior High School, from those just entering to those just finishing. It therefore had a certain continuity, a third or half of the children entering each year and an equal number leaving. All children remained with the same "advisory" teacher throughout their Junior High School experience. This teacher got to know each child well, to know his parents and his home. If he had difficulty in another class, the teacher of that class discussed the problem with the "advisory" teacher, who in turn discussed it with the child, his parents, or the school psychologist, and helped the other teacher to understand the child better.

It is the "advisory group" that formed the self-governing unit of the Junior High School. It met one period a day with the teacher. This period was used for study, for individual counseling, and for group decisions on school policy. It elected two representatives to the school council.

That council was the legislative body for the school as a whole and appointed committees for the execution of its decisions. It was conducted by the children (with a faculty advisor) in parliamentary form. Its discussions were vigorous and usually much more intelligent, thoughtful and in better spirit than those of their adult counterparts in government.

In all the Winnetka schools there were school assemblies. Some of these were for the transaction of business brought before the assembly by the classroom units in the elementary schools, or by the Council (representing the "advisory rooms") in the Junior High School. Other assemblies were for entertainment or general instruction—dramatizations, concerts, motion pictures, lectures, assembly singing, and so on.

It was in the assemblies that one felt the heartbeat of the entire school.

In Summary

The individualization of the tool subjects requiring mastery of skills by everyone at the appropriate stage of his development resulted in sufficient economy of time and effort to make possible an extensive program of group and creative activities. As we have just seen, these included long, continuous projects in the elementary schools and economic enterprises in the Junior High School. They included art, music, dramatic expression, electives, clubs, physical education and recreation, school practice of citizenship and democracy, and the school assemblies. In all of them, the ideas, the special interests, the talents and the abilities of each child had scope. In almost all of them (art is a partial exception) each child learned to coordinate his special interests with those of his fellows and to cooperate with other children toward a common end.

While separated from individual work on the timetable, the group and creative activities (incidentally, but never at the expense of spontaneity and freedom) gave motive to the individual work and gave application to the skills developed individually. The partial separation of group and creative activities from individual work was the major cause of criticism of the education in Winnetka. Yet it is this very differentiation of functions that enables each child to master essential skills at his own rate and at the appropriate stage of his development, and that allows time and opportunity for the group and creative activities unhampered by the necessary mechanical aspects of learning.

In life itself there are many such separations of activities. Our eating, work, and recreation may be and usually are quite separate aspects of our living and it would be artificial and undesirable to try to combine them. Integration takes place within the individual—food gives us energy to work, work gains us the means to recreate, recreation refreshes us for work, and both recreation and work give us appetite. The fact that when we eat and recreate we don't necessarily think of work, or vice versa, does not destroy the inward integration of the three activities.

In like manner, the individual mastery of skills can, and must at times, be separated from group and creative activities. Yet the two complement each other and interact, and within the individual they are integrated into his life.

If any part of the education of Winnetka can legitimately be called "The Winnetka Plan" it is this principle of distinction between (*a*) individual mastery of skills and (*b*) group and creative activities, and the techniques for developing both *and* assuring their interaction.

CHAPTER EIGHT

Mental Hygiene and the Educational Clinic; Education for the Deaf

In 1919 there was in Winnetka as in many American cities a "special room" for children of retarded mental development and others who for one reason or another could not do the regular classwork. The teacher was an efficient tutor who, with a much smaller class than the average, could give individual attention to each child, and who supplemented academic work with handicrafts. When she left, a year later, to teach in Chicago, she was replaced by a woman (Mrs. Helen Brenton) who was less a disciplinarian and more a warm, motherly person. It was she who, a year or two later, said:

"I don't think we should have a special room for these children. They and their parents consider it a disgrace for them to be so segregated, and the other children look down on them. Now that our work in Winnetka is individualized, why can't these children be grouped with others of their own age, and be assigned the individual work that they are ready for, even if it is much simpler than the work of others in the same class? Instead of teaching the special class, I could go to the classes where these children are and give them and their teachers extra help."

This idea had a strong appeal and we decided to try it. Everyone was happy about the result. Mrs. Brenton, however, left Winnetka a year or two later, and was replaced by Florence Brett, a Junior High School teacher of literature who had shown special sympathy for children who were difficult, and who had understanding and skill in helping them.

During the next two or three years Miss Brett frequently said, "I am not the right person for this work. Many of the children I am trying to help need the expert services of a person trained in psychology and mental hygiene."

Since she was doing excellent work with the children we at first thought she was simply self-deprecatory. But we needed a new principal for one of the elementary schools and Miss Brett was the person best qualified for that position; so we made her a principal and replaced her, in 1926, with a psychiatric social worker, Frances Dummer (the sister of Katharine Dummer Fisher who instigated the experiment in postponing formal learning).

Miss Dummer's work and the light she shed on the problems the teachers were facing were so successful that the demands on her time became inordinate. Then the teachers themselves requested an additional social worker. They said, "We know there is no money in the budget for another staff member, but we will gladly accept an additional child or two in each class so that one regular teacher can be replaced by a social worker who can help all of us. The extra child or two will not add to our work nearly as much as another social worker can help us."

There were always some teachers leaving at the end of each year—to marry, or have a child, or because a new teacher did not prove successful and had to be dropped at the end of the year. The next autumn, therefore, with the consent of the Board, one teacher who left was not replaced, there was some reorganization of classes and a second social worker was added.

Origin of the Educational Clinic

At about that time Miss Dummer recommended urgently that highly specialized help be obtained for the more severe cases of emotional disturbance among children. With her professional insight she recognized situations that required study and treatment by a psychologist and a psychiatrist. In Chicago there was a well-known child guidance clinic, the Institute for Juvenile Research, which Miss Dummer's mother, Mrs. William Dummer, had helped to establish some years previously. "Why don't we ask the Institute to help us?" Miss Dummer suggested.

The Winnetka schools were by then very well known as an experimental center. The Institute was desirous of spreading the idea of helping children in the schools, and thereby preventing many cases from developing delinquency or psychosis. It therefore gladly sent one of its own psychologists for two days a week and one of its psychiatrists one day a week to work with us, the Institute for Juvenile Research paying their salaries.

But they—and the two social workers—needed the report of a pediatrician on each child who was to be intensively studied. A very well known pediatrician (Dr. C. A. Aldrich, later of the Mayo Clinic) lived in Winnetka and was a great friend of the schools. (He later served on the School Board six years.) He was much interested in what we were attempting to do for difficult children and volunteered his services as pediatrician.

Thus we had a real child guidance clinic, which we named the Department of Educational Counsel. And up to this point the Board of Education had not had to spend any money beyond the usual budget for the schools.

Soon the part-time services of the psychologist were insufficient— the more we studied the needs of children the more needs we found. The Board of Education was having difficult times financially both because of the economic depression and because of the rapid growth of the schools. So I asked the Wieboldt Foundation in Chicago for a grant to employ a full-time psychologist for two years. The Foundation agreed to give us half the amount needed if local citizens would subscribe the other half. By going to one home after another among the wealthier citizens, I soon got the matching funds and we employed a psychologist.

By the end of two years, when we had used up the grant, the Board of Education was convinced of the value of the Clinic and the psychologist became a regular member of our staff. In time, we added two more social workers and a full-time psychiatrist. By 1939 the Department of Educational Counsel was at its zenith—a psychiatrist, a psychologist, a volunteer pediatrician, and four psychiatric social workers—by far the most extensive child guidance clinic, for the number of children served, in any public school system anywhere.

How the Department of Educational Counsel Functioned

When a teacher found that a child was showing symptoms of maladjustment—over-aggressive, antisocial, too quietly conforming, seemingly lazy, lying, stealing, over-absorbed with sex, unable to progress with some or all aspects of school work—the problem was discussed with a social worker. The social worker made a preliminary study, interviewed the parents, the principal and the child's previous teachers. If the case seemed sufficiently serious to warrant a full study, the child was then examined by the pediatrician to see whether there were organic causes involved. He was thoroughly tested by the psychologist as to both school achievement and intellectual capacity. He was interviewed at length by the psychiatrist to determine the emotional factors behind the behavior. The psychiatrist also usually interviewed the parents. Then a staff meeting was held. At this the entire staff of the Department of Educational Counsel, the teacher of the child, and often the principal and superintendent of schools were in attendance.

At the staff meeting all reports were given, the teacher adding what she had observed and what methods she had been using to cope with the problem. The psychiatrist then summarized the whole and indicated both the apparent cause of the problem and the general direction of necessary treatment. The teacher and principal worked out a plan of action as far as the school was concerned and the social worker undertook to help the parents in providing the necessary home situation, as far as that could be done.

Effect on Teachers

Since, sooner or later, every teacher had one or more cases for such intensive study, every teacher was actually receiving training in mental hygiene in a very effective way, seeing the principles applied by all the specialists to a problem with which he or she was grappling. This intensive training was supplemented by a seminar for teachers conducted by the psychiatrist. New teachers were required to attend this seminar when they were first employed; others attended it voluntarily. And all did considerable reading.

It was not, therefore, as strange as it first seemed when the social workers came to me one day in about 1940 and said, "What is the matter with us? Teachers used to be calling on us all the time and we could hardly carry the work. Now they call on us less and less often. Three of us could easily carry the load. Are we failing?"

"No," I replied. "You have succeeded too well. In the first place, we have caught up with the many problems that had accumulated before we had a Department of Educational Counsel; so now we are getting just the normal number of new ones. In the second place, you and the rest of the Department staff have trained the teachers so well that much of what you used to do they can do themselves. Now they can detect problems in their incipiency and deal with them before they become severe. And besides, our whole school program has been steadily improving. The knowledge of mental hygiene has permeated everything we do, so that we know much better how to help children to meet their needs for self-expression, how to give them greater emotional security, and how to help them to coordinate their personal lives with those of their fellows, how to work together toward common goals."

Consequently, the next year we did not replace the social worker who resigned that spring, nor, a year or two later, another who accepted a position elsewhere. The Department of Educational Counsel began to shrink, not because it had in any way failed, but because it had succeeded so well that a much less elaborate staff was able to carry out most of its functions.

Now, in 1963, the Educational Clinic consists of a psychologist, a psychiatric social worker and a specialist in reading.

Class for the Deaf

Our concern with mental hygiene naturally embraced *all* children. But even the Department of Educational Counsel could not provide adequately for children with severe physical handicaps. Fortunately there were not many such children in Winnetka. The only ones for whom we had to make special provision were the very few who were deaf and hard of hearing.

When I was a little boy, in about 1896, my mother and Mrs. Charles Crane managed, against strong opposition from institutions for the deaf, to get a certain law passed in Illinois. It was, I believe, the first law in any state to provide free special classes for the deaf in public schools at the expense of the state. It provided that where three or more parents of deaf children requested it, public schools must provide a special class to teach them to speak and to read lips, and to give them general education. (The law was later followed by similar laws in most states.) Thirty-seven years later, we were able to make use of that law in Winnetka.

One of the six children of an influential citizen of Winnetka was deaf. He wanted her to have the benefits of the education in the Winnetka Public Schools. There did not seem to be enough other deaf children in Winnetka to make such a class feasible. But in the neighboring suburbs there were several, and arrangements were made to have them enrolled in the Winnetka schools. The class was organized in 1933 under Fern Hagen, a specialist in the education for the deaf, whose salary was, at first, paid by the father whose concern gave the plan its start.

The individual work in Winnetka was a great advantage in making the work of the class successful. In the class itself, Miss Hagen, and later her successors, trained the children in lip reading and in speech, and helped them with their individual work. But for group and creative activities the children attended regular classes. The other children were very helpful and protective, guiding them through games and dramatizations, demonstrating in manual activities, making them feel at home in the group. It was good education for the hearing children and it accustomed the deaf and hard-of-hearing children to associate freely in normal social activities.

The purpose of such a class, as distinguished from an institution for the deaf, is to enable children to lead a normal home life, a normal life, as far as possible, among hearing children and later in adult society. The class in Winnetka is unique in the large amount of time that the children spend in free association with hearing children. While their technical training in speech and lip reading is probably as good as can be found in the best institutions and day classes for the deaf, the continuous experience of working and playing with normal children is as unusual as it is valuable.

This provision for deaf and hard-of-hearing children in Winnetka has continued without interruption to this day. Children with serious visual or physical handicaps are sent to special rooms in the Evanston public schools, six miles away. As will be seen in Part Two of this book, such inter-school cooperation for special education has recently been greatly extended.

CHAPTER NINE

Nursery Schools

Early in 1926 I happened to be lecturing in Chicago on the same program with Mrs. Rose H. Alschuler, who lived in Winnetka and whom I knew casually. In her lecture she described a nursery school she had organized (and financed) in one of the large public schools of Chicago. At the close of the program I said to her, "You live in Winnetka. Why don't you start a nursery school in one of our public schools?"

"If you, as Superintendent of Schools, will take the lead, I will be glad to support you and help you in any way I can," she replied.

I had been interested in nursery schools for some years and had visited some of the best in the United States—there were very few at that time. The frequency with which the causes of maladjustments could be traced to early childhood made it very clear that the years before a child entered school or even kindergarten were the most important ones for helping children adjust to themselves and to the world. We had, of course, a free public kindergarten for five-year-old children as part of each elementary school, but no provision for children three and four years of age.

So Mrs. Alschuler and I began an educational campaign in Winnetka, speaking to many organizations and explaining the value and importance of a well-conducted nursery school. Many people opposed the idea—a nursery school, they said, was merely a way of letting lazy mothers get rid of their children. Nursery schools, or day nurseries, in impoverished parts of England and France, and even in the United States, might be a necessary service for mothers who had to leave the home to earn a living. But in suburban Winnetka few mothers really had to work for wages full-time while their children were very young. Mrs. Alschuler and I found that it was not easy to help people see the *educational* value of the nursery school. We tried, however, to show the importance of an environment planned for young children, of supervision by a teacher trained in psychology and mental hygiene and in the best ways of helping young children's development, the advantages to children of having playmates of their own age, the value of daily medical inspection, and the important part a nursery school can play in educating parents.

Enough mothers were convinced to assure a full enrollment for the first year. Then with considerable difficulty the Board of Education was persuaded to allow us to use an unoccupied room in one of the elementary schools. (It had been a kindergarten but was too small and we had added a new and larger kindergarten in the building.)

First Nursery School Opened

So, in the autumn of 1926, our first nursery school was opened, the parents paying a modest fee to cover the cost of the teacher and her assistant. The 20 children were three and four years old. The school nurse made the daily medical inspections.

Our use of the room was very tentative. The Board of Education had stipulated that it would be taken back for classroom use as soon as there was need for it. And the room was not large enough, nor did it have the kind of equipment that was needed. Nevertheless, the nursery school was well conducted under Mrs. Alschuler's supervision, and was highly successful. There were far more applicants for enrollment for the next year than could possibly be accommodated.

Then Mrs. Alschuler and her architect husband (Alfred S. Alschuler) made a public-spirited offer: They would build an addition to the Junior High School, at their own expense, to house two nursery schools—one for three-year-old children and one for four-year-olds, with a small room where a child could be isolated, an office for the staff, a kitchen for preparing the lunches, and an observation space where visitors could watch the children without being among them. In the same wing they would include a suite of offices for the embryonic Department of Educational Counsel, and an office for research.

There was considerable discussion in the Board of Education before this generous offer was accepted. Some members were still unconvinced of the value of a nursery school. Some felt that taxpayers could object to the use of public funds for the cleaning, heating and maintenance of a nursery school, especially since children would have to pay tuition to cover the cost of the teachers. But finally the Alschulers' offer was accepted. And when the truly beautiful nursery schools were completed, the Board held a public reception in them in honor of the Alschulers.

Why in the Junior High School?

The educational purpose of putting the nursery schools in the Junior High School building was to use them as a laboratory for the Junior High School students in connection with their study of family living. Children just coming into adolescence needed to look toward the time of becoming parents. Sex education had been a part of the biology course for all children in the Junior High School from its beginning. To move directly from the biological explanation of reproduction to the psychological and social aspects of family responsibility seemed to us eminently desirable. The nursery school gave us an ideal laboratory in which the boys and girls of the Junior High School could see the meaning of parenthood and could learn to deal with little children—with their younger brothers and sisters just now, with their own children later.

Mrs. Alschuler selected the teachers and, as a volunteer, supervised the program. She had weekly staff meetings in her home, attended also by the superintendent of schools, where problems were studied, plans made, and, in time, research undertaken. Later, as research projects grew, she employed a research assistant (first Dorothy Van Alstyne, then Laberta Hatwick). Besides a number of articles, two books were published as a result of this research (*Two to Six*, William Morrow Co., and *Painting and Personality*, University of Chicago Press). The Winnetka Nursery Schools became known as among the best in the United States.

Free Public Nursery Schools

Still, I was not satisfied. Parents by now were clamoring for nursery schools for their children. Inadequate private nursery schools sprang up to meet this demand. While we had organized a Nursery School Board for our own two nursery schools and this Board raised money for the tuition of children whose parents could not afford the modest fee, we still did not have a free public nursery school, and the two units in the Junior High School took care of only 35 children—15 three-year-olds and 20 four-year-olds.

Finally, in 1941, we saw our opportunity. The lower birth rate which began in 1929, and the geographical limits of expansion for the adult population resulted in our having, by 1940, an empty classroom in each school building. A plan was devised whereby our school building bonds could be refunded over a longer period of years at a very low interest rate and thereby save considerable annual expenditure from current taxes. With this saved money and the empty classrooms it would be possible, without increasing tax rates, to open a free nursery in each of the elementary schools, in addition to the two nursery school units in the Junior High School.

Then came my most difficult struggle with the Board of Education. Three of the seven members were unalterably opposed to the plan—they wanted to use the money saved by refunding bonds to decrease taxes and they could not be convinced of the value of free nursery schools as part of the public school system. There were no such free public school facilities for very young children anywhere in the United States. Three other members were equally in favor of the plan. The seventh member, the president of the Board, was undecided. We had discussion after discussion at Board meetings.

I spent evenings in their homes talking personally with the opposing members—all good friends and fine people—and with the president. Finally we decided to devote an entire meeting to the subject. Arguments waxed strong and the opposing sides failed to convince each other. I used every fact and theory at my command to no avail.

Then the president of the Board of Education thought of his own little girl. She had been drowned and his grief had been great. He remembered the happiness she had had in nursery school. For her sake, he could not deny this happiness to the children of others. At midnight he cast the deciding vote. The free public nursery schools for four-year-olds were established in each elementary school and exist to this day. The nursery school units in the Junior High School likewise have continued to serve their special functions of pre-parental education.

Effect of Nursery Schools

The nursery schools affected all the education that followed. First they transformed our kindergartens, suffusing them with a new spirit and imparting to them many of their techniques. Then the influence spread up into the first grades, and from these, less conspicuously, crept into the upper grades.

For nursery schools at their best are the most perfect education we have today. Coming into being after the work of Freud was well known, after educational psychology was well developed, after pediatrics had become a highly specialized science, and after sociology and anthropology had begun to shed light on education, nursery schools combine and apply all these sciences. They are untrammeled by tradition and by parental ambition for academic learning by their children. They are built and equipped to meet the needs of growing children. They are taught by carefully selected teachers with some understanding of the contributions of modern science to the education of young children, teachers who also have a warm and tender understanding of little children. Their primary, all-inclusive purpose is to help each child to develop naturally, wholesomely, happily. They recognize that no two children are alike and try to help each one, in accordance with his special design of growth, to achieve mastery of his own faculties and to coordinate his activities with those of other children and the surrounding adult world. The child's physical, intellectual, emotional and social well-being are seen as an interdependent and integral whole.

Such nursery schools become laboratories for research in child development and a center for study by teachers of all levels, by parents, and by students preparing to teach.

CHAPTER TEN

Selection and Education of Teachers

From the beginning, we recognized in Winnetka, as all must recognize, that good teachers are the key to good education. Since no one to this day has been able to define with sufficient precision for measurement just what constitutes a good teacher, we had to rely on recommendations by people who knew the candidates and on our own impressions from personal interviews. We selected with the utmost care, seeking teachers who were not merely qualified in terms of training but who were the kind of educated human beings whom we should want to associate with children and who could command the the liking and respect of parents. We wanted teachers who loved and understood children, teachers who had ideals and vision.

Most of our choices proved right. But about one new teacher out of ten was unable to adapt to our situation and had to be dropped after the first or second year. One or two others, out of ten, needed so much help that we would not have employed them if we had anticipated the difficulty of helping them to become really effective, yet showed such potential for growth that they were retained. Not infrequently, these came to be among our best teachers.

Training New Teachers

The principals of the schools were those who gave most time and help to new teachers. But the group meetings and the meetings of the entire staff of each school with the principal were exceedingly important parts of their training. Working side by side with their colleagues in planning and revising curriculum and materials, participating in research, and, later, takng part in staff conferences with the Educational Clinic and visiting the nursery school, teachers received a continuous and effective education.

Nevertheless, there was considerable expenditure of our time and effort in the first year a new teacher was with us, and the children of the new teacher often had a less educative year than they should have had. We therefore first required new teachers to come a week before school opened to get as much training as possible in the techniques of individual work and familiarity with self-instruction materials. And we organized seminars for them in group and creative activities, before school opencd and during thc school year.

In 1928 we conducted a six-week summer training course at the University of Minnesota, with demonstration classes taught by some of the best Winnetka teachers. We required all new appointees to the Winnetka schools to attend this course. The course proved so very succcesssful, that thereafter, for the next 12 or more years, we conducted it independently in Winnetka as "The Winnetka Summer School for Teachers." This was open to teachers from any schools, but was required of all new teachers appointed to the Winnetka schools.

Even then we were not fully satisfied. It was impossible in six weeks of lectures, seminars, and observations to undo the habits and techniques learned by teachers trained for dealing with classes rather than with individuals, to teach them to organize group and creative activities, to give them insight into the causes of undesirable behavior of children and how to deal effectively with children who exhibited such behavior.

The Graduate Teachers College

In 1932, therefore, we organized "The Graduate Teachers College of Winnetka." To do this I sought the cooperation of two well-known private schools with a philosophy similar to ours. One was the Francis W. Parker School of Chicago, the other the North Shore Country Day School in Winnetka.

The Francis W. Parker School was named after its original head and organizer, Col. Francis W. Parker, who, it will be remembered, had been called by John Dewey "the father of progressive education." As a child I had gone to school under him when he headed the old Cook County Normal School (now the Chicago Teachers College) and again in the school that was later named for him.

When I was attending the fifth grade there, the older brother of my best friend was Perry Dunlap Smith in the sixth or seventh grade. He remained in the Francis W. Parker School under Miss Flora Cooke until he entered Harvard University, then returned to teach there. When I came to Winnetka in 1919, I found that Perry Dunlap Smith was coming at the same time to organize and head the North Shore Country Day School. (There were, and are, still some parents in Winnetka who wanted their children to attend a private school, and especially who wanted their children's secondary education, up to the university, to be in a private, rather than a public institution.) Fortunately Perry Smith and I had common ideals, and there was always warm friendship and cooperation between us. Many of the children who attended the Winnetka Public Schools moved on into the senior high school at North Country Day.

In establishing the Graduate Teachers College of Winnetka it was natural, therefore, to turn to Flora Cooke and Perry Smith for cooperation. They would strengthen the training of our students, would give variety of experience, and, very important, they would provide training for senior high school teachers.

So the three of us became "Educational Directors" of the Graduate Teachers College, and induced members of our respective boards to become the legal corporation to establish and maintain the college.

How the Graduate Teachers College Functioned

The most important member of the staff was to be a full-time dean, since none of us Educational Directors could give the time and attention that the students would need. We fortunately found the ideal person for this key position in Mrs. Frances Murray, an outstanding teacher in the Junior High School in Winnetka. She had the energy, vigor, and enthusiasm we wanted. She had great understanding of young people. She was a first-rate organizer. From its foundation (1932) to its end nearly a quarter of a century later (1954), Frances Murray was the dean—and the heart—of the Graduate Teachers College.

The rest of the staff were members of the staffs of the three cooperating institutions—the Francis W. Parker School, the North Shore Country Day School and the Winnetka Public Schools. We three heads conducted successively through each year the seminar in the philosophy of education. The psychiatrist and psychologist in Winnetka gave the courses in mental hygiene and psychology. Other specialists on our three staffs gave courses in their specialties. But the most important part of the training was in the classrooms.

Each student was assigned to one of our best teachers. The student spent the entire school day with that teacher, understudying him or her, helping, and gradually taking full charge of the class—first with the teacher present, then alone. That teacher met with the student as soon as the children left, discussed the day's work, planned the next day's work, and suggested reading assignments.

The seminars were all held in the late afternoons and evenings. We needed no special buildings, since the school classrooms were all available during those hours.

Since the students had to do a great deal of reading we developed, largely by contributing the most useful books from our personal libraries, supplemented by purchase of the most important new books, a small working library in an anteroom of the Junior High School library. And we arranged with Northwestern University and the National College of Education, six miles from Winnetka but easily reached on the electric railroad, for the free use by our students of their very large collections. A similar arrangement was made to borrow books from the specialized library of the Institute for Juvenile Research in Chicago.

The students were selected with the same care as were members of our respective staffs. They all had to be graduates of universities, but there was no requirement as to the field of their specialization. It was their general foundation of education and their quality as persons and potential teachers that concerned us. If a student wished to become a secondary school teacher of a subject in which he had not had sufficient specialization in the university, he was required to make up his deficiency by taking courses at Northwestern University, which agreed to accept such students without undue formality.

After one or two years, according to the needs of the individual students, the degree of Master of Education was conferred upon them by the Graduate Teachers College—we obtained the necessary authority from the state of Illinois.

We accepted only a small group of students each year. (The maximum, I believe, was 18 and the average about 12.) Among them were always some foreign students from European countries, Australia, Canada, China, or India. For these we raised money by private contributions to award fellowships. Because we had had visitors from all these countries, and because I had visited and lectured in most of them, we had friends in many places in whose judgment we could trust and to whom we turned for recommendations. The Vienna psychologist, Alfred Adler, and the Swiss psychologist, Jean Piaget, were among those who sent us students.

Some of our graduates later made distinguished contributions to education. Perhaps the most influential was Anathnath Basu of India. He organized and headed the faculty of education at the University of Calcutta, and then developed and directed the Central Institute of Education in Delhi. On retirement from this in 1957, he took charge of the training of teachers at the University founded by Rabindranath Tagore at Santiniketan.

While Basu was probably the best known example of the success of the Graduate Teachers College, practically without exception those who were awarded its Master of Education degree found good positions and acquitted themselves well. Two of the foreign students (Alfred Adler, from Austria, a kinsman of the psychologist of the same name, and Lenore Boehm of Germany, who had been recommended by Piaget and later took her doctorate under him) are now on the staff at Brooklyn College.

The three cooperating institutions of the Graduate Teachers College selected for their own staffs some of the students who proved most able. These students, after completing their training, took over their classes with confidence and skill. Not one of them, as far as I know, failed to do a really fine job as a teacher.

Time and circumstances, however, brought an end to the Graduate Teachers College of Winnetka in 1954. Flora Cooke retired in the earlier years of the College (1934), her immediate successor (Herbert Smith) in 1956. I left Winnetka to become Director of Education for the Allied Military Government and Allied Commission in Italy in 1943, and was followed by five successive superintendents. Perry Smith retired in 1954. Those who had conceived the Graduate Teachers College were therefore no longer available to attract students and guide its destiny.

At the same time the education of teachers throughout the United States was greatly improving. Students were receiving a much broader liberal foundation and courses in education were improving markedly. Much of what distinguished the Graduate Teachers College of Winnetka could by now be found in large, well-known institutions. The need for the Graduate Teachers College had diminished.

So, after 22 years of distinguished service, the Graduate Teachers College of Winnetka ceased to be.

CHAPTER ELEVEN

Teachers' Salaries

In 1919, Winnetka, like many small communities
at that time, had no salary schedule for teachers.
Each teacher's salary was determined by the Board
according to the amount necessary to get his or
her services or to keep other schools from enticing
a much-appreciated teacher away. One teacher
might be paid twice as much as another with
equal training and experience if one had received
very tempting offers elsewhere.

Within the first month of my arrival I had
induced the Board to establish at least a basic
minimum, below which no teacher would be employed. During the next year I worked out a
graduated schedule of automatic increments based
on (a) amount of education beyond the two-year

normal school, (*b*) the number of years of teaching experence, (*c*) the number of years taught in Winnetka, and (*d*) an efficiency rating. With variations (always upward) in the amounts of the increments, and in their relative weights, the schedule continued in operation essentially unchanged for the next eight years, but the efficiency rating became gradually obsolete. We found no way of objectively determining efficiency. The rating started out to be in three degrees—A, B, and C—as determined subjectively and from observation by the principals, supervisors and superintendent. Those rated B got a somewhat smaller increment than those rated A; those rated C were on probation for the next year and got no efficiency increment. Any new teacher rated below C was dropped at the end of the year. The distinction between A and B was, however, very tenuous, and the B rating or fear of it was bad for morale. Gradually every teacher whom we wanted to retain got the A rating, until the rating system became meaningless and was dropped when the schedule was revised.

It was in about 1928 that a complete revision was made. The idea of automatic increments over a minimum base was retained, as were the elements of relating the increments to amount of education, years of total experience, and years of experience in Winnetka, although the weights given to each were changed, as were the increments themselves. Educative travel was counted, if approved as really educative, as equivalent to an equal number of weeks or months of full-time study in a recognized institution. What was more important, and in some ways unique, was a group of what might be called in labor parlance, "fringe benefits." These were:

(*a*) *Sabbatical leaves of absence.* A *right* to a sabbatical leave of absence every seven years, for the purpose of study or educative travel, was almost unheard of in elementary schools at that time. During such leave the teacher received half pay. This was, however, given *ex post facto*, during the next two years after the teacher's return to Winnetka— a not too desirable arrangement from the teacher's standpoint but politically expedient if the community was to be reconciled and the existing state laws complied with. The community was insured of profiting by the teacher's growth during the leave, since she had to return for two years to collect her sabbatical pay. From the state standpoint, we did not pay a salary to the teacher while not actually teaching.

(*b*) *Health insurance.* The Board agreed to pay a teacher's full salary for up to a month of absence due to illness. *And* the Board arranged with an insurance company to pay for protracted absence a flat monthly rate of $100 up to a year of absence due to illness. At first this included pregnancy, childbirth and absence following childbirth; but a record five pregnancies occurred during the first year, and the insurance company insisted on dropping that part of the insurance thereafter.

(c) *Annuities.* The Illinois state pension at that time was absurdly low—about $400 per year. So the Board agreed to supplement it for Winnetka teachers by buying for each teacher when he or she had been with us 10 years an annuity that would pay $100 per month for life after the age of 60.

(d) *Early retirement.* To avoid the problem of elderly teachers kept on because of long, faithful service but past the age when they could bring freshness, vigor and enthusiasm to the children, we required, under the new schedule, that every teacher (including the superintendent) must retire at the age of sixty. Being 38 years old at the time, I thought of sixty as "elderly." With the Winnetka annuity, the state pension, and the teacher's own savings made possible by the greatly improved salary scale, the teacher would be free to travel and to find new ways of life while still young enough to enjoy them and make adaptations. On the whole this worked out very well. We lost, it is true, some of our finest teachers, still young in spirit and with much still to contribute to the children, when the age limit was reached. But we were able to retire humanely many others who were no longer a real asset to the schools. Those who still wanted to teach and had the health and mental vigor to do so found new outlets in other schools or in college teaching. (National College of Education and Roosevelt University proved eager to employ a number of these over the years, and still do.) Some went to private schools or to public schools with less rigorous restrictions on age. Many used their early retirement for travel, recreation, and easier living.

This salary schedule, with all its "fringe benefits," applied to all professional personnel. With modifications (*e.g.*, retirement at age 65) it applied to all other personnel—custodians and office force—but at a somewhat lower rate.

At the time of its adoption this schedule made Winnetka one of the highest-paying communities in the country. When the great depression came, all agreed to accept a 20 per cent cut in cash salary, and this was only very slowly restored in later years. The sabbatical leaves, health insurance, retirement annuities, and early retirement remained intact.

One feature of the schedule, and of the one preceding it, caused considerable dissatisfaction and criticism: It provided a bonus of $600 to $1,000 for men. My theoretical argument got nowhere with the teachers. It was to the effect that normally the man had to support wife and children, and that in our type of society a higher rate of pay for men was the way society subsidized the social value of motherhood. Teachers argued that many wives worked, that some men were unmarried, that most women teachers had dependents. We appointed a committee of teachers to try to work out an acceptable substitute in terms of allowance for dependents, but the problem became too complex. Other members of a family who were helping support an aged mother, for instance, could easily shift the responsibility to the teacher on the ground that she could get extra pay by assuming the full support of the mother; there was the question of who could legitimately be counted as a dependent. The committee found no solution and was dissolved.

The one answer that came anywhere near satisfying the critics on the faculty was that of practical expediency—no one wanted to have an all-female faculty. We could not recruit or keep men with the salaries we were paying women, even at the relatively high level of the new schedule; for a man with a wife and several children could not support the family decently at this rate. To raise the salaries of all the women by $1,000 a year was beyond the power of the Board under existing legislation in the state. To cut men (only 10 per cent of the faculty) by $1,000 would raise each woman's salary only $100 and would lose the men. To that argument the teachers gave reluctant assent.

But the strong labor movement for equal pay for equal work won the day after I left Winnetka, and the state legislature made it compulsory to drop the differential. One of my successors had, therefore, the problem of equalizing the salaries. His struggles, between Board pressures and teacher pressures, and the new law, occupied most of his time and energies during his administration and was a contributing factor in his accepting a university position at the end of three years. Thereafter little improvement was made in the salaries of Winnetka teachers. Meanwhile salaries over the country kept going up after World War II, until the Winnetka salaries instead of being among the best became relatively low.

It was not until Sidney Marland became superintendent that anything was done about the situation. Then, with a stroke of genius, he did the magnificent job of organizing, with the Board's help, a citizens' committee to work out a new schedule (of which he tells in Part Two of this book). One of his greatest contributions has been his much fuller use of the citizens of the community. For instance, the salary schedules during my superintendency were of my own making almost exclusively, agreed to by the Board and faculty. Sidney Marland's remarkable, daring and excellent schedule was the work of citizens of the community—inspired and helped by the superintendent but going far beyond what any superintendent would have believed possible or any Board would have been likely to accept if it had been the superintendent's brain child.

Yet even the new schedule incorporated some of the best features of that of 1928.

CHAPTER TWELVE

School Buildings

and Equipment

An educational program has to be housed. While under the best of teachers a good program can be effective even with poor housing and meager equipment, all teachers and children work more effectively in pleasant, well-lighted, sanitary, and well-adapted schools and classrooms, and with suitable equipment.

Early Buildings

This fact was recognized in Winnetka before 1919. The Hubbard Woods school, built in Winnetka in 1915, was, for its time, a long step in advance of the traditional, rather formidable square schoolhouse of several stories. It was (and is) a one-story building, spread out on a reasonably ample site, fitting into the landscape of a residential district, and equipped with movable furniture rather than screwed-down desks. The Skokie Junior High School, built in 1922, but planned in 1919, was of similar architecture on a much more adequate site.

As our educational program developed in Winnetka, we began to make more and more demands on building and equipment. We replaced the screwed-down desks in the older schools with movable furniture. We redecorated all schools with brighter, more cheerful colors. The parents of children in the oldest and largest school (Horace Mann) themselves painted the furniture and made curtains and flower boxes, transforming it to a gay and homelike place for their children.

The number of activities of our children and the informality of the classroom atmosphere made us conscious of the fact that most classrooms have considerable reverberation, magnifying the noise. One classroom in particular, in the Hubbard Woods school, always seemed noisy and teachers had great difficulty in maintaining any semblance of order. It took us years to recognize that the trouble was not inefficiency of the teacher but the acoustics of the classroom. We put acoustical tile on the ceiling to absorb reverberation and the room was transformed. That room became the quietest and pleasantest of all classrooms. Discipline ceased to be a problem.

This started a trend. Little by little every classroom was given acoustical treatment, and as we built additions to the schools to keep up with growth of school population, we used acoustical plaster in all ceilings. As far as I know Winnetka was the first school system to have acoustical treatment in all its rooms. The cost, spread over the years, was inconsequential. The effects were almost magical.

Not only did we gradually add all kinds of desirable equipment to the classrooms, we also equipped the school playgrounds adequately. The most interesting addition to the playgrounds was the jungle gym, which originated in Winnetka. The story of its genesis is interesting:

It was about 1920. Edward Yeomans, who, it will be remembered, had been a member of the original Board of Education that was trying to make the Winnetka public schools as good as possible, had a dinner party in his home. The guests included Perry Dunlap Smith of the North Shore Country Day School, a man named Theodore Hinton, myself, and our wives. After dinner I was talking to Hinton and he told me of a climbing frame he planned to build in his yard for his children.

"When I was a boy," he said in effect, "we lived in Japan. My father was a mathematician and especially interested in the mathematics of the fourth dimension. He had a theory that the reason most people had trouble in conceiving a fourth dimension was that most of their experience was in two dimensions only—we live and move on planes. Let children become used to living three-dimensionally and the step to an understanding of the fourth dimension will be easier. We children of course knew little of this and what we knew bored us. But to put his theory to the test, father built a framework of bamboo in our garden, the poles crossing each other to outline many cubes. He named the horizontal poles than ran one way X1, X2, X3, etc. The horizontal poles that crossed these at right angles he named Y1, Y2, Y3, etc. And the vertical poles were Z1, Z2, Z3, etc.

"Then he would have us children race to get to a given intersection —he would say 'X2, Y4, Z3, Go!' We had to visualize the point of intersection and climb through the frame to reach it, each trying to be first.

"The game was rather fun, but what we liked best was, after father had gone, to climb around in the frame, hang by one hand or by our knees, play tag in it like monkeys chasing each other. None of us ever gave a hang for fourth dimension, but we had more fun on that frame than on any other thing I can remember. So I am going to make one for my children."

I was enthusiastic about the idea, and said, "But that is an ideal piece of school playground equipment. It can take care of many children in a small area. It satisfies every child's desire to climb. It exercises all the muscles." I called Perry Smith over, and he immediately caught the idea and became enthusiastic.

After the party Perry Smith and I went to Hinton's house and worked with him far into the night scheming how this framework could be made into a practical piece of equipment for school playgrounds. The first experimental and rather crude frame, made of iron pipes, was erected at the North Shore Country Day School and became as popular as we had predicted. The flaws in construction became evident, and a new, much better designed frame was erected in the yard of the Horace Mann School.

Hinton incorporated a company and began the manufacture of the frames for school use. He called them "Jungle Gyms." They are now in use all over the world—they and later modifications. But very few people know that their origin was in Winnetka.

The Crow Island School

From 1919 to the present there has scarcely been a two-year period in which there was not activity in school construction or reconstruction in Winnetka. Most of it, however, has consisted of additions to existing schools, or alterations. Only two entirely new buildings have been constructed—the Skokie School, or Junior High School, which was already planned by the architects in the spring of 1919 (it opened in 1922), and the Crow Island School, built in 1940. The Crow Island School has had such a profound influence on American elementary school architecture, and its genesis is so unusual that its story is worth telling:

As we constructed additions and made alterations in the various schools we were always hampered by the existing architectural forms and limits. We wanted a school that was built to fit our educational philosophy and methods. We wanted it to be beautiful and functional. We wanted it to be the architectural embodiment of our ideas and ideals.

It was evident that the oldest of our buildings, the Horace Mann School, built in 1899, was completely out of keeping with modern school construction. We gave it various "face liftings," but nothing could change its basic form satisfactorily. Furthermore, it was in the center of the town and commercial stores had grown up around it. Its site was inadequate in size even when we bought a little adjacent land. But the cost of buying a new site and constructing a whole new school was for many years a prohibitive obstacle.

There came a time, however, when we were able to buy a beautiful site of about five acres, three-quarters of a mile west of the Horace Mann School, adjacent to a wood called "Crow Island," owned and preserved in a natural state by the Winnetka Park District. We then managed to sell the land on which the Horace Mann School stood to the United States government for a new post office. Meanwhile we began a search for an architect for our new school building.

Many architects wanted the commission—the Winnetka schools were by then very well known and to build the new school would give the architect prestige. The competing architects submitted ideas to the committee on buildings of the Board of Education and to the Superintendent of Schools. Many had good features but none had daring, vision, and an adequate recognition of the new demands of education.

Then one day Lawrence Perkins came into my office. His father's firm (Perkins, Fellows and Hamilton) had built two of Winnetka's schools, Hubbard Woods and Skokie, but Lawrence was just starting a firm of his own. He pleaded with me to give this new firm a chance by recommending it for the contract.

"But, Larry," I exclaimed, "this is to be our dream school. For years we have been thinking about it. We want it to be the most functional and beautiful school in the world. We want it to crystallize in architecture the best of our educational thought and to house appropriately the best educational practices we can evolve. We can't trust this to a group of youngsters who have only built one house and one small church!"

"Don't you recognize," Perkins replied, "that a young firm, knowing that its whole future is at stake, will give more time and thought to this school than any old, established firm could give? Don't you see that we would not be limited by old habits but could see the problem with fresh eyes? We would study every activity in your schools, we would read everything you have written, we would confer with your teachers and principals. We would fit the school to your own educational ideals and needs."

I saw the force of what he was saying, but enthusiasm was not enough. "Larry," I said, "what you say is true. But we want the best, and experience and past performance are necessary guarantees. If we could combine your zeal with the experience of a really great architect, that would be ideal."

"What do you mean by a really great architect?" he asked.

I aimed at the sky and said, "Well, a man like Eliel Saarinen."

"If I can get Eliel and Eero Saarinen to take me and my firm as partners for building this school, would you agree?" he asked.

"I think it would be marvelous. Can you do it?" I replied.

A few days later he had obtained Saarinen's consent. The committee of the Board of Education and I went to see Saarinen and the breathtaking beauty of the Cranbrook school he had built near Detroit. The decision was made.

Perkins lived up to his promise and Saarinen to his reputation. Perkins visited classes, read our writings, talked with teachers, supervisors, principals, school custodians. He made sketches and discussed them with all of us. Gradually the basic classroom units began to take shape. Then he made a table-size model of a classroom, with miniature furniture, and placed it in the corridor of the Horace Mann School for criticisms and suggestions. There was no lack of these, and the model was altered accordingly.

The Winnetka teachers were accustomed to thinking for themselves and expressing themselves freely. They knew just how much cupboard space they needed, how much space for books, their need for room for activities of all kinds, their need for a place where children could hammer and saw and do experiments in science, the need for space on the walls where children's work could be exhibited, and so on.

Frances Presler, in charge of group and creative activities, knew what kind of stage children needed in an elementary school assembly hall, what kind of lighting, what amount of storage space. She conceived, also, a "pioneer room" in the basement that would be a replica of the homes of early American pioneers, where children from all three elementary schools could take turns play-living pioneer life when they were studying it in their classrooms. Near the "pioneer room" she conceived a general work shop for manual activities too large for the classrooms. And hers was the idea for a children's museum and for visual education—all these things she worked out for the basement of the one-story building, requiring little extra cost.

Myrtle Craddock planned the art room, with enough sinks and faucets so that children without crowding and wasting time could mix their paints and wash their brushes—and hands. Jean Duffy, the physical education teacher, had plans for the gymnasium and playground. Ben Helke, the custodian, had valuable suggestions for more sanitary provisions for custodians and better ways of preventing floors from getting soiled. Hazel Gethman, principal of the Horace Mann School who was to be in charge of the new school, had many suggestions to give. And so on. Everyone made contributions.

The architects were sometimes at the point of distraction. Never had they been asked to satisfy the demands of so many people. Coordination of the requests by the Superintendent of Schools helped a little.

But he and the Board of Education kept, at the same time, continued emphasis on economy. This multiple—and highly democratic—pressure on the architects was particularly exasperating while the building was under construction: teachers had after-thoughts of how something could be better done; the architects had misinterpreted some of their ideas; this work would have to be taken out and the right work substituted.

The seating equipment and other furnishings were designed by Eero Saarinen, son and partner (later, successor) to Eliel. Lillian Swan, then Eero Saarinen's wife, made the ceramic decorations.

In due course the building was completed and equipped. It was simple, beautiful, very colorful, and almost ideally fitted to its purpose. And the cost was no more than that of a traditional building with equal floor space. It was named the Crow Island School.

The principal American architectural magazine, *Architectural Forum*, gave the leading 16 pages of an issue to photographs and plans of this school. Altogether, it was written up in 30 magazines. Visitors swarmed to it from far and near.

Fifteen years later, the *Architectural Forum* published an article on "Crow Island Revisited." The article began: [1]

> Back in 1940, Crow Island was an astonishing building. Architects Eliel and Eero Saarinen and Perkins, Wheeler & Will, working with a highly creative school administration, designed this building almost as if no school had ever been designed before. For the first time, modern elementary education—incubated in plants a colonial schoolmaster could have understood perfectly—got a house to fit it.
>
> In 1955 Crow Island appears, if anything, more significant than it did 15 years ago. Time and use—not only here but in many hundred later schools—have proved out the workability of its innovations to a degree that only the wildest optimism in 1940 could have conjectured. The national debt owed Crow Island for ideas large and small is staggering.
>
> But the most exciting thing about Crow Island in 1955 is the lessons it still can teach. Mainly these are lessons in atmosphere, compounded partly of scale, partly of materials, partly of detailing, infused with a loving, patient perfection, inspirited by the civilized, humanizing values of calmness and warmth.

Lawrence Perkins and his firm (now called Perkins and Will) got contract after contract for schools in other cities and are now among the best known and busiest school architects in the United States. Elementary school architecture all over the United States has been influenced markedly by Crow Island School, and even in Victoria and Tasmania, Australia, there are schools patterned after Crow Island.

---

[1] *Architectural Forum*, Oct. 1955, pp. 130-137.

■

CHAPTER THIRTEEN

Relations with

the Community

■
■

From the time when Edwin Fetcher first proposed that the Winnetka public schools should
be made so good "that we will be proud to send
our children to them," the parents and other citizens of Winnetka have been, basically, responsible for the progress made in the schools. It is they
who elect from among themselves the Board of
Education—at least one new member, on the average, every year. It is they who must be satisfied with the education of their children. It is
they who must vote the taxes which support the
schools.

Ever since Fetcher and his friends cam-
paigned to get a Board of Education that would
be dedicated to making the schools as good as

they could be made, committees of citizens have sought each year the best men and women to fill the vacancies in the Board. Such vacancies are caused by the ending of members' terms of office (members are elected for a three-year term, and by common agreement do not serve more than two terms each). When the committee (called the Caucus Committee) has found suitable candidates and obtained their consent, these candidates are submitted to the voters in a special election. Of course any other group of citizens could nominate other candidates. But so careful have the successive Caucus Committees been and so eminently fit the candidates they have proposed, that opposition candidates have rarely been presented.

There have been two exceptions. It will be remembered that there was, in 1920, a great division of opinion in Winnetka as to whether the new Junior High School would be placed in the center of the town, by adding to the old Horace Mann school, or whether it should be placed on the ample new site the Board had selected. That year the opponents of the Board's plan put up three candidates who represented their viewpoint, in opposition to the Caucus Committee's candidates. The caucus candidates were overwhelmingly elected.

Then in 1933, when the Depression was rocking the whole country and the dominant Republican party had just been overthrown by the Democrats with Franklin Roosevelt's election, an opposition party was organized in Winnetka. This group was opposed not only to the Caucus Committee that nominated Board of Education members but also to the corresponding committees of the same caucus that nominated all other elected officials of the local government—the Council, the Park Board, and the Library Board. The opponents of the Board of Education consisted of people who wanted the tax rate lowered; of people who wanted the schools to return to the traditional education concentrating on purely academic studies and rigid discipline; of people opposed to the liberal tendencies in the social studies program which, they felt, should be made to indoctrinate children in what they called "Americanism"; and of parents whose children, in spite of our best efforts, were not learning as much as their parents thought they should. All these elements united for a battle to change the character of the Board of Education, to get rid of the Superintendent of Schools whom they held responsible for the evils, and to alter the kind of education in the schools. They fought valiantly for their candidates, but were defeated by a majority of over 70 percent of the voters. (The defeat of the opposition for the other branches of the local government was even more impressive.)

Without this solid support from the great majority of citizens we could not have made the progress we did in all aspects of education. Nor could we have got the necessary financial support for improved salaries for teachers, for specialists ("advisors") in group and creative activities, art, music, the Educational Clinic, etc., and for ample equipment, the improvement of buildings and grounds, and new construction. Many times during the past 40 years the Board of Education has asked the citizens to vote, in special elections, the required authority to increase their taxes and to issue bonds. Not once have the citizens failed to vote favorably on these proposals, and by very large majorities. We would not have had such support if we had not worked closely with the parents, kept the community fully informed of all we were doing, and given the children both happiness and a demonstrably effective education.

Our two chief means of working with the community were the Parent-Teacher Association and, of course, the Board of Education.

The Parent-Teacher Association

There was already in 1919 a Parent-Teacher Association in Winnetka. From that time forward this was strengthened and enlivened. The resulting organization came to be as follows: The parents of the children in each classroom elect one of their number as "room chairman" and meet at least once a month (usually in the evening so fathers can be present) with the teacher. There is a program of simple entertainment, explanation by the teacher of what the children are doing and the purpose back of it, and an opportunity for parents to ask questions and express themselves.

When, as often happens, a parent speaks of the difficulties of his particular child and when his (or her) elaboration and complaints threaten to consume a disproportionate amount of time, it is the responsibility of the chairman and the teacher to suggest a personal conference between the teacher and that parent to discuss this personal case, and then to direct the discussion to problems of more general interest. Sometimes, however, many parents have comparable problems, and the teacher must use this situation to help the parents understand just what the school is trying to do about them and how this is being done. If the teacher is wise, he or she listens open-mindedly, admits bafflement at times, and agrees to give the problem careful consideration in consultation with the principal and the school specialists. The teacher learns much from these meetings and parents, too, are educated.

It is in these classroom meetings that parents plan what they can do to make the classroom more attractive for their children—perhaps plants for a window box, perhaps curtains which certain mothers agree to make, perhaps a special piece of equipment that fathers can make.

In such meetings, too, the teacher can draw on special interests, skills, or talents of the parents to contribute to the children's work. This mother has been in the Netherlands and has pictures she can bring to class and experiences she can relate when the children are studying the Netherlands. Or, in another class, a father has a hobby of astronomy and can stay away from the office one morning to talk to the children about the stars or can invite them some evening to look through the small telescope he has in his yard. A mother is a singer and can come some day to sing to the children. A newly arrived immigrant gets status for herself and her children and can contribute to all the class by coming to school to tell of the country from which she came and her adventures in reaching America. A storekeeper can invite the children to visit his store. The possibilities are endless. The resources of the community are made available to the children, and the parents have a feeling of participation in the school program.

The chairmen of the classrooms and the school principal form the Board of the School Parent-Teacher Association. All parents of the school elect the officers of this organization. These officers, with their Board, decide on what general meetings and programs there should be for the school as a whole—lectures, concerts, study groups. They may also raise questions to discuss with the superintendent or Board of Education.

Each school Parent-Teacher Association sends delegates, always including its president and the school principal, to an all-Winnetka Board of the Parent-Teacher Association, of which the superintendent of schools is always a member. It is this Board that coordinates the work of the four school Parent-Teacher Associations, suggests activities, and clarifies the role of the Parent-Teacher organization in relation to the roles of the professional body of the teaching staff and to the Board of Education.

It is essential that a Parent-Teacher Association keep to its own role. It must not interfere with nor try to dictate school program. It is primarily a lay body without professional competence to decide what should be taught and when and how. These are responsibilities of the professional staff. Neither is it the duly elected legal body to appoint, promote, and dismiss school personnel, to levy taxes, to set educational policy—these are the roles of the Board of Education. Neither must it enter into political questions. Its members, being all the parents and teachers, have various opinions on these questions, and no officer or majority of members of the Parent-Teacher Association has a right to speak on political matters in the name of the Association.

Yet, within these limits, the Parent-Teacher Association has an important role. Here are the parents of all the children. No one knows as well as they whether the children are developing satisfactorily and happily. Problems and difficulties and questions can, when they are representative of the experience of a number of parents, be brought to the attention of the principals and superintendent, and of the Board of Education. The Parent-Teacher Association has, also, the responsibility of keeping its members informed as to the progress of educational thought and practice, and interpreting the program of the schools to all parents. New families moving into Winnetka need to be amalgamated; the Parent-Teacher Association arranges for a meeting in each school in the autumn where the superintendent or principal can explain to new parents the aims and practices of the schools. And, as mentioned before, the parents, through the Parent-Teacher Association, can contribute to both the physical environment and the educational program.

The clarification and interpretation of this role is the responsibility of the Board of the all-Winnetka Parent-Teacher Association. It is also through this Board that suggestions and questions may be directed to the Board of Education with effectiveness. And to this Parent-Teacher Association Board, the Board of Education turns for help in giving all parents an understanding of its policies and needs.

The comprehensive Parent-Teacher Association usually has an annual meeting for all parents, with an important lecture, and with a social program—often a picnic for the parents, teachers and children of all the four schools.

In general, the Parent-Teacher Association in Winnetka has been an invaluable asset to the schools. It is the most important and widespread means of maintaining contact, understanding and cooperation between the schools and the community.

The Board of Education

From the beginning of this book it has been made clear that the keystone of the education in Winnetka, as in any other city, is the Board of Education. If the people of the community select and support some of the ablest, most far-seeing, intelligent, and public-spirited citizens as members of the Board of Education, the foundation is laid, as it was in Winnetka, for good schools getting ever better. Winnetka, for half a century, has elected such people to its Board of Education.

This Board, with all its changes in membership, has been consistent in working continuously to make the schools fulfill their function as effectively as possible, to help the children of Winnetka to develop physically, intellectually, emotionally, and socially, in an atmosphere of beauty and happiness. It has selected successive Superintendents of Schools with great care, and, as long as each retained the Board's confidence, has supported him in his work and recommendations. It has looked to the superintendent for professional leadership and been educated by him to an understanding of modern educational goals and the procedures for reaching these goals. It has given him great freedom in the selection and placement of teachers and other school personnel and in the development of the program, and given the necessary legal sanction to his acts.

During the 24 years (1919–43) when I was superintendent, I had many battles with the Board; these were, however, always the clashes of opinion among people holding a common ideal but differing as to the ways of realizing it. We worked so closely together that we were all personal friends. We had high mutual respect. Arguments were never petty or personal. I learned much from the Board of Education and was kept from letting my enthusiasm carry our program forward too fast for assimilation by the community. And it was my responsibility to help educate the Board, to keep it aware of the advances of educational science and philosophy, to maintain sympathetic and understanding support and to familiarize it with what we were doing in the schools and why.

It was, however, my responsibility and that of my successors to see that the Board did not step out of its role and interfere with the detailed administration of the schools, or try to substitute lay judgment for the professional decisions of the teaching and supervisory staff of the schools. The selection of personnel and their assignments, from custodians to principals, was a professional matter. So were the selection of textbooks, the planning of curriculum, the decision as to methods. For these matters the Board must trust the judgment of the superintendent and support it—or else get a new superintendent whom it can trust. On the other hand, with the type of responsible and intelligent men and women who served on the Winnetka Board, blind trust was out of the question. The superintendent must justify and interpret his decisions to the Board so that their confidence in his judgment is based on understanding and knowledge.

Legally, the Board of Education has all power, the superintendent none. But the Board, if it is wise, delegates most of its power on all professional matters to the superintendent—and this the Winnetka Board of Education has consistently done.

In the matter of budget, tax levy, and school construction, the work of the Board and the superintendent is cooperative, their roles being combined. The superintendent prepares and recommends a budget each year, then discusses it at length with the Board, making such modifications as are necessary. The Board, representing the citizens, decides whether certain expenditures can be justified and whether the people will be willing to meet them with tax support. The Board is very sensitive to the public pulse. The Board then levies the tax, within legal limits set by the state, to raise the money needed for the budget. On school construction the superintendent brings the needs to the attention of the Board and makes recommendations as to how they can be met. The Board takes active part in deciding all major matters of school construction and alteration.

These relationships did not exist in Winnetka before 1919. There was no real Superintendent of Schools until 1913, and then the superintendent did not long retain the confidence of his Board, which therefore took over many of his functions. But from 1919 onward the respective roles of Parent-Teacher Association, Board of Education and Superintendent of Schools became more and more clarified, and there was rarely any usurpation. As will be seen in Part Two, Dr. Marland has wisely added carefully selected Citizens' Committees as a means of further involving the community in the schools. These were—and are— organized for specific, well-defined purposes. They supplement the roles of P.T.A., Board of Education, and professional staff, without taking over any of their respective functions.

It is the recognition and respecting of the various roles, and their coordination and cooperation, that have kept the people of Winnetka so nearly united in their understanding support of the total educational program.

CHAPTER FOURTEEN

Recognition

and Influence

The experiments, the research, and the techniques of Winnetka were written up and published in professional periodicals and in periodicals for parents and for the general public from 1920 onward, first in the United States, then in countries over the world. Books (or chapters in books) describing Winnetka's experiments and principles have been published in England and Australia, and in many languages, among them French (in Belgium and France), Spanish (in Spain, Argentina, Ecuador, and Chile), Italian, German, Finnish, Danish, Polish, Czech, Arabic, Chinese, Japanese, and Bengali. The Winnetka schools rapidly became known on all continents. Our first work was, as we have seen, in the adaptation to individual differences—the provision and techniques for permitting each child to progress at his own rate of speed. The early experiments in Winnetka seemed to be an answer to the problems presented by a demonstrated range of children's abilities.

Consequently, universities, institutions for training teachers, superintendents of schools, and boards of education and teachers all focussed attention on Winnetka. They called our work "The Winnetka Plan." As I have said before, we never used or liked this appellation. We were not trying to set a pattern for all schools, nor did we have a fixed plan—we were continuously revising and improving our work, and the techniques of individualizing instruction were only a first step in the total aim of providing children with the best education that research and experimentation could help us to give. This objective has remained unchanged right up to the present.

Nevertheless the name "Winnetka Plan" has persisted to this day.[1]

Countless visitors came, and still come, to Winnetka, from all parts of the world. Teachers' associations and universities in all sections of the United States and in Canada and abroad called on members of the Winnetka staff to give lectures, summer courses and demonstrations.

In 1924, A. J. Stoddard, then Superintendent of Schools in Bronxville, New York, a suburb not unlike Winnetka, asked if he could borrow a Winnetka teacher for a year to teach a class and demonstrate there the Winnetka techniques. We were glad to cooperate and we selected Marion Carswell. She was one of the first teachers we had employed in 1919 and was young, attractive, vigorous, efficient, and gracious. She had participated in our experiments from the beginning and had conducted a highly successful summer demonstration of Winnetka techniques at Teachers College of Columbia University.

Her work in Bronxville went very well. Consequently, two years later, when Stoddard decided to leave Bronxville to become Superintendent of Schools in Schenectady, he and his Board of Education de-

---

[1] The "Winnetka Plan" has often been confused with the "Dalton Plan." The "Dalton Plan," first worked out in her Children's University School in New York by Helen Parkhurst, was tried in the public high school in Dalton, Massachusetts, beginning in 1920. It had, at first, one thing in common with our work in Winnetka. It did, during the earlier years, provide for individual progress of the children. I shall not attempt to describe the Dalton Plan—Miss Parkhurst herself has done so fully in books and periodicals, with translations in several languages. It had many merits

cided that they would like to have someone from Winnetka as Superintendent of Schools. Stoddard came to Winnetka and discussed the matter with us. The man they wanted was Willard W. Beatty. Beatty and I, it will be remembered, had been colleagues under Burk at the San Francisco State Normal School, and he was invited to Winnetka to head our new Junior High School and be assistant superintendent. He wanted to head a school system himself, and especially one like Bronxville, which though smaller than Winnetka, incorporated the senior high school as well as the elementary school and junior high school. So he gladly accepted the Bronxville offer and took with him several of the Winnetka teachers. Years later, after Beatty had left Bronxville to take charge of the education of Indians for the United States and its territories, one of the teachers whom he had taken to Bronxville from Winnetka (Howard Funk) became the Bronxville Superintendent of Schools until his retirement in 1957.

A year after Beatty went to Bronxville, the International School in Geneva, Switzerland, asked for a Winnetka teacher to help reorganize that school in accordance with some of the practices in Winnetka. Again we selected Marion Carswell. She worked there for two years (1927–29) and when we called her back to resume the principalship of one of our elementary schools (Hubbard Woods), she was succeeded in Geneva by a series of other Winnetka teachers, each for one or two years.

A few years later (1934), the American School in Tokyo asked for similar help. Mildred Hughes of Winnetka went first and was followed by from one to three teachers every year until the Second World War threw Japan into the enemy camp.

A similar arrangement was made with the American School in Beirut, Lebanon.

The international educational organization, the New Education Fellowship, has had representatives of Winnetka on its program for almost every international congress it has held since 1925. The American

---

and it had very wide vogue, especially in the British Commonwealth (its first fame was in England), in the Netherlands, in the early days of the USSR, and in the Orient. It differed markedly from the work in Winnetka in that it was never characterized by research, by the preparation of self-instructive teaching materials, by the scientific construction of curriculum ("The Dalton Plan," Miss Parkhurst said, "is a vehicle for any kind of curriculum"), or by techniques for group and creative activities.

Section of the New Education Fellowship, the Progressive Education Association, elected the Superintendent of the Winnetka Schools as its president (1936–40) and later he became president of the international body for eight years (1948–56).

As soon as Winnetka became well known there was a demand for our self-instructive teaching materials. We therefore incorporated a small non-profit publishing company, the Winnetka Educational Press [2] in 1925. This distributed, at cost, literature on Winnetka and the materials we were using in the schools. It actually saved money for the Board of Education, which gave it a basement room in which to operate, because it published (usually in mimeographed or multigraphed form) all the materials the teachers prepared, in quantities much larger than the Winnetka schools alone would need, thereby distributing the cost to other schools which used the material. For experimental purposes, however, the quantities published were much too small to attract commercial publishers, and, from a commercial point of view, we revised them too often as our experience and research progressed. The Winnetka Educational Press served a useful function for 27 years (1925 to 1952).

Textbook materials that were of more permanent character and likely to have wide use were published by commercial publishers. Altogether more than 30 volumes, small and large, of such textbook material were commercially published between 1919 and 1943 in the fields of spelling, primary reading, reading for retarded children, arithmetic, science and social studies. These were in addition to the many publications of the Winnetka Educational Press.

The Influence of Winnetka on Education

There is always a gap of time, often of two or more generations, between the formulation of educational principles and their application in a large number of schools; there is a similar lag between obtaining definite results from research and the full use of research findings. A historian, writing 30 years from now, will be better able to assess Winnetka's influence than anyone can do today; and even he will be unable to say how much of the progress in the direction which Win-

---

[2] First named "Individual Instruction Materials, Inc."

netka has pointed is due to Winnetka and how much Winnetka merely illustrates and expresses in action a more universal trend.

A few very direct effects of the work in Winnetka can, however, be demonstrated, even now:

1. The work on arithmetic, by the Committee of Seven, which originated and centered in Winnetka, has demonstrably influenced school curriculum and textbooks, especially in the United States.

2. The postponement of formal teaching of reading and arithmetic in a great many American schools can be traced to Winnetka's original research in this field, although that has been supplemented by much confirmatory research and is part of a larger stream of influence.

3. "Workbooks" are now used extensively throughout the United States. These are exercise books in which children work individually. The first of them were directly and consciously adapted from the Winnetka self-instructive teaching materials.

4. Some 549,460 copies of the self-instruction textbooks in English grammar and composition, based on the Winnetka *Functional Grammar* and written for the armed forces by a Winnetka teacher, Agnes Spangler, were used by members of the American armed forces for teaching themselves.

5. The "Jungle Gym" climbing frame, which originated in Winnetka, has been and is still used on the school playgrounds of a great number of schools not only in the United States but in countries over the world; somewhat similar frames, adapted from the original "Jungle Gym," are also very widely used.

6. One of the most spectacular influences of Winnetka has been the revolution in the architecture of American elementary schools as a direct result of the Crow Island school.

These specific results of the work in Winnetka are, however, less significant than those which have so merged with other influences that Winnetka's part in the progress cannot be sharply identified. Where, however, Winnetka was the first, or among the earliest of the public school systems to focus on a problem or demonstrate a solution of a problem, it can be safely assumed that the subsequent attention to the problem by schools, universities and educators generally has been influenced considerably by Winnetka. For example:

1. The recognition of the wide range of differences among children and the need for adapting, in one way or another, to these differences.
2. "Programmed" instruction. While we never called it by that name, Winnetka was probably the first school system to use what is today called "programmed instruction." The self-instructive, self-corrective teaching materials and tests were necessarily "programmed," and were the prototype of "teaching machines" as now beginning to be used.
3. The individualization of the teaching of reading. In New York City, for instance, the individualization of reading is now an officially recognized part of the program. The same is true increasingly in many other cities.
4. The more accurate grading of children's books to fit various stages of reading ability.
5. The wide use of manuscript writing in the earlier classes.
6. The publishing of school textbooks better adapted to self-instruction, written more simply and interestingly.
7. Psychological and psychiatric services for the schools and the training of teachers in mental hygiene.
8. The general trend in the United States toward integrating in a comprehensive series of courses, known as social studies, what were formerly separate courses in history, geography and civic education.
9. The wide use of "projects" and other forms of group and creative activities.
10. The extensive use of the resources of the community—parents contributing to the schools from their own experience, trips by the children to observe the various activities of the community, etc.
11. The incorporation of nursery schools into the public school system.
12. Democratic school administration, including full participation of the teachers in planning curriculum, preparing textbooks, and carrying out research.

13. The direct action of the citizens of many communities in efforts to improve and support their schools.

We have tried here to single out specific ways in which the Winnetka venture his influenced education. But it is the totality of the venture that is more significant. Winnetka has shown that where citizens, the board of education, the superintendent of schools and the teaching and supervisory staff of a public school system work cooperatively toward making the schools as effective as possible and use research toward this end, a public school system can become an educational laboratory and center of demonstration, valuable not only to its own children but also to countless others.

Yet because of tradition and inertia and the consequent long lag of practice behind knowledge, much that was found effective and valuable in Winnetka is still not utilized in most schools. In time these things will be rediscovered and gradually, usually without reference to Winnetka as such, will help teachers to adapt their work in the classrooms to the widely varying maturity, intelligence, interests, needs and capabilities of the children.

The educational significance of Winnetka is not a thing of the past, a brief episode in the history of education. It is a continuing influence. It is a stream which got its identity from three converging streams—the resolution of the parents in Winnetka to make their schools so good that they would be proud to send their children to them; the work of Frederic Burk and his associates; and my own early experience. But these streams themselves had earlier origins, from Rousseau, Pestalozzi and Froebel, from William James and G. Stanley Hall, from Francis W. Parker and John Dewey.

And it is a center, a convergence of many influences. Influences have come in continuously: from Freud, Adler and Jung; from Piaget and Gesell; from William H. Kilpatrick; from European pioneers in the "activity school"; from Decroly and Montessori; and from innumerable researchers in psychology, sociology and anthropology.

As a growing organism assimilates many elements, selecting and using what it needs and recombining them, so Winnetka has freely used the ideas and experiences of many people over the world and made them a part of itself. Then, in turn, it has become an element to be assimilated by others, losing its identity in proportion to its assimilation.

Winnetka was, and is, an integral part of the whole forward movement of education. For more than 40 years it has been a center in which many influences have coalesced. Put to the test under practical public school conditions, modified by research and experience, these influences have gone forth again into the educational world as a new unity. The American poet, Walt Whitman, expressed well the idea I am trying to convey when he wrote:

> O strain musical, flowing through ages and continents,
> Now reaching me and America,
> I take your strong chords, intersperse them, and cheerfully pass them forward.

Transition

In April, 1943, I accepted a call from the Army.
During the next 13 years there were four successive Superintendents of Schools, as will be seen
in the next chapter; so progress was somewhat
uneven.

The main retrogressions, as seen from my
viewpoint, were the diminution of the Department of Educational Counsel; the abandonment
of the Winnetka Educational Press; the cessation
of all research activity; the slowing down of production of instructional materials, and the disso-
lution of the Graduate Teachers College. On the
other hand, the four principals remained in their
posts and carried on effectively. The actual work
in the classrooms went forward much as before

with some improvements. No basic, solid principles were abandoned.

Then, in 1956, came Marland, determined to stay to see the job through. With vigor, dedication, vision and courage he revivified the whole program. What he has done and why, form Part Two of this book.

With no idea of uprooting what was best in the first quarter century, but rather with the determination to use that as the basis for new growth, doing such pruning as was desirable, he started the renascence of the schools.

PART TWO

Sidney P. Marland, Jr.

CHAPTER FIFTEEN

C. W. and I

This chapter title is not the abbreviated name of a mythical midwestern railroad. It is, rather, a short way of introducing Carleton Washburne and me as I view the two individuals in their relationship to education in Winnetka. For the reader to have a fair understanding of what is to follow and its relationship to what has gone before, this chapter should be used as a transitional bridge between Washburne and Marland. The continuing evolution of education in Winnetka should be viewed in its light.

* * *

I must risk presuming upon the reader, in recording certain autobiographical notes and an

excessive use of the personal pronoun. Their purpose is to afford something in the nature of an administrative diary which may be useful to
the student of educational administration. Further, it seems fitting that
the energies and influences and motivations, modest though they may
be, which I have brought to my work in Winnetka, be viewed in some
kind of juxtaposition with those of Dr. Washburne, whose achievements
(also somewhat autobiographical) have been recorded in the preceding
chapters. For, without feigning false modesty on the part of either of us,
administrative leadership is a crucial ingredient of education. I can state
with great conviction that the quality of instruction depends very largely
upon the competence and commitment of the teacher, and with almost
as much conviction, I can state that the quality and competence of the
teacher rest heavily upon the effectiveness of the system-wide leadership
and the building leadership.

The Co-Author's View of Washburne

Dr. Washburne (referred to frequently as C. W. after this) devoted considerable attention in the early chapters to his personal background and orientation for his subsequent work in Winnetka. These are
important passages, for they reveal in large measure the extraordinary
dimensions of this man.

The observation should be made at this point that, all appearances
to the contrary, this book is not a collaboration. It is a tale in two parts,
written by two quite different individuals. This permits me to compliment my partner without embarrassment, and, I trust, disagree with him
if I find it appropriate. By having the last word, I enjoy something of
an advantage—such advantage being partially or totally offset by the
fact that in dealing with the present tense, my colleagues are still close
at hand to keep me honest.

I met C. W. for the first time in the spring of 1956, soon after I
had accepted the invitation to be Superintendent of Schools in Winnetka the following fall:

> Dear *Dr. Marland:*
>   I was delighted to learn [* * * etc.] Hearty congratulations to you and to
> the Winnetka Board.
>   I should like very much to have a talk with you sometime this spring. I think
> I might be able to give you some tips and some general orientation.... You
> are going into a challenging and potentially highly satisfying experience, but
> one which ... has its pitfalls and roadblocks. ...

This cordial note led to our first meeting at C. W.'s apartment in New York City. (He was then Professor of Education at Brooklyn College.) An increasing friendship has ensued. But it may be revealing to observe here that at least two members of the Winnetka Board of Education at that time were considerably distressed to learn that I had been to see Dr. Washburne. They appeared either to mistrust his influence or my independence, or both. One member wrote to me:

> We invited you here because you were different from Mr. Washburne. We trust we were not in error in this judgment.

They were not in error. I am very different from C. W., but possibly not in the directions hoped by the uneasy Board member. Washburne is an intellectual giant; I am a garden variety working superintendent. Washburne is fundamentally, by nature and by training, a scientist; I am, if anything, a romanticist, a pragmatist and a very modest student of the humanities. Washburne was and is an indefatigable writer of very important educational works; I find that the essential written work of my day-to-day obligations to communicate with the Board of Education, the faculty, and the community, together with more speech-making than I truly enjoy, command more time than I have to give. Washburne is possessed of an extraordinary personal magnetism that after 50 years of heavy and very genuine usage shows no signs of wearing thin; any comparison in this category leaves me far behind. Washburne's brand of instructional leadership, as I see its evidence in Winnetka, was a hip-deep kind of personal immersion in educational innovation, in which he not only conceived the ideas, but did some of the actual teaching, wrote and edited the necessary texts, calculated the statistical outcomes, and published the learned papers deriving from the exploration. My kind of instructional leadership leans heavily upon the creativity of others, draws upon the resources of faculty and community, and occasionally starts minor or major fires of inquiry that are spread by smoldering embers rather than by gales or explosions.

It is true that we were working in different times, and with a different set of circumstances. Washburne was called to Winnetka in 1919 to make it the best possible school system in the country, starting from scratch. He had nowhere to go but up. His faculty and student enrollment, while steadily growing, were roughly half the dimensions of today's numbers. We are still a small school system, however, with roughly

2,300 pupils and 150 staff members, including all personnel. But changing times have brought a changing faculty; the faculty stability of
C. W.'s day has culminated in swift and sudden turnover, as the elder
statesmen reach retirement age.

But apart from sheer numbers of teachers and children, C. W.
lived and worked in Winnetka at a time when educational leadership
(for all of his honest devotion to democratic administration) was considerably more status-oriented than it can be today. Just as the evolution of personal dignity and freedom has flowered in business, in industry and on the university campus, it has caught up the public school
teacher since the mid-1940's, and rightly so. This condition, calling for
less authority in the "status leader," with correspondingly greater dignity
and freedom in the teacher, produces a slower, more complex, more
volatile context for educational advancement. But it is nonetheless effective, and very likely more effective than the conditions prevailing in
1920–44 in the United States.

C. W. will undoubtedly quarrel with the foregoing passage which
endeavors to illuminate differences in the *settings* in which we have
worked. He would, with much justification, declare that he was a sensitive, democratic administrator. But it is not he that I am considering;
it is the teacher, and the posture of teachers in general toward administration in general that has changed. Even in my brief span of 25 years
in education the change is radical—suggesting only that educational innovation has been re-oriented, and probably, in the long run, been
improved by the enlarging "status-leadership" of the teacher. This does
not diminish the greatness of C. W.'s work in Winnetka. On the contrary, it underscores his personal and individual strength as the leader
of that period. And it rationalizes a different kind, a slower kind perhaps, or less colorful kind, of leadership demanded today.

The Evolution of Leadership

Calling attention to the evolution that has taken place in the role
of superintendent of schools, the *Encyclopedia of Educational Research*
(1950) states:

> The superintendent of schools has come through a gradual development
> to occupy a most significant place. . . . The opportunity for a superintendent of
> educational enterprises, rather than for a superintendent of instruction or schools,

grows constantly larger as our societal organization continues to grow more and more complex. . . . It constitutes a challenge to all the resourcefulness, intelligence, patience, tolerance and tact an individual has.

The changing nature of leadership in education is examined further by MacKenzie and Corey: [1] A "recognized leader" is "a person who is seen by individuals or groups as helping . . . to provide the means *they* desire to use to identify or attain *their* goals." Notwithstanding C. W.'s personal humility and his repeated protests that the great creative work of the Winnetka Schools was the work of the faculty, in truth, the Winnetka Schools were Carleton Washburne's schools. His desires and his goals motivated the faculty and the community. In MacKenzie and Corey's definition this would not be workable today.

I noted earlier that C. W. came to Winnetka to plow a relatively fallow field, with high expectations and support. The high expectations and support remain strong and vital today. The field, however, is rich, heavily plowed, harrowed, planted, and rewardingly harvested. One might almost say that while C. W. came here with nowhere to go but up, I came here with nowhere to go but down. One might *almost* say this—if he did not know the nature of education.

The Sensitive Role of the School Administrator: A Case Study

It may be discernible to the reader by now that I have begun my part of this book with more than one purpose in mind. It has been our original intent to examine the Winnetka Schools as an educational experiment, spread over some 40 years, to include the present. This I shall endeavor to do, contributing testimony for the past seven years.

But beyond this primary objective, I hope also to inject into this historical drama a useful sub-plot that reveals the role of school administration in a dynamic, demanding school system and school community. Accordingly, as a device for introducing the numerous educational enterprises that have been perpetuated, discontinued or inaugurated in the past seven years, I shall, where appropriate, attempt to describe the administrative or leadership setting in which educational evolution took place. This sub-plot may serve for good or ill those aspiring adminis-

---

[1] MacKenzie, Gordon N. and Stephen M. Corey, *et al.*, *Instructional Leadership*, Bureau of Publications, Teachers College, Columbia, New York, 1954, p. 209.

trators who wish to venture upon this exciting and rewarding but sometimes uneven road.

I cannot go all the way with the MacKenzie-Corey definition mentioned earlier. I use it simply to underscore the changing character of school leadership in the 1920–1963 period. If I thought that my only function was to arbitrate, negotiate, balance, and help *others* (including society as well as faculty) to achieve *their* goals, there would be no joy in my work. Indeed, the school leader, while giving earnest attention to the hopes and fears of the community and the faculty, as well as the Board of Education, and responding to those hopes and fears, *must have some hopes and fears of his own concerning children and education, for which he contrives creative solutions.*

To accept MacKenzie and Corey is to immobilize the administrator's creativity. To undertake, on the other hand, what I believe was C. W.'s personalized leadership in a context of benevolent, centralized, administrative firmness would be impossible today, at least in a proud faculty. Hence, with unaccustomed neutrality I stand between these extremes, advocating high prominence to the initiative and freedom of the teacher, but, at the same time abdicating none of my own responsibilities for initiative and innovation. The initiative of the democratic leader is limited only by his ability to convince others of the worth of the undertaking he has in mind. The likelihood of unity and broad consensus in a faculty in the 1960's is considerably less than it was in the 1920's, when the status leader was not necessarily expected to "convince" the faculty.

I hasten to add one point: C. W.'s high commitment to, and demonstrated practice of, the ideals of democratic administration flourished ahead of their time. And, with many other innovations that took form in Winnetka, democratic leadership, *per se*, undoubtedly contributed to the wholesome evolution of school administration at large.

So far I have examined differences between Washburne and Marland as individuals, and as instruments of their respective periods in our educational evolution. But there are ways in which our roles have been alike. For example, we have both found in Winnetka a community of citizens heavily committed to educational excellence, and willing to make sacrifices of dollars and energy to insure good schools. We have been consistently favored with distinguished, broad-visioned boards of education whose differences, if any, were of unselfish and non-political origin. We have both been blessed with the means to attract and retain in Winnetka teachers of high competence and unsurpassed devotion to children.

More specifically, as individuals we both seem to have good health and energy, with more than ordinary tolerance of long hours. (My work week, including evening obligations of a professional or public character, runs in the neighborhood of 65-75 hours. I am sure the C. W.'s was as much or more.) We both hold very high our devotion to the dignity and sacredness of individuals, whether child or adult, swift or slow, large or small. We both believe deeply in freedom, and the schools' strategic place in freedom's processes. Interestingly, we both came into education by the back door, neither having followed the conventional pattern of teacher preparation. (I was nearly disqualified from my earlier superintendency for lack of certification requirements, and was held in legal limbo until I had taken the necessary courses. Lest this be construed as a disparagement of the professional requirements for teaching and administration, let me hasten to add that I subsequently continued my graduate work in education with high intellectual stimulation and satisfaction.) Both of us had been identified one way or another by our betters as "good teachers" before entering administration. Washburne's field was science, mine English. We both enjoy good stories, either as listeners or tellers; we are both possessed of a certain amount of "ham," as many teachers are.

We both have great faith in people, both those in immediate association with us and the more remote.

There are doubtless other ways in which we brought similar characteristics to our duties in Winnetka. But likenesses aside, the job itself when approached in 1956 possessed many contradictions. My first visit with C. W. revealed a few.

Some Contradictions

He said: "You have doubtless heard of the Winnetka Plan." I nodded, hoping he would not press for details, and he went on. "There is no Winnetka Plan; there never was. It is and was a spirit, a condition, an attitude of teaching, but never a fixed plan. Our educational theorists of the day enjoyed attaching names to things, so what we were doing became known as the Winnetka Plan."

My next contradiction took form when I had been in Winnetka
only a few weeks and realized that so far as many members of the faculty
at that time were concerned, there was a very definite Winnetka Plan,
and it was a good plan, even though in some respects it had not changed
in 25 years. C. W. would have deplored this, but of those who still
venerated his memory in 1956 (and there were a good number), a few
still took joyful consolation in keeping things "just as Carleton would
have wanted them."

After Washburne left Winnetka, some who were his ardent followers
overlooked one of his deep convictions, as expressed in his classic work,
A *Living Philosophy of Education:*

> As each child is ᴤ new creation, as life is ever growing, ever changing, so
> must education, if it is to nourish the living child, be ever developing, never
> finished.

Carrying my contradictions a bit further, I had occasion to speak
before the Woman's Club not long after joining the community. After
the meeting, a more-than-middle-aged lady whom I did not know then,
but later recognized as a community force of substantial proportions,
took me aside over our tea. "I don't have any children in your schools
now," she said, somewhat redundantly. "We're so glad to have you here.
We hope you stay longer than the others. My children were in school
when Carleton Washburne was Superintendent. Of course he just about
ruined the schools. But he was the *nicest man."*

I continued to receive ardent opinions about C. W., trying to
remain objective, and trying to remember that "under the tree that bears
the finest fruit will be found the most sticks and stones." One of the
teachers during those early months paid me what I know she felt was
the highest possible compliment: "You said that just as Carleton would
have said it!" (I gagged, doggedly remained neutral, in a community
and faculty that had no other neutrals on the subject of C. W.)

Being one's self as a school leader under these circumstances was
awkward. I took on a steadily increasing respect for the men who had
been superintendents in Winnetka between C. W. and me. After 13
years (and four other superintendents), C. W.'s authorship was still
prominent on the covers of the textbooks; his name was on many lips;
his bust, even, held a prominent place in one principal's office; his
writings were still being distributed by the central office, though in some

cases they were yellowed 20-year-old reprints from journals, sent in response to those who asked for current information about our schools. My secretary, who had also been Dr. Washburne's, occasionally made a slip of the tongue in reference to me, such as a telephone bit, one side of which I heard: "Just a moment, I'll let you speak to Dr. Washburne." (Meaning *me*.) This, after 13 years!

In all seriousness, the splendid shadow of C. W., diminished, I am sure, by 1956 when I arrived, may have had a significant influence on the rapid turnover of the good men whom I also count among my predecessors.

Other Winnetka Superintendents

Rae Logan, who had been junior high principal and associate superintendent under C. W., assumed the post initially in 1943, remaining until his retirement in 1946. Following him came Dr. Harold Shane, who remained until 1949. His contributions to Winnetka in that period were significant, including major salary and personnel improvements, and a substantial effort toward curriculum development. Harold continued to live in Winnetka, occupying a professorship at Northwestern University, and providing warm friendship and counsel to me until 1959 when he accepted the post of Dean of the School of Education at Indiana University. He, too, enjoys a national reputation through his major contributions to professional literature and his leadership at Northwestern and Indiana. Following him came Dr. William M. Alexander, who, after a short period, went on to achieve an increasingly distinguished place in American education. He is now nationally recognized as a leader in curriculum development from his professorship at Peabody College.

Gilbert Willey followed Alexander, continuing to move forward with curriculum development during his tenure between 1950 and 1956. Unhappily, he was overtaken by illness at this time, and has retired from active work in education. He continues to take a keen interest in our accomplishments, and responds warmly and enthusiastically to progress reports which we send him from time to time.

Each of these very able men went out of his way to encourage my acceptance of the superintendency in Winnetka, and to offer good counsel during my freshman period. They have all contributed to whatever may be good in Winnetka education; it is emphasized here that if this book appears to pass over the years between C. W.'s time and mine, it is because I must limit myself to the things I know.

Teachers and "the Administration"

There were other influences in Winnetka beyond C. W.'s lingering image that produced contradictions. One derived from my first interview with a faculty committee before I had been invited to the post. I had asked the committee, which had been elected by the faculty to share in interviews of candidates for the superintendency, what they were looking for primarily in the new superintendent. With one voice they had declared, "leadership." It is no secret that leadership means different things to different people. But the corporate faculty, strongly and proudly organized in the Winnetka Teachers' Council, seemed wary of this new-comer, leadership notwithstanding. Reduced to the simplest terms, the Board of Education was looking to the new superintendent to bring about change; the corporate faculty (as distinguished from individuals) was uneasy lest the superintendent attempt to bring-about too much change too soon.

The wariness in the Teachers' Council was normal, and could be expected to prevail in some degree in any good school system upon the induction of a new superintendent. In this case the teachers seemed to be mindful of the frequently changing superintendents they had known for 13 years. Correspondingly they seemed to be guarded in their initial acceptance of anything that might suggest another change. Their loyalties to a nominal leader had, perhaps, been too often dislodged to permit quick and easy transfer. Indeed, a quick and easy transfer would have been unworthy of this faculty. I am sure that I added unwittingly to the uneasiness by making noises like a new superintendent during those first weeks.

But I had not come to Winnetka to be a ballot counter for the teachers' association. Nor had I come to brandish my authority as the "senior officer present." I knew well that anything good that might lie in the future of the Winnetka Schools would be the result of heavy faculty involvement and consensus. Changes in a school system, if they are to be forward-moving and enduring changes, must be the product of hard work by all concerned, especially classroom teachers. Superintendents may help teachers move forward, but the moving is done by the faculty. It became important to me to demonstrate my belief in this principle lest the friendly wariness in the Teachers' Council change to coolness.

My purpose in noting here what to me was an unfamiliar watchfulness between the organized faculty and the administration is to point up the possible relevance to education leadership at large. My message, therefore, to faculties and boards of education is to be mindful of this circumstance as changes in leadership occur. Loyalty to the symbol (not the person) expressed by the Superintendent of Schools is highly important to an effective school system. Communication, unity of purpose, security, efficiency and corresponding morale hinge crucially on the genuine acceptance of the nominal leader, but this acceptance must be earned by performance.

Not long after taking office, I resolved that one of my first and most important trials would be to make a happy partnership between the Teachers' Council and the superintendent, without diminishing the strength and dignity of the Council. I knew that I could not be successful in Winnetka as long as any defensiveness or anxiety prevailed between the organization of the teachers (again distinguishing between individuals and the corporate faculty) and my office. I had long felt that a strong professional teachers' organization was essential to a good school system. I wanted the Winnetka Teachers' Council to flourish, and I wanted to be a useful and constructive part of it. For one thing, I knew that a strong professional organization with conventional state and national affiliation was the most certain safeguard against teacher unionism. I knew that teacher unionism and I would be uneasy partners. But, more important, I knew that in a strong Teachers' Council there would be established channels, organization and procedures with which I felt I could relate systematically in doing my job.

This was much to be preferred over a listless or non-existent organization having no paths I might follow or doors at which I might knock. The chapter following will deal in some detail with the processes we employed in finding a constructive partnership.

Summary

I have sought to describe in this first chapter of my contributions
to this book the monumental qualities of Carleton Washburne as a
great pioneer in American education. It has been my purpose to create
a framework within which to view the subsequent educational evolution
in Winnetka, in which Washburne's earlier work has come under
scrutiny in my time, with certain ensuing reaffirmations, and certain
major departures.

Washburne's influence, for all its greatness as a force in the schools
of the United States, has been in itself a substantial handicap to his
successors. Even within the first Board of Education with which I
worked, all of whom were, of course, new since Washburne's time, there
were those who said, by implication if not in so many words, "We look
on you to preserve the character of these schools as Dr. Washburne
conceived them." There were others who felt quite the contrary; one
said quite specifically, "Your first job is to destroy the Washburne
image."

In any case, I believe that Carleton Washburne possessed genius,
that he was a man of wide-ranging intellect and capacities, that he
possessed extraordinary courage, and that he has earned an enduring
place for himself and incidentally for Winnetka in international educational history. Yet, in the changing administrative scheme of things,
where less prominence resides in the nominal leader, and more in the
individuals of the staff, I believe education in Winnetka today possesses
the qualities of greatness, of innovation, of a sense of destiny and
creative productivity that it possessed at the peak of C. W.'s tenure. We
shall speak of these things as other chapters unfold.

CHAPTER SIXTEEN

A Mechanism

for Democratic

Administration

NOTE: This, and subsequent chapters, will deal with various specific aspects of education in Winnetka which may be considered as contributing to educational evolution. Some of these chapters will relate to the earlier experimental contributions of the 1920–40 period, tracing current practices as they have grown out of the original explorations. Some of the chapters will deal with wholly different explorations now current. They will not be limited to the instructional program, for which Winnetka was most widely recognized, but will undertake to view the whole spectrum of the schools, including administrative innovations, personnel considerations, facilities, and philosophy, as well as instruction.

In each chapter, a central theme of educational contribution, which may be considered useful to others, will be developed. No claim is made that the "contributions" are by any means exclusive with Winnetka. The justification for exhibiting them here rests in the frequency with which inquiries are received from other schools, both in the United States and abroad, for information on the subject at hand. It is very likely that other school systems are doing as much or more than we on many of the topics to be considered. However, this is an account of Winnetka.

Some Initial Impressions

As noted in the preceding chapter, a major need for understanding appeared to exist in Winnetka between the corporate faculty and the administration. Just where the Board of Education came into this uncertain arrangement was not clear, differing with the viewpoints of the Board members. Some were dissatisfied and frustrated with the relatively ineffectual role held by the Board in terms of bringing about educational change; some were only slightly aware of the condition, possibly assuming it to be normal. In any event, the Board made it very clear to the new superintendent that they wished "a major re-evaluation of the curriculum toward giving a much larger emphasis to scholarship and standards."

My preliminary study of the curriculum and the grade level expectations had suggested that Winnetka, by choice, had departed substantially from the norm in postponing or deferring certain learnings from lower to higher grades. This, in itself, was not necessarily wrong, but it warranted further study. Perhaps of more serious concern, however, was the impression in the community (which doubtless influenced the Board) that the schools were preoccupied with non-intellectual activity, and that academic discipline was out of vogue.

This impression, while exaggerated, was not altogether without foundation. During the early weeks of the "new superintendent's" tenure, he asked a question of one of the junior high teachers concerning the academic record of one of the pupils whose parents had called for some advice. The teacher replied, "You should know that the word 'academic' is a bad word around here. We call it 'growth.' " While the foregoing anecdote is not a fair indicator of the faculty's position, it gives support to the doubtful public relations circumstances of the Winnetka Schools in 1956.

Just as Dewey had been out-Deweyed by his disciples and his over-zealous interpreters, so, I believe, had C. W. been out-Washburned by many of his teachers once he had departed. Knowing C. W., he would have placed high prominence on the "academic" obligations of schools, call them what he might. But the zealousness with which the *other* aspects of child growth and development had been pursued by the Progressives, not only locally but nationally, had left the impression with many lay observers that the intellect had been overlooked. This seems to have been the case with at least a significant element of Winnetka school patrons and, correspondingly, the Board of Education.

I had arrived in Winnetka in August of 1956 with a month of useful time prior to the opening of schools in September. As noted earlier, it was my privilege to have Miss Jessie Knox as my secretary, whose IBM-like memory extended over all of C. W.'s years, and who was capable of reproducing large and small details upon request. I was also fortunate in having Miss Marion Carswell, long a close associate of Washburne, as Assistant to the Superintendent during my first three years in Winnetka. Both of these very competent individuals were available for orientation in depth during my first month, fortifying or refuting the many informal or accidental conversations which came my way from Board members and citizens at large. I began to view preliminary admonitions with larger understanding. Nearly everyone, including teachers and custodians, had earnest advice for the new superintendent—and it all pointed toward change.

Communication Between Superintendent and Faculty

Before undertaking any major consideration of curriculum, I knew that I had to earn the goodwill and support of the Winnetka Teachers' Council, for it *was* the faculty at that time. During the ensuing years I believe that the two identities, if indeed there need be two, have become more clear: the *Teachers' Council*, concerned with matters of welfare, legislation, social activities, public relations; the *Faculty*, concerned with the transcending affairs of education—instruction, curriculum, research, and philosophy. In any case, I had to earn some kind of a position of recognized worth quite apart from "appointed status" if we were to succeed. Accordingly, I aimed my opening day address at declaring my position, for good or bad, go-for-broke.

That address in part is reproduced here, with periodic interruptions to explain the relevance of my statement to the problem as I saw it. Subsequently in this chapter, I will offer what is intended to be its "contribution" to education, evolving from the struggle for compatibility between administration and faculty. The pages immediately following are offered as a case study of the newly arrived administrator confronting a distinguished and very proud faculty for the first time on the day before the children arrived for classes.

Following opening remarks which included a brief prayer,[1] and some modest attempts at relevant humor, the message began:

> Standing before you today for the first time, I realize that I may succeed or fail as your superintendent, or be only half good, depending upon the extent to which I convey to you the thoughts that will bring us together for the good of children in this community. Knowing myself and having a fair knowledge of how I tick, I know that as time passes I will come to possess each of you in varying degrees as a friend, and to hold you in deep affection as a colleague. And, knowing this, words do not come readily as I speak to you as strangers. For one does not say the same things to strangers that one says to friends.
>
> When a new leader joins a successful and vigorous organization or institution, there is bound to be a watchfulness and concern on the part of the membership, lest something be upset, lest he threaten established personalities and customs. No matter how earnestly he might protest his intent to respect the status quo, the very fact that his is a new face, a new voice, a new set of ideals is bound to cause concern. There is a normal anxiety over the unknown. I might observe that this anxiety is not limited to the "membership"!

As I read this seven-year-old address, I must confess an embarrassment in imposing my own lengthy quotations upon the reader. A note of rationalization seems warranted. This was a frank wooing of a faculty at an extremely sensitive moment in its history. I had determined that a happy marriage between the teachers and the administration was imperative. The first impressions of the new superintendent, I felt, were

---

[1] After the address one teacher quietly advised me: "I don't think much of prayer in teachers' meetings. You'll find we're not much of a praying faculty." I have found the reverse to be true, and have continued to offer an appropriate brief prayer on subsequent occasions.

crucial to eventual success for both. Therefore, the marriage ceremony, in all of its breast-baring intimacies, is recited here, not because of my pride of authorship, but because we are engaged in a case study of complicated forces at work.

My address, therefore, with some deletions, but no corrections, continues, hoping for the reader's tolerance of the first person singular. I was walking a narrow course between consideration for the revered past, and my own declared commitment to an evolving future. It was important to be very honest, though courting.

> It therefore seems fitting for me to take this time today to endeavor to tell you of myself, for good or bad, so that you may know what I believe about education at this moment. It may well be, and should be, that what I believe about education will change, for if I do my work well, you will change me and I will contribute to changes in you. . . .
>
> I have implied that we will change as time passes—that education in Winnetka will change. For, in all honesty, we must acknowledge that no school system stands still. No philosophy of education is static. The science and art of education are dynamic. Therefore, we either go forward or we go backward. But indeed we change. It is the *mechanism for change* that is important, and the direction we point as we move that is important. It is the *extent to which all concerned make their contribution to change* that is the telling criterion of how effective the leadership has been, and how enduring the change will be.

Exchange of Faith

This passage was intended to reveal my concern about the loss of forward movement in education that I had detected. It also laid the groundwork for what would later provide a mechanism for "all concerned" to share in designing forward movement.

Continuing:

> I have been a teacher just short of 20 years, allowing time out for the war. This is my ninth year as a superintendent of schools. And perhaps it is timely here to observe one characteristic of my make-up which I believe dominates all others. I have an overwhelming confidence in the *exchange of faith* among human beings. This is a force which in our relationships must find its place if I am to be successful as your leader. I cannot demand that faith from you, for you have no basis at this time on which to offer such faith. This can come only as I work with you, and you come to know me. But faith works two ways—in this exchange of faith. It must have equal force in both directions. My faith in you is fully as important to success as your faith in me. My presence here today is a declaration of my faith in this faculty and this Board of Education and this community. For I came here from a school system and community and faculty

that I had come to love very deeply—where years of hard work had brought much satisfaction and reward to all of us, where the trials and frustrations of growth and change had produced happy outcomes, and where I might have looked forward to long years of relative composure and productivity.

But I was impressed with the dedication of the members of this Board of Education whom I met here. I was impressed with the stature and world reputation of these schools. But mostly I was impressed with those members of the professional staff with whom I talked who told me of the things they were looking for in their superintendent. I believe I am not violating a confidence to report to you that while being interviewed by our Board of Education I stated that if I were selected for this office, my first responsibility would be to the professional staff. I believe I said that I could serve the Board and this community best by serving the faculty first. I do not know whether they hired me because of this or in spite of it.

This latter passage was not a shallow attempt to seek favor or to ingratiate myself with my listeners. The longer I work in education, the more I am certain that if the superintendent's loyalties must be declared (and it will be unfortunate if conditions demand such extremes very often), then he must throw his weight in support of the faculty. His is a delicate and complex role, serving as the Board's executive, and the community's interpreter (in both directions) and as the faculty's leader. But his commitment to the faculty must ultimately transcend his other obligations if the occasion demands the taking of positions.

The foregoing passage gives prominence to "exchange of faith." I hold heavily to its meaning in school administration, whether in large or small situations. There were those in the faculty audience that day who, true to their love for semantic speculation, found occasion later to question the exchange of faith idea, saying "trust, yes; mutual respect, yes; faith, no." Trust, respect, faith, I find them only as different as beige is from buff, and both depend upon the light in which they are viewed. I like *exchange of faith* as carrying a note of action and affirmation, and I place high store in it; I discipline myself with it, as a joyful obligation I carry at all times toward others with whom I work. I think it is essential to modern leadership.

I have said that I have yet to win your loyalty and faith. I do not expect to win it by speech-making and easy talk. I hope that I will earn it by the things I do. The earlier I can achieve that goal, the more effective I will be. Knowing myself, I am certain that if I find myself unable to earn it, I will not want to remain here as an obstacle and hindrance to good education for children. But I am looking forward positively, and have high expectations that we will shortly become an effective team. We must learn the signals from each other; we must learn who carries the ball on what plays; some may think we should pass instead of run off tackle, and we must find ways to resolve such differences. I believe we will do all of these things—not overnight.

This passage was offered as further introduction to what was to become the Planning and Advisory Committee of the Faculty, which will be developed later in this chapter. It was also offered to reveal my awareness of the endless debate and "democratic" arrangements that had existed in the teachers' organization, leading often to inconclusive and frustrating perpetuation of the status quo.

A Sketch of Educational Beliefs

I then went on to describe some of my own personal background and beliefs, leading up to my views about modern education. I did not dwell long on Progressive Education, as such, for there were still some teachers in Winnetka in 1956 who counted themselves proudly among the Progressives of Winnetka's illustrious past. I shared the feeling of the greater part of the faculty and principals that Progressive Education had had its day and was no longer a meaningful term. But I gave and still give high prominence to the good things that came of it, in Winnetka and elsewhere.

I believe I understand the good things that came to pass in the 30's and 40's. I also have learned to be watchful of the weaknesses. I think a poorly conceived and sloppily executed activity program is worse than the most hidebound program of formal learning ever perpetrated on a child. Some teachers never really understood a good activity program. Too many still believe that activity must limit itself to physical activity and that "experience" must be practical rather than intellectual. To this I do not hold. But for all its varying degrees of success and failure, the child-centered-activity program destroyed forever the cult of uniformity. To this I do hold. It was the belief of some teachers that uncontrolled freedom for children in school was good. And inadequate teachers, unable to distinguish between a free educational environment and chaos took shelter in the cult of permissiveness.

Then I went on to review the historical sequences which had affected education in the United States, noting the contributions which had derived from experimentation in Winnetka.

I describe this over-simplified vista of education in my adult lifetime to tell you of the things that have influenced me, for good or bad, to make me what I am. Where does this evolution find us today? I think education is in a period of maturing. I think that many of the good things to which we have attached pedagogical names have always been practiced by good teachers, whether they were adherents of a particular school of educational philosophy or not. I think we are, in this decade, reconciling the strengths of the past 30 years and discarding the weaknesses. I think that great teaching today cannot be neatly catalogued as of this or that pedagogical cult. I think that great teaching is a product of a given teacher, at a given time, with given children, and it possesses characteristics of the child-centered theme and "integration" and "community," and certainly it possesses what we once disparaged as subject matter and academic discipline.

We hear less today about whether a teacher is conservative or liberal pedagogically, but rather whether or not he is a good teacher. A good teacher is too complex a creature to be neatly classified or typed. Perhaps this tells you what I feel about education. What has happened is this: For some years we have been evolving under various theoretical schools or philosophies. These philosophies dominated the teacher—he was expected to conform to whatever the current pattern might be if he was to be considered modern. We now find the teacher emerging as the dominant character—the person rather than the idea. And this person is expected to teach as best he knows how, drawing upon the resources of our past, and upon the whisperings of his own heart. Whatever his methods, whatever his techniques—be they of 1910 or 1960—his is the obligation and privilege to determine. He is expected to produce results within the framework of a mutually conceived curriculum. I will take my chances on a hundred or a thousand free and unfettered teachers, well-informed, diverse, and dedicated to their task, rather than endeavor to mold a dozen teachers to a pattern that might have unity and consistency for all.

I am old-fashioned enough to be profoundly concerned with scholarship—and I believe most teachers are. I am fully aware of the abundance of corollary goals and ideals which the schools must serve. We must be concerned with the emotional, social and physical attributes of children, in all their complex and trying aspects; but to stretch the mental resources of every child to his greatest fulfillment is our primary task. To some of you this may sound like reactionary talk. Until you know me better, please take on faith my respectful advice that the last thing I would be called by those who know me well is reactionary.

These statements, I knew, would be hard for some of my listeners to take. But, since this was my go-for-broke day, the statements had to be made if I were to be honest.

I passed on to less immediately dangerous but equally important territory, school-community relations.

We have, as a profession, lost some of the faith of our society, the kind of faith I spoke of earlier. And we need that faith now more than ever before, as we face unprecedented crises in public education. By calling attention to the newer and better things that were happening in education, and by shrouding them in unclear names, we have failed to call attention to the basic accomplishments in academic proficiency. We, ourselves, may have been caught up in our own fascination with a process rather than with a child and his needs.

There is no witchcraft in teaching. There is hard, hard work. There is much harder and far more complex work for the effective teacher of today than there was even 10 years ago. It is to this condition that I would call the attention of our people, rather than sit in endless debate over Deweyism or paternalism or Progressivism or socialization, or the whole child. The public schools, through a million and more teachers, have affected the thrust of this nation to the peak of world prosperity and leadership more than any other resource we possess.

The indivisibility of the whole child is an essential and well documented concept in modern education. But in our fervor to serve the whole child we have given such ardent verbalism to his emotional, social and physical parts that our lay audience believes we have omitted the part about which we are most competent and concerned, his intellect. In this we have done ourselves, as teachers, and education in general, a disservice.

I then went on to speak more specifically of the responsibilities deployed among the various components of education in a free society, dealing first with the teacher. I sought here to acknowledge, possibly prematurely, without prior clearance with the Board of Education, my concerns over the salary situation as I viewed it in Winnetka. A subsequent chapter will deal with the outcomes of this inference.

We have chosen a way of life that is outwardly often thankless and ill-rewarded. But we have chosen a way of life that we believe in and in which we find great joy and satisfaction. If we do not, we should separate from it as quickly as possible—for we cannot be good teachers if we look upon this work as drudgery. Most of us could quickly command more worldly goods elsewhere than in teaching if goods are what we seek.

The superintendent's primary task is to clear the tracks so that the teacher may teach at his maximum efficiency. This means not only the resources of staff and facilities—but peace of mind, economic security and dignity. I have dedicated my small life to the enhancement of the teaching profession, and shall not relax as long as I am fit. I know that we shall in our lifetime find really good salaries for teachers—find dignity and prestige consistent with our responsibilities. But we shall not find these things easily.

We shall not prosper as a profession so long as we make our ranks too safe for the mediocre. We shall not prosper so long as the superior are rewarded equally with the inferior, and I know full well the pitfalls of this assertion. We shall not prosper so long as we assume the unbecoming posture of coal miners or teamsters huddled in collective security. We are a proud and dignified profession with a glorious history of accomplishment in this land.

But we must achieve our growth and dignity and prestige by the intrinsic worth of our work and by the demonstrated excellence of our product, proudly. We will not be recognized except with tokens, by demanding recognition and telling of our sorry lot.

The latter part of this passage I know raised a number of hackles. To this day, some of the teachers who once found solace in unionism, and whom I now count among my dear friends, refer half-jokingly to my unkind comparisons with teamsters. They knew what I was saying; I had to say it. I think it was a good gamble.

The Arrangements Between Schools and Society

I moved on to the community as one of the instruments for education. It had been my early impression, an impresssion not substantially modified, that the faculty had come to view the role of the community as an element of educational organization in a considerably dimmer light than I believed was right. High prominence was given at that time, and continues to be given, to the parent-teacher relationship, but the *corporate* body of citizens was another thing. The atmosphere of critical and sometimes antagonistic feeling among many citizens toward the schools undoubtedly conditioned the attitude of teachers. But it was clear that a feeling of defensiveness existed. This was to be revealed more specifically later when lay advisory committees were activated. The condition will be examined in a subsequent chapter.

> We have dedicated ourselves to the service of society, that each succeeding generation may be something finer, and more nearly fulfilled than the last. And no matter how proficient we may be or how skilled, we are still the servants of society. It is true that we must influence our culture and help it make the right choices, for that is part of our obligation as professional people. But the circus parade cannot go faster than the elephants. We may coax them into a trot now and then, but in the long run the parade moves at their pace. But it moves, and it reaches its destination.
>
> To say it another way, I believe that the schools of this nation held themselves apart from the people too long. Some of our communities have been set back 25 years in their educational progress when confronted with an angry and ill-informed public. We have begun to return the schools to the people. We cannot succeed without their understanding and support. Paradoxical as it may sound, we the teachers have our right and duty to teach what we believe, how we believe—anything less is academic slavery. At the same time, as servants of society we have no right to declare what children shall learn and what they shall not learn. We have no monopoly over the hearts and minds of children, for this is academic totalitarianism. Instead there must be a joining of the strength of the community and the strength of the teacher in the mutual determination of what children shall learn. There is a big place for the exchange of faith in this process. It can be realized.

This passage, at the time, did not provoke the reactions (pro or con) that might have been expected. It probably was as important as any other part of the paper, as a bellwether of events to come in Winnetka. It may have usefulness for other schools. It commands a very large obligation from the administration, if the schools are truly to share society's destiny with society, and at the same time fulfill professional hopes and ideals.

The Place of the Board of Education

Last among the elements of educational organization, following the teacher and the community, I described my concept of the Board of Education. This seemed especially important at the time, and still does, as busy and creative teachers pause to take note of the political arrangements our society has designed for its preservation and extension.

The legal and moral voice of society is the politically elected or appointed Board of Education. The Board of Education is probably the most truly democratic creature of our governmental system. For these men and women, speaking for society, determine what the schools shall do. And what the schools do determines the course that our culture will follow. In recent years Boards of Education have become more and more concerned with the mechanical and fiscal affairs of the schools, and less and less concerned with the primary functions of education. This is a dangerous condition, brought on by the pressures of time, dollars and numbers. While it may be simple for us as teachers to go our way and let the Board of Education spend its time and energies laboring over bond issues and salary schedules, we must find ways to rectify this condition. It is against the nature of democracy.

The superintendent as the executive officer of the Board of Education must keep the Board wholly informed of the education program, either directly or by calling upon experts within the faculty to assist. He must provide the materials for the Board to evaluate the effectiveness of what is happening in the education program, good or bad. He must, with the aid of the faculty, draft programs, plans and procedures for the Board's consideration and adoption. But the right of decision on major educational issues is society's through its agent, the Board of Education. We are the instruments for proposing and for carrying out policy. We are not the deciders in this democracy. I might add that in a fair number of years of dealing with Boards of Education with widely varying moods and tempers in their membership, I have yet to find a Board reject a wisely conceived and selflessly presented recommendation of a faculty.

I hope that in the interests of good order, our Board of Education will relate itself to the faculty through the superintendent—and conversely. As time passes and I learn the wishes of the Board, a majority of day-to-day decisions will probably be made within the framework of our administrative organization. The superintendent will normally determine what actions must be deferred for Board consideration. Until I know how the Board wishes to function, I shall probably err in the direction of passing more matters to its attention than it wishes. On the subject of faculty participation in general planning affecting the schools, I hope to find workable processes by which staff members may share actively in the formulation of policies affecting their lives, their teaching and their welfare.

The closing note of this passage again made reference to a *mechanism for democratic administration* which I felt was the immediate need. The passage also endeavored to emphasize the high place of the Board of Education, at least in my view, as an essential partner in the educational process. It also tried to declare diplomatically that voting on educational policy in the Teachers' Council was out of place.

And finally:

> I accept my responsibilities as superintendent, knowing that I must at times make unpopular choices, and depart from the advice of respected colleagues. That is one of the unhappy obligations of my job. While I shall always seek counsel with you in important matters, it will not be my practice to make decisions by counting ballots. I shall preserve at all costs the teacher's right to his freedom to share in deliberations, but I shall not abdicate my own responsibilities as I see them—responsibilities to the Board of Education, the faculty, the community, and, fundamentally, the children.
>
> To you who are veterans of many years' teaching, I salute you most respectfully as my betters, and envy you your joy and composure as you reflect upon the many citizens of this land whom you have nourished. You who are new in this profession, I greet with warmest welcome. We need your strength and vision and critical scrutiny. To all of you I offer what talents I possess to make your life happy and productive. Of all of you, I ask your help and patience as I fumble my way during these beginning months of my office.

There it is, no world-shaking testament, yet a first step in relating myself with the very able, and justifiably proud, faculty of the Winnetka Schools. I am sure I upset some teachers; I believe I gave reassurance to many, for they took the trouble to express their feelings one way or another in the moments or the days that followed. One teacher said, "You made half of us angry, and you won the everlasting support of the other half." This batting average, if true, was better than I had expected.

* * *

A Mechanism for Democratic Administration

The burden of this chapter is to describe a contribution to education. Therefore, "what's past is prologue."

Within a few weeks after delivering the opening address, a faculty workshop was scheduled. This event, following a brief general session to state its purposes, was organized by grade and subject matter sub-groups of 8–12 teachers, each with a chairman and recorder. It was the purpose of the workshop to provide an opportunity for all teachers to express and record their concerns, their uncertainties, their questions, their dissatisfactions—in short, to describe their feelings toward the instructional program in total. They were encouraged, if appropriate, to express satisfaction or reaffirmation. There were no identifications made of who said what, or how many agreed or disagreed. It was simply a design for releasing and channeling what I had felt was a considerable amount of static in the system, for study, and, where appropriate, for the launching of corrective measures.

Eleven closely-typed pages of uncertainty and concern resulted from the workshop. They constituted the beginning of change, and led to steps which have been taken during the ensuing seven years. They will be treated in the next chapter.

Authority and Responsibility

But before we could proceed in an organized way to resolve the uncertainties and concerns, there had to be a systematic arrangement of authority and responsibility for the deployment of the staff among the jobs to be done. We had to decide what tasks came first, what problems could be readily resolved by administrative decision, what problems might take years to resolve by labored faculty involvement.

This need gave rise to the Planning and Advisory Committee. The function of this committee, as a *mechanism for democratic administration,* is the "contribution" offered by this chapter. This committee is probably not greatly different from many like it in school systems throughout our country. If it is different at all, the difference may rest in the very high degree of selfless commitment which the members give to their work in the committee, to the status and prestige which appear to attach to being a member, and to the unlimited and very candid agenda which the committee is encouraged to share.

Shortly after the revealing faculty workshop I met with the Executive Committee of the Teachers' Council and described my beliefs about democratic administration. I gave high emphasis to the effectiveness of small working groups, charged with key responsibilities *in depth,* and given heavy respect by the remainder of the faculty once their findings and recommendations were submitted. I described my own experience with a central advisory group serving as a closely knit forum for regular counselling with the superintendent. In the course of that meeting, the Planning and Advisory Committee, as it now exists, took initial form. There was at that time a committee known as the Planning Committeee already established in the schools. Its membership was a carefully balanced composition of five teachers and five administrators, tacitly revealing the intramural skepticism then current. The committee's duties had been primarily concerned with planning in-service activities. Therefore, rather than name a new committee, we enlarged the scope and the membership of the existing group, and modified the name to Planning and Advisory Committee.[2] The increase in membership was intended to provide a larger complement of classroom teachers. It seemed desirable, particularly in the interest of disarming those who might fear administrative domination of the committee, to have the faculty at large elect four additional teachers to the ten-member group then existing. We also agreed to add the Assistant Superintendent of Schools. The ratio, while it has now lost its importance as the years have passed, was nine teachers to six administrators. Most of the faculty seemed to be pleased by this demonstration of faith.

Scope and Purpose—Planning and Advisory Committee

Not long thereafter the newly conceived committee met, began immediately to function effectively, and does so to this day, meeting every two weeks at the close of school. Soon after the first meeting the superintendent drafted a *statement of scope and purpose* and put it before the committee for suggestions. The committee felt that it could better view itself at the end of a year of trial. Accordingly, the statement was tabled until the following June. As the draft was studied, a few good revisions were made, and the statement was endorsed and forwarded to the Board of Education for formal adoption as a matter of policy.

---

[2] There had been corresponding central advisory bodies over the years in Winnetka, the most recent of which was the Committee of 28, which included lay members and Board members. This committee had become only moderately active by 1956, and, with the advice of the Teachers' Council Executive Committee, it was dissolved.

The Board of Education made further minor changes in which the committee concurred, and the statement was published as follows:

STATEMENT OF SCOPE AND PURPOSE OF THE PLANNING AND ADVISORY COMMITTEE

Name:

The name of this committee is the Planning and Advisory Committee of the Winnetka Faculty.

Scope:

The scope of this committee is virtually unlimited as to subjects appropriate to its interest. All matters which relate to the education of children or the effectiveness of teaching are matters of concern to this committee. It advises the superintendent, at his request, in matters requiring his action; it calls to his attention matters it considers of importance to the superintendent or to the Board of Education; it serves as a channel of communication between the superintendent and the faculty to bring better understanding in both directions about matters affecting the schools and the teachers.

The committee plans activities relating to the in-service training of teachers; to curriculum design; to the improvement of instruction. It identifies general problems or needs, and counsels the superintendent as to the delegation of tasks, the membership of operating committees within the faculty, the designation of duties to be performed in the carrying out of Board of Education policies and programs.

Purpose:

It is the purpose of this committee to provide the highest quality professional counsel to the superintendent in all matters which he places before the group or which it determines, in its wisdom, to call to his attention. Such responsibility calls for the election of teacher members whose professional stature, insight and wisdom are such that they enjoy the respect and confidence of their colleagues in dealing with matters affecting education in Winnetka.

The committee falls far short of its purpose if it assumes the role of a grievance committee or becomes a delegation to carry instructions back and forth between the faculty and the administration. To the extent that the committee as a whole can come to grips with major issues in quiet counsel and arrive at sound conclusions in concert, it succeeds. To the extent that it becomes an "inner sanctum" of the administration, it fails. To the extent that its findings receive the faith and confidence of the faculty and the Board of Education, it succeeds. To the extent that it is felt to be an instrument dominated by the Board of Education, the faculty, or the superintendent, its primary function is unfulfilled.

The Planning and Advisory Committee is not a legislative or a decision-making body. It advises and recommends. The Board of Education, or its executive officer, the superintendent, acting within policies laid down by the Board, must accept by law the responsibility for making decisions.

Even though the membership is a cross-section of the faculty, members of the Planning and Advisory Committee function in a larger framework than that of a representative body limited by directives from those groups represented. Members are expected to communicate fully and freely with those they represent. The wishes and opinions of their group should be given high respect and full consideration. But, in the deliberations of the Planning and Advisory Committee, it is their unbiased opinion and mature judgment which members owe to themselves, to their group, to the schools of Winnetka.

Membership:

The size of the committee is kept small enough to insure effective meetings, yet large enough to represent the viewpoint of various elements of the professional staff. The membership includes:

Superintendent of Schools
Assistant Superintendent
All principals (4)
Representative of Department of Educational Counsel
    (Psychologist)
Representative of the Special Teachers
President of the Winnetka Teachers' Council
Immediate past president of the Winnetka Teachers' Council
Representative of the Creative Activities Consultants
Four classroom teachers

Rotation and Election of Membership:

The members who serve on the Planning and Advisory Committee by title remain members while holding the position giving them the title.

All other members serve for a three-year period.

The membership held by a representative of the Department of Educational Council is rotated among the members of that department.

The membership held by a representative of the Creative Activities Consultants is rotated among the members of that department.

The elected memberships are established so that one member is replaced every three years, two members the other years.

*   *   *

The Planning and Advisory Committee has been the largest single force for bringing about an "exchange of faith" between the faculty and the administration during the ensuing seven years. Its meetings are packed with vital and important issues. Rarely is an agenda completed at adjournment time, normally 6:00 P.M. There are occasional evening meetings following a potluck supper at the superintendent's or a member's home. A weekend winter retreat about every two years at a state park lodge has provided a fruitful setting for the study of long-term goals. (An outcome of one retreat will be reported in a subsequent chapter.)

Every significant action which the Winnetka Schools have taken during the past seven years was first weighed and examined in the Planning and Advisory Committee. Its work is never hurried. If there is insufficient time adequately to explore an issue, it awaits the next meeting, or it can be the subject of a special meeting. There is never any voting. Either we have a broad consensus, or we put the issue on the "back burner." There is really no chairman, although the superintendent logically brings the larger bundle of items before each meeting, and more often than others presents issues to be considered.

Out of the deliberations of the Planning and Advisory Committee, one of three things can normally happen:

a. The superintendent makes an administrative decision and puts the wheels in motion for necessary action. An example might be the selection of a central topic for a faculty in-service workshop.

b. The Planning and Advisory Committee names a subordinate committee to perform a given task over a period of time. An example might be the activation of a curriculum committee in the language arts, including the designation of chairman.

c. The superintendent puts a major policy matter before the Planning and Advisory Committee, for initial study and exploration. Upon endorsement by the committee the issue is presented to the Board of Education for formal consideration. An example of this process might be the launching and eventual adoption of a major overhaul of teachers' salaries.

The existence of the Planning and Advisory Committee appears to have removed, or at least substantially reduced, the sensitivity or defensiveness detected earlier in the Winnetka Teachers' Council toward the administration. The Council now addresses itself to appropriate matters with vigor. The superintendent participates actively in its deliberations. But the Planning and Advisory Committee has absorbed the deliberative function that was once felt to be the full faculty's prerogative in the teachers' association. The frustrations that accompany balloting on issues only lightly known to the members is past. A deeper and more worthy kind of democracy functions through the *representative* process of the Planning and Advisory Committee. No balloting, but sober and prolonged study of issues brings good solutions to both the faculty and the administration. The membership of the president and the immediate past president of the Teachers' Council in the Planning and Advisory Committee give assurance that there are no administrative secrets. There is frequently a need for confidentiality within the committee membership, particularly during the development of major considerations in their premature stages. But this is quite different from secrecy. Incidentally, during the seven years of its existence no breach of confidentiality by members of the committee has been known to occur, in spite of the extreme delicacy of some subjects under study. Those who know the ways of teachers may marvel at this condition. I have. This is a part of the exchange of faith mentioned earlier.

A Deeper Kind of Democracy

This chapter has dealt with the theme of *leadership*, and its deployment among many people in a school system. The happenings reported here have been offered in evidence to suggest that the superficial or outward manifestations of democracy, such as balloting, total participation, and petitioning, are not necessarily satisfying or productive in a school organization. The faculty had asked for "leadership," yet had guarded itself closely against leadership actions that implied "authority." As Halpin has noted, these are "value-laden concepts, charged with much emotion."

Halpin observes that efforts at shallow "democracy" in school administration have "immobilized school administration." He continues:

> In applying human relations principles, we must be sure that we do not overlook the responsibility imposed upon every leader by the institutional realities ... of which he is a part. ... Let us remember ... that the primary responsibility of a leader is to lead, and that by doing so he becomes no less democratic.[3]

A considerable amount of attention has been given to the *setting* and *mechanism* for the exercise of instructional leadership through a design calling for deeper democratic practices than meet the eye. The continuing educational evolution to which Winnetka is endeavoring to contribute rests largely on the *instrument* through which educational leadership flows from the status leader to the other equally important or more important leaders of the moment. The Planning and Advisory Committee in Winnetka is such an instrument. The educational scheme in Winnetka, including the reaffirmation of some practices conceived in the 1920's and the development of new concepts currently on trial, is wholly the product of this body of teachers and administrators as they release and reflect the creativity and labor of the full faculty. Subsequent chapters will record the details of these developments.

Summary

The student of school administration must be aware of the need for establishing a cordial working environment in which the faculty and the adminstration can relate systematically to each other. It must be assumed that effective educational leadership (at whatever level it springs) must be leadership *for* something; it follows that change or forward movement is a function of instructional leadership. There were individuals in the

---

[3] Halpin, Andrew W., "The Behavior of Leaders," *Educational Leadership*, Dec., 1956.

Winnetka Schools in 1956 for whom forward movement or change was unthinkable. These teachers, few in number, but effective, were bemused with Winnetka's past, pleased and proud of its present, and unmindful of the inevitability of a changing future. To some degree, the corporate power of the teachers' association became the setting for those few who like Lot's wife preferred to look fondly backward. Administrative authority implied change, and therefore hostility.

While most school systems would not find themselves in the unique circumstances of Winnetka in 1956, the fact remains that the *mechanism for democratic administration* (call it the Planning and Advisory Committee, or by any other name) is an essential to good school organization. Without it, my leadership in Winnetka would have been futile. With it, we have set exciting ideas in motion. We will tell of them.

CHAPTER SEVENTEEN

What About the

Winnetka Plan?

A philosophy of education, evolved by those who are living among children, helping them, and being taught and guided by them, is itself living, and like all living things it is ever-changing.

—WASHBURNE in A Living Philosophy of Education, 1940

As the faculty and administration change, it is important that all concerned, periodically, have a hand in establishing new goals and procedures. Otherwise, something
less than whole-hearted commitment is likely to follow.

—MARLAND in an address to
the Winnetka faculty, 1957

The reader is reminded that during my first
visit with Carleton Washburne he declared that
there was no such thing as a Winnetka Plan.

He emphasized his distaste for the static implications of the word *Plan*. He declared that the theory underlying his work in Winnetka was one of thoughtful and considered revolution, as revealed in his quotation above. He declared that instead of a *plan* there was a *spirit*, a way of thinking, a way of behaving, a way of living within the faculty. I believe this is true. I also believe it was a source of greatness—and I believe it was a source of weakness. So long as C.W. was present as the inspirational force, the revolutionary, the interpreter, the sharp questioner, the scientific appraiser, Winnetka's design flourished. As his personal influence became diluted in subsequent years, and as fewer and fewer teachers *who had possessed intimately the creation and implementation of the design* remained at hand, the dynamic or revolutionary spirit diminished. Thus, the design, dependent upon a "spirit" of change, exploration, and discovery became, to a degree, a "plan" in the non-dynamic sense. This was wholly contrary to Washburne's ideal. In 1956 there were in active use, for example, locally written instructional materials originally published in the 1930's, and periodically reproduced without major change. They were ardently defended by many teachers who had developed extraordinary skill and creativity in their use. Yet newcomers to the faculty, lacking the original spirit, and having had no hand in the exciting processes of creating the materials, found them obsolete, incompatible with their training, and difficult to use effectively. I was not of much help to them, for, like them, I had not been a part of the original spirit of revolution, and had not "internalized" the unique and sometimes puzzling instruments which 30 years earlier had so successfully shaken American education out of the rigid lock-step of uniformity.

Stated another way, those of us who were "new to Winnetka" found ourselves coloring in the line drawings created by other artists. In spite of our earnest respect for the other artists, we found this process something less than creative, and certainly not revolutionary.

At this time, 1956-57, the faculty presented an interesting profile of differences, relating largely to their longevity in Winnetka. Of a total of 106 teachers and principals, 38 had worked with C.W., at least briefly, and could be classified as a part of the original design. Interestingly, these teachers, for the most part, were among those most eager for change and most responsive to suggestions for a new spirit of inquiry. They seemed most ready to return to the frontier of discovery, once a fair case was made for a given investigation. They became the backbone of exploratory developments which were to follow.

There was then what might be called a "middle group," consisting of some 37 teachers who had not known C.W., but had thoroughly and effectively mastered the techniques of teaching within the Winnetka design. Risking a generalization, I found these teachers for the most part heavily committed to the design, very successful in its pursuit, and, initially, less inclined toward change. They had had the advantage, even though Dr. Washburne had left, of working intimately over a number of years with a great majority of teachers who had been a part of the period of discovery, and who had taught its outcomes to them effectively.

Finally, there were the relative newcomers to Winnetka, among whom I counted myself. These might be grouped as those teachers who had been in Winnetka less than three years, who had been caught up in the diminishing influence of the retirement of older interpreters in the faculty—a thinning of the ranks of C.W.'s colleagues, a diluting of the original "spirit." These teachers, including myself, trained and experienced in more conventional teaching processes, were confused. Too often an elder statesman in the faculty would counsel an able and experienced newcomer, "But we never say that in Winnetka!" or "In Winnetka we never do that!" Well-intentioned though the counsel was, it flowed squarely against my own ideals concerning the freedom, individuality, and creativity of teachers. I believe it flowed against C.W.'s beliefs, too. But he had been long gone, and the Winnetka Plan, that was never a plan, remained.

The "Plan"

There is a steady flow of visitors to Winnetka from all parts of the United States and from abroad. While many of our guests appear to be chiefly concerned with interesting things we are doing in the here and now, one may fairly regularly expect the question, particularly from our international visitors, "What about the Winnetka Plan?" To refresh some readers, and to inform others, an over-simplified description of the plan is quoted from the *Encyclopedia of Educational Research:*

> This is a thoroughgoing attempt to break the class lock-step procedure which characterized the graded elementary school of the past. . . .
> The individual instruction, or Winnetka technique, is primarily a method of

curriculum organization. The course of study is divided into two parts, the "common essentials" and the "group and creative activities." The former consists of the knowledge and skills which presumably everyone needs to master. The group and creative activities include the development of appreciation of literature, music, and art, playground activities, assemblies, handwork of various kinds, projects which are an end in themselves rather than a means to the mastery of subject matter, group discussions, and much of the color, material and background of history and geography. The school program is arranged so that one-half of each forenoon and afternoon is given over to the individual work in the common essentials and the other half of each session is given to group and creative activities. The individual work is carried on through the use of specially prepared individual-progress materials.

. . . Surveys showed that, in terms of such tests as were available, the Winnetka schools were doing distinctly effective work—work which on the whole was more efficient than that done by comparable schools which used class methods of instruction. In academic achievement 23 out of 30 comparisons of comparable mental-age groups were favorable to the Winnetka students. The study of high-school students showed that the pupils who had graduated from the Winnetka elementary schools were above the average of students in the township in scholarship in all five major subject fields and led in participation in extracurricular activities and in the proportion of offices held in various pupil organizations.

This rather objective, bare-bones definition of Winnetka's design is an over-simplification, when weighed against the wealth of descriptive material published during the 1920-40 period. The earlier chapters of this book tell the tale much more completely, as viewed by the architect of the design.

During the period of my orientation in Winnetka, I asked Frederick Reed, one of C.W.'s brilliant close associates during his Winnetka years, to define for me *his* view of Winnetka's uniqueness. Mr. Reed had been for many years principal of Greeley Elementary School, and remained for three years in the post after my arrival in Winnetka, before being overtaken by retirement.[1] Reed's statement follows:

First, old tradition yielded the center of the stage to the spirit of science. Educational practice was re-oriented toward the goals which were agreed upon by the faculty and checked by as objective measurements as could be applied.

New values encroached upon older ones. Reason took a higher place than authority. The happiness of the child became more important. Conformity more often gave way to concepts of justice or fair play.

Fostered by scientific and humanitarian ideals, several specific educational trends found expression in Winnetka, roughly in this order:

---

[1] Frederick Reed continues to serve education as a member of the faculty of Brooklyn College, New York.

> Individualized instruction materials, embodying pre-tests, practice exercises, practice and final tests.
>
> Much emphasis upon individual creativity, and, a little later, upon group enterprises involving the planning and execution of both short- and long-term projects by children under teacher leadership.
>
> New attitudes and beliefs concerning human behavior with less faith in punishment and more in "mental hygiene."

C.W.'s early chapters in this book, together with the foregoing amplifications of the "Winnetka Plan," should provide the reader with renewed assurance that the "Plan" was indeed meant to be a spirit rather than a thing. I came upon it first hand with much to learn about it. As I look back over seven years in Winnetka, I believe I can answer those who ask the question, "What about the Winnetka Plan?" My very short answer would be this:

> *"The spirit of faculty inquiry and experimentation, the high concern for individualized instruction through locally written materials, the encouragement of creativity among children, the emphasis on social learnings and attitudes, the devotion to good mental health practices, self-instruction and responsibility for self-discipline on the part of pupils—all remain powerful and specific characteristics of these schools. The principles and underlying philosophy remain substantially unchanged. The methods, objectives, procedures and techniques have in some cases been retained, but in some cases have been substantially modified."*

Comparisons and Contrasts

The following paragraphs are offered as my understanding of the key characteristics of the educational design created by Dr. Washburne and the Winnetka faculty during 1919-43, and my judgment of the corresponding circumstances today. (The table picks up the topics and sequence of Washburne's chapters.)

The tabulation (*pp. 200-206*) concludes a comparative appraisal of Washburne's chapters in this book. Using C.W.'s chronology and chapter headings, I have endeavored in the left-hand column to appraise the various elements of education in Winnetka as I saw them upon arrival there, and then to relate briefly the changes or reaffirmations that have ensued.

KEY ELEMENTS OF WINNETKA EDUCATION,
THEN AND NOW

CHARACTERISTICS, AS CONCEIVED 1919-1943	AS VIEWED BY THE SUPERINTENDENT, 1963

Individualizing Arithmetic

(*See* Chapter Two.) Self-instructive materials, locally developed work books; progression through content, irrespective of grade; deferred grade placement of some content, as prescribed by Committee of Seven; speed tests for mastery. Teaching for "meaning"; relevance to group and creative activities. Little or no use of commercial textbooks.

We continue to individualize arithmetic. (*See* Chapter Eighteen.) We have revised the grade level objectives considerably above the expectations declared by the Committee of Seven, developing our own textbooks accordingly and utilizing good commercial textbooks where appropriate. We continue, with good success, to follow the self instruction, self-correction, progression pattern, but we expect more learning at all grade levels. We have clarified "mastery" and "speed." We give high importance to *understanding*, as corresponding to Washburne's "meaning." We give high importance to relating arithmetic to group and creative activities. We have been experimenting with wholly new approaches to the world of numbers in the context of modern mathematics for Grades I—VIII during the past three years, utilizing teaching aids and materials developed by the faculty.

Reading

(*See* Chapter Three.) Introduce at mental age of 6.5; rely actively on intelligence tests for readiness; sight reading, followed by phonics; small groups, rather than individuals; right book for right child (interest); controlled word list; remedial attention, especially to emotionally disturbed.

Our present reading program is not formally and individually articulated with mental age; entrance age (chronological) to Grade I at no younger than five years, nine months, predicts general readiness; grouping follows, with 3-4 reading groups in a room; intelligence testing is administered at Grade I rather than Kindergarten, based on greater validity and reliability of results; sight words and phonics, as generally practiced in modern reading program; very high emphasis on right book for right child; no basal readers, but wide variety for teacher selection;

Reading (cont.)

decreased emphasis on controlled word list, toward encouraging discovery; very high emphasis on library; speed, pacing and comprehension drill at Junior High.

Postponement of Formal Learning

(*See* Chapter Three, p. 58) Arithmetic grade placement of certain content deferred year or two later than customarily taught; impressive experiment in delaying reading and arithmetic learning beyond Grade I; deferral of formal grammar until Grade VIII; no foreign language instruction; science learnings below Grade VII treated as subordinate element of social studies; manuscript writing continued at all levels, with cursive at Grade V upon request by parent.

Much of our present spirit of inquiry leads in the opposite direction. We are searching for the teaching techniques and learning expectations that will provide intellectual fulfillment and satisfaction, (without loss of efficiency) at earlier rather than later ages. (*See* Chapter Twenty, Mathematics, Chapter Twenty-One, More Curriculum Evolution.) High attention to balance between creative activities and formal learnings. Partial segregation of gifted; emphasis on differentiation of content consistent with individual ability; new curricular objectives in mathematics, language arts, science, foreign language, social studies. Cursive writing (use optional) taught to all at Grade VI.

Language Arts

(*See* Chapter Four.) Penmanship relied largely on manuscript writing; spelling based on selected word lists, with much initiative for creative teaching left to teacher; composition emphasized creativity, with mechanics of secondary priority; individualized instructional materials for teaching mechanics of expression; grammar instruction deferred until Grades VII or VIII; technical terms, such as *verb*, avoided in elementary grades by using term *action word* if reference was necessary. Indirect or functional teaching of grammar in Junior High.

Manuscript writing prevails; cursive taught quickly to all at Grade VI in departmental organization of Junior High under specialist. Spelling, vocabulary and composition continue in much the same character as described at left. (*See* Chapter Twenty-One, Curriculum.) Individualized instructional materials rewritten in conformity with revised curriculum. Grammar continues to be taught functionally, but larger expectations for grammar and other mechanics of expression being established in Grade III and up, rather than deferred to Grades VII and VIII. Creative writing still very high priority; verbs are called verbs. Library services and

Language Arts (cont.)

functions continue to be a key element of language arts; also creative dramatics; listening; literature. (These latter were clearly an unspoken part of the earlier design, but are systematized under Language Arts currently.)

The Social Studies

Early leadership in weaving the social sciences together for wholeness in learning history, geography, citizenship, economics, etc.; important articulation with socialized activities. (*See* Chapters Five, Six.) Research on published "allusions" gave scientific undergirding to content; sharp departures from "norms" of content, with heavy emphasis on Old World backgrounds; fairly limited individualization (except in mechanics), consistent with group process in teaching the social studies. Included modest attention to science as a part of social studies.

Of all current Winnetka instruction, very likely the work in the social studies remains least changed. A major curriculum overhaul (*see* Chapter Twenty-One) re-evaluated and largely reaffirmed the broad as well as the specific objectives of the earlier social studies design. Heavy emphasis on attitudes and values; much attention to creative activities and realistic pupil enterprises; slight trend toward "spiral" arrangement of grade content, as distinguished from vertical or chronological. Still relatively slight individualization of social studies learnings. Science is now separate and of equal "status," all grades.

Group and Creative Activities

(*See* Chapter Seven.) A very basic and unique element of education in Winnetka at the time, a key to the full understanding of the Winnetka design, creative activities afforded a balancing or complementary force running parallel to the fundamental learnings. Washburne gives very strong emphasis to the autonomy of the Group and Creative Activities—or the incidental nature of their relationship to academic learnings. High importance given to creativity, human relations, self-discipline, citizenship, fair play, honor, self-government, economic enterprises and the practices of cooperation.

One could read Washburne's Chapter Six, digest his numerous colorful examples, and find virtually the identical kind of group and creative activity flourishing in corresponding classrooms today. (*See* Chapter Twenty-One.)

The one large difference between the design that C.W. has described and that of the current period is that group and creative activities often grow out of, and are clearly and consciously related to academic learnings. They often motivate, stimulate and give meaning to the fundamentals. They are believed to be no less creative.

This element remains a vigorous (though now less unique) foundation of education in Winnetka.

Psychological and Special Educational Services

(*See* Chapter Eight.) The pioneer work undertaken by Winnetka in mental health of pupils, as early as the mid-1920's, has had an everlasting and constructive effect on education in the United States. The concept that disturbed or otherwise handicapped children deserved equal educational opportunities with normal children called for courageous and vigorous leadership at the time. Psychiatric, pediatric, psychological and social work staffing and services, as well as specially trained teachers for the deaf, were inaugurated. Heavy emphasis on the induction and in-service education of teachers toward mental health principles and practices; understanding of the extremely nonconforming child; close cooperation between teachers, clinic staff and parents, toward appreciation of disturbed or handicapped child's needs.

These services continue to occupy a vital and dynamic place in Winnetka education today. While education in the United States has moved markedly toward recognizing the need for psychological services, and Winnetka is correspondingly less unique in this respect, the high degree of mental health orientation on the part of teachers and parents remains a paramount characteristic of the program.

Increased attention to the handicapped, including all types of handicaps as well as the deaf and hard-of-hearing, is currently evolving. Present staff consists of psychologist, two social workers (we still call them counselors), a speech therapist, a hearing therapist, and a remedial teacher. Current experimental programs with academic underachiever and perceptually handicapped, now in their fourth and third year, respectively, show promise.

Local community resources have greatly improved with the establishment of a mental health clinic, a warm and cordial association between the schools and local pediatricians, and, as C.W. notes, a much greater competence on the part of classroom teachers to confront and respond to the needs of atypical children.

A cooperative program of special education is shared by 23 area school systems where provisions are made for all types of handicaps reciprocally.

Nursery Schools

Initially motivated to develop a setting for the pre-kindergarten child, as a quasi-private element of the public schools, C.W. succeeded first in creating the experimental program for a limited number, tuition-supported, in the junior high school. Washburne's

Both of these instruments—the quasi-public, tuition-supported nursery school for limited numbers of 3-year-olds, and the school-wide 4-year-old junior kindergarten program—remain active today.

The present administration, less in-

Nursery Schools (cont.)

high interest in and commitment to the pre-school child led to junior kindergartens, publicly supported, available to all children, in all elementary schools.

The quasi-private element, located in the Alschuler facilities of the junior high school, continues, and remains today, as a pre-school setting for 3-year-olds. The proximity of the small children to the junior high classes provided extraordinary opportunity for child study and human growth learnings for the early adolescents of junior high school. (*See* Chapter Nine.)

formed, and admittedly less ambitious for the pre-school child (an acknowledged weakness), is less energetic in stimulating this dimension of Winnetka education than was C.W. The 4-year-old kindergartens are strongly supported by some very competent kindergarten teachers, and are the object of cautious reservation by other, equally competent kindergarten teachers. Parents endorse them heartily and willingly pay a $50 a year tuition toward $300 a year costs for four half-days a week.

The 3-year-old group continues to flourish as a largely tuition-supported nursery school, with active and enthusiastic lay government by a board of directors.

The two incidental by-products of the nursery school are of largest interest to me: the opportunity provided for the induction, counselling and preventive mental health instruction of pre-school parents; and the convenience of a living laboratory for those junior high children who need the experience of relating with small children in a systematic setting.

Selection and Education of Teachers

(*See* Chapter Ten.) Responding to a clear and urgent need at the time, the Winnetka Graduate Teachers College served as a resource, not only for limited numbers of graduate students for posts in the United States and abroad, but for the training of teachers in the revolutionary ideas, techniques and processes of the Winnetka Schools. In connection with North Shore Country Day School and Francis W. Parker School in Chicago, the graduate school provided a unique service to education from 1932 to 1954.

No longer in existence when I reached Winnetka, the graduate school had left a clear and favorable record. Several members of the current faculty were its product. As I sought to acquaint new teachers (not to mention myself) with Winnetka's ways, I often wished the graduate school had not been dissolved.

Yet, as C.W. states, teacher training institutions, including the large university graduate schools, had by this time come a long distance in recognizing the processes of modern pedagogy.

Selection and Education of Teachers (cont.)

The disparity between "conventional" teacher education and Winnetka teaching, while still significant, was diminishing.

In selecting teachers for Winnetka, we are now able to attract strong, experienced teachers from systems not unlike our own, or to engage young, beginning teachers of high promise who have performed their student teaching obligation with us. (We are affiliated with Northwstern University, National College of Education, Knox College and Roosevelt University for student teaching programs.)

A substantial orientation program, yet in no way comparable with the Winnetka Graduate Teachers College, is conducted for newly appointed teachers, consisting, among other features, of Saturday morning seminars during the fall months.

School Buildings and Equipment

(*See* Chapter Twelve.) Winnetka's population doubled during C.W.'s administration, resulting in the need for new schools and additions. Skokie Junior High School, planned before Washburne's arrival in 1919, remains today a complete and splendid plant. But the crowning glory of the period, insofar as facilities are concerned, was Crow Island School, a product of many able minds, including C.W.'s.

The courage, vision, and creativity which characterized Winnetka's instructional program of the period was no less evident in the design and development of Crow Island School.

Winnetka has stopped growing, except for a very modest trend toward increasing family size. The basic school plant (three elementary schools and one junior high school) has not changed in 20 years. However, interior adaptation, renovation and modernization are almost constant. A few additions have been built in the past several years, but the plant, now 50 years old in its oldest element, is functionally modern.

Plans are currently before us for the design and construction of a *learning laboratory* as an element of Skokie Junior High School.

Relations with the Community

C.W.'s treatment of this subject (*See* Chapter Thirteen) is an excellent monograph on the respective roles of the P.T.A. and the Board of Education.

The relationship of both to the superintendent is also an excellent account of the sensitive balance and the "exchange of faith" upon which good administration rests.

C.W., as in many ways, was ahead of his time in the degree to which laymen were encouraged to identify with the schools. Even so, he described the P.T.A. as "a lay body without professional competence to decide on what should be taught and when and how."

Winnetka's schools continue to enjoy the general goodwill and support of the community. Citizens of the highest ideals and competencies are chosen without political alignment for Board of Education service. The P.T.A.'s remain active, supportive and effective. The Central P.T.A. Board, filling what might be called the role of Lay Council, continues to meet monthly with the superintendent, and performs a vital function.

There is one substantial difference today over the earlier period, again accounted for in large part by the changing nature of the social order surrounding the schools, as well as a changing philosophy of leadership. C.W.'s quotation, opposite, runs contrary to present practice. Taken literally, the statement is probably true. Yet, the involvement of numerous lay advisory committees, working at the invitation of the Board or the superintendent, has had a broadly constructive effect on education in Winnetka during the past seven years. Beyond C.W.'s P.T.A. and Board of Education, the additional dimension of *lay advisory committees* on virtually all major issues and their successful performance constitute a significant change over the earlier years.

But this is not enough. If we were merely to "keep school" or adjust the program here and there, as reflected above, this book would be badly mistitled. If, indeed, Winnetka is an "Experiment in Education," we should do more than tinker with the creative innovations of the 1920's and 1930's. Accordingly, much of the remainder of the book will be devoted to the spirit of inquiry, trial and error that continues in these schools, irrespective of the Winnetka Plan that-was-never-a-plan.

Summary

Taken item by item, and viewed in 1963 (as distinguished from 1920), the creative contributions to education which Carleton Washburne has recalled may not seem to be of heroic proportions. The reader may well say that most of these characteristics of Winnetka's revolutionary period are to be found in any good school today. Indeed, this is true; it is also a vast compliment to the imagination of devoted teachers and administrators who, in a span of 25 years or so, in a small Illinois community changed the course of education in the United States and abroad.

In a number of significant categories we are different today:

1. While C.W. was heavily committed to the proposition that academic disciplines, broadly speaking, should be deferred to the years later than orthodoxy prescribed, we are probing in the opposite direction. Giving full heed to the social, emotional and physical parts of the child, and capitalizing on Winnetka's momentum in these categories, we suggest that the schools have never remotely begun to release and fulfill the intellectual potentials of the child, Kindergarten through Grade XII. Much of our current activity is concerned with this hypothesis.

2. A second departure, which I am sure will not be wholly accepted by C.W. as a departure, is the extent to which we have sought and welcomed the layman in the affairs of education, including the curriculum. Very high prominence is given to drawing the community into the studies affecting education, without implying abdication by either the faculty or the Board. We do not assume that laymen know more about education than we do. But we assume they have the right to know in detail what we are up to and why, and to make their contributions to the process.

3. We no longer labor the subject of the "whole child" in our communication with our patrons. We assume that parents and teachers now comprehend that a youngster comes to school in all his parts—emotional, social, physical and intellectual. We give unremitting attention to all these parts, but we accept as our unique and primary concern the development of the intellect. I think this has always been true in good schools, but there was a time when we were so busy explaining the other parts that our patrons thought we had forgotten about the intellect.

4. Creative activities, as will be noted in a later chapter, have remained a major heritage from the "Winnetka Plan." The principal difference today is that, instead of compartmentalizing them into autonomous periods of work, separate from academic learning, we now deliberately blend activities *with* formal learnings so that an observer can hardly tell where one begins and the other ends. Activity gives reality and purpose to learning. It was one of the great innovations of earlier Winnetka.

Classifying these "differences" today and pointing to the ways in which we have changed is not particularly rewarding or productive. We are truly not conscious of "differences," because the process has been an evolutionary one in which all concerned have shared. Indeed, I had to think quite earnestly on the subject to discover these differences. But since the questions is often asked, "What is different?" these are the answers. They *are* substantial differences, but they are the result of faculty deliberation and consensus. They are not born of fire, explosion or pronouncement.

One never hears of the Winnetka Plan today in Winnetka, except from strangers. But, if, as C.W. declares, it is a *state of mind*, then it is with us. We shall describe the explorations upon which this *state of mind* is now engaged.

CHAPTER EIGHTEEN

Something Old,

Something New

There are no past things for
which one should long—
There are only eternally new
phenomena being shaped from the past.

—GOETHE

While a few of Winnetka's teachers by 1957 still
mused over "past things for which one should
long," the general temper of the faculty was one
of readiness for forward movement. The unique
characteristics of the educational philosophy and
design which Washburne relates in his chapters,
and which are briefly sketched in Chapter Seven-
teen, had grown thin. Well over half the faculty
by this time had never known C.W. The unique
process of instruction had become a diminishing

folk lore, handed on by a diminishing number of faculty veterans.

There were no curriculum guides. The content outlines of grade expectations were implied in the goal cards, but these were not curriculum guides. The steady hands in the faculty needed no curriculum guides. There was no statement of general goals of the schools. When one inquired about a statement of philosophy or goals, he was referred to C.W.'s *Living Philosophy of Education*—all 585 pages of it, copyrighted in 1940. (Any other questions?)

There was something called the Black Book. It was a start made some years earlier toward curriculum construction that I believe had not quite come off. But curriculum construction meant change. And change meant a questioning of past and present practices. And a fair number of superior teachers deeply and sincerely believed that any change would be for the worse. I greatly respected these teachers, and count them among the master professionals I have known. One of them, after two or three years, said to me, "Aren't you ever going to give up this curriculum development idea?"

Faculty Concerns

Yet the majority of teachers were uncertain about what the Winnetka Schools were attempting to do. The faculty workshop held in the fall of 1956 revealed such questions as these, some of which were frighteningly revealing of the uncertainty of the philosophy of the schools:

a. Why do we not have curriculum guides?
b. Why may we not use commercial texts?
c. What is the balance between individual and group instruction?
d. What basic skills do we expect to establish at each grade level?
e. Can we disregard the goal cards?
f. How can I get help in Winnetka techniques?
g. Should creative activities take so much time?
h. Is enrichment all we can do for the gifted?
i. Is not grouping better than individual progression?
j. How much homework at Junior High?
k. How do we get a decision on materials of instruction?

Such questions as these went on for 11 pages, as submitted by the recorders of the several workshop groups. Yet, in spite of these uncertainties, a high quality of education was being carried on in Winnetka. Four distinguished principals headed the four schools (three elementary and one junior high) and each had been a vital and deeply involved part of Winnetka's period of innovation and research. James Mann at Hubbard Woods School is one of the quiet giants of elementary education; Donald Cawelti, principal of Skokie Junior High School, who later became Assistant Superintendent, possessed as deep an insight into teachers and children of the junior high as any other educator I have known; Frederick Reed, a philosopher and scholar of first rank, who had done much curriculum work with C.W., was principal of Greeley School; and Edna Olson, while not of as long tenure in the principalship as the others, was the effective mistress of Crow Island School, following many years of distinguished classroom teaching in Winnetka. These leaders were able to preserve a high order of educational excellence during the period of changing superintendents. And closely allied with them, and with me during my first three years, was Marion Carswell, who had served for many years at all levels of the Winnetka Schools, and who had a firm grasp of Washburne's ideas. As I looked at the service records of these champions, I was shaken to discover that their ages were such that retirement would claim them all too soon.

Something Old

It was clear to me that an overwhelming need of the Winnetka Schools at that time (second only to the creation of a working relationship between the administration and the faculty) was an all-out commitment to curriculum development. But for me simply to have declared this, and to have hoped for results, would have been foolhardy. Further, I was becoming deeply impressed by the unique historical processes of teaching in Winnetka when executed by a master teacher. These processes, as I saw them and came to appreciate them, possessed these chief characteristics:

Individual pupil progression through extensive use of locally prepared instructional materials, with corresponding exclusion of commercial textbooks in some subjects at some grade levels. The justification for the locally prepared books rested in the proposition that self-instruction was the highest form of teaching artistry, and that conventional textbooks were not adaptable to self-instruction and individual progression.[1] Over a period of time, I came to accept this proposition, slowly, I am sure, for I saw the anxiety and ineptness in new teachers joining our schools, who had learned their profession in more conventional ways, as I had. The term "commercial text" became a *cause célèbre* that year, as sides were taken and forces joined.

But amidst the debate, one thing became clear to me: individual progression was right and good; it presented a very demanding task for the teacher; it epitomized all that we believe about individual differences; its effective application in Winnetka at the time was widely variable. Yet, as the fundamental worth of individual progression as a concept became clear to me, I had to ask, *progression in what?* Were we as a faculty satisfied that existing grade level content expectations, irrespective of individual progression, were compatible with what we knew children could learn, and should learn? I had felt from my first day that the intellectual fare was thin. Many teachers concurred. But individual progression, and, where appropriate, locally prepared instructional materials, were reaffirmed as far as I was concerned, and that decision was behind us.

We did liberalize the commercial textbook issue, however, making available, particularly to new teachers, selected commercial texts at appropriate grade levels to supplement or replace the locally prepared materials that had by that time become older than some of the teachers.

The Goal Record Card. If one comprehends fully the meaning of individual progression as it was, and is practiced in Winnetka, the question of bookkeeping becomes staggering unless the goal record card or goal card is also comprehended. Even though many teachers, especially those relatively new, found the goal record system quite forbidding, it appeared to me to be absolutely essential to the individualized design. If, as stated earlier, we were to reaffirm the idea of individual progression, it followed inevitably that there had to be a mechanical system

---

[1] Currently we are hearing much about programmed learning or teaching machines. While less sophisticated, and possessing no hardware, the early Winnetka instructional materials, long before the term became familiar, were devices for programmed instruction.

of record keeping that would support it. For example, a third-grade teacher could very likely, within the Winnetka design, have 25 children all at different stages of progress in arithmetic. There would be three or four finishing off the goals of Grade II, three or four probing independently into the goals of Grade IV, while the remaining 15-18 children would be located at various stages of the expected content of Grade III. This is not to say that all instruction in arithmetic is totally individualized at any grade. Periodically, the teacher undertakes the introduction of a new concept with the entire group, or with say six or eight children moving more swiftly than the others, or more slowly. But most of the instruction is on a one-to-one basis, as each child works his way through the *goals*. Accordingly, it is essential that the instructional materials (locally developed or commercial) be reasonably consistent in scope and chronology with the goals. For a child at Grade III has his goal card in hand, knowing what is expected of him for the year. As he fulfills, to the teacher's satisfaction, the sequential goals (see more on this in Chapter Twenty-One) in a given subject, as demonstrated by a test for *mastery*, the teacher dates the pupil's card, for example opposite "Knows Roman Numerals to 20." At the same time the teacher posts her master goal record book with the same notation. With 25 or more children all progressing at different rates, the goal record becomes an indispensable bookkeeping instrument.

Thus, it was resolved that the goal card would remain. But again, I mistrusted the *content* of the goals. It was desirable that children should progress at the rate of which they were capable. But the very existence of a goal card, say at Grade III, with established, specific academic expectations aligned chronologically for the majority of grade three children (allowing overs and shorts for a few) implied that this *was* the content to be learned. Even though some children in Grade III proceeded to the work of Grade IV or even V (and took their goal cards with them the next year), many of us felt that much more could be expected of the majority of the class, and still have individual progression into the even more demanding fare of the higher grade. In any case, the *idea* of goal cards was reaffirmed.

Emphasis On Individual and Group Creativity. Schools at large have come a long way since C.W. first inspired his staff toward a major emphasis on creativity. His earlier chapters reveal the intensity with which this phase of education in Winnetka was treated. But C.W.'s beliefs, and those of some of the remaining teachers, held that certain types of creative activity should exist for their own sake, quite apart from other elements of the more formal instructional program.[2] As I viewed the situation my first year there were widely varying degrees of effectiveness in what was still called the creative activities program— or, by the more esoteric term, the socialized activities program. Washburne's term had been "group and creative activities program."

The high concern for creativity in the original Winnetka design is a further mark of Washburne's remarkable insight. Only recently, in 1960–61, as scholars such as Jackson and Getzel [3] and others roll back the edge of knowledge about children, is American education beginning to systematize the hunches that C.W. and his teachers were pursuing.

Individual and group creativity as seen by Washburne did not necessarily articulate with other, more formal academic instruction. In this we would differ. For example, if the social studies curriculum at Grade IV called for an exploration of early Egyptian culture, and if time and energy is to be devoted to creative activity at a given day or hour, it seems desirable to reinforce the learnings of early Egypt by drama, art, crafts, etc., as creative instruments *which produce intrinsic outcomes in themselves,* and at the same time build upon and stimulate the academic learnings at hand. I doubt that we could justify today the pupil time and teacher energies called forth for an activity that had no relevance to the curriculum. For I believe the desired cultural and mental health gains and satisfactions take place in children if the activity is well planned and executed, even though academically relevant.

As will be revealed in a later chapter, the Winnetka Schools for many years have had specially qualified teachers in each elementary

---

[2] "The purpose of group and creative activities is never academic. There is no attempt to teach subject matter through these activities. . . . Such correlation as exists is incidental and unforced." Washburne, *School and Society,* January 12, 1929.

Actually, C.W. had conceived two types of creative activities for pupils, one of which he classified as Creative Group Activities, of which he says further, "Now such activities have no academic purpose whatsoever. . . . The teacher . . . will not interrupt or warp this activity to drag in subject matter." (See pp. 288, 289, *A Living Philosophy of Education.*) But he goes on with his other classification, which he called *ad hoc* projects: "In the teacher's mind such an activity is a means to a specific end in the field of the acquisition of certain units of knowledge or skill." (P. 289, *A Living Philosophy of Education.*)

[3] Philip W. Jackson and Jacob W. Getzel, educational psychologists at the University of Chicago, have been producing some remarkable findings in the field of creativity in children. *University of Chicago Reports;* Vol. II, No. 1; Oct. 1960. See *Creativity and Intelligence,* published by John Wiley, 1962.

building concerned with creative activities. I became heavily impressed with the extraordinary power of this resource. I found that in actual practice, the group and individual creative activities were, indeed, largely related to the formal curriculum, and were often deliberately guided in this direction by the creative activities teachers, notwithstanding C.W.'s earlier convictions.

Thus, another of the fundamental concepts of the early Winnetka design was reaffirmed. Emphases may have been modified; articulation with the academic program became more conscious; the role of the creative activities teacher (which apparently had been somewhat tenuous) became affirmative and clear.

The Spirit of High Devotion in the Faculty. While there is nothing in the "Winnetka Plan," past or present, that prescribes the high commitment of the professional staff, this ingredient was clearly implicit in all that C.W. did. It is an ingredient that is indispensable to the execution of the demanding task of teaching within this design. The deep devotion to children, and all their needs; the willingness and even eagerness to invest many extra hours in parent consultation; the readiness to undertake demanding and time-consuming in-service experimentation or action research on many fronts—all characterize this faculty, past and present. These qualities pervade the faculty, and flow from one member to another with a happy infectiousness. Without these qualities much that was and is Winnetka education would be impossible.

These were the unique elements that I found in my early months in Winnetka that were the heritage from the earlier years of innovation. Perhaps more knowing observers would question my discernment, saying there were other, more subtle things that distinguished these schools. Perhaps so. But as offered above, the essential distinctions, which were *distinctions in degree* from other schools I had known, were my judgments at the time, and remain so today. But in noting *distinctions* in degree, I must add that the degree was very marked, even after the passage of years and the passing of many people. Washburne's shadow is still long and clearly etched, and this school system is indeed a community of teachers and families who place education uppermost in their arrangement of values.

One might go on listing other unique qualities of these schools, to which my administration fell heir. There would be, well up on the list, mental hygiene of pupils and teachers, self-discipline, economic literacy, extensive student participation in organizational responsibilities, high community expectation and support, extensive special staff support for the classroom teachers, and a selfless and highly literate Board of Education. But these latter qualities, while very significant in drafting a profile of education in Winnetka, were not as decisively unique, or as marked in their degree of emphasis, as those described earlier. They are essential to understanding Winnetka teaching as it was, and they are essential to an understanding of education in Winnetka today. For they constitute the key features of the Washburne period that have been reaffirmed, revived, built upon, and implemented in the present. I would hope that, with the passage of time and experience, we have improved on them. I list them again—the reaffirmations of the Winnetka design:

Self-instruction
Self-correction
Locally developed books, compatible with the above
Individual progression by pupils through content, irrespective of grade
Goal record system for academic accounting
High emphasis upon group and individual creativity

While much has been done to modify the instructional program in Winnetka over the past seven years, with broad and deep changes in curriculum content, the key characteristics of instructional technique, itemized above, have been preserved. They have stood the test of time; they have been examined and re-examined, evaluated and re-evaluated; discarded, and reactivated by teachers, both old and new to Winnetka. Given a year or two for induction, with freedom to accept or reject the design, new teachers joining us now generally take readily to the demands of this kind of teaching. Some move on, either at their initiative or ours, if they are incompatible with these techniques. Teaching in Winnetka is very hard work. Good teaching is hard work anywhere.

Something New

It is important to make clear at this point that, while much of this accounting is recorded in the first person singular, consistent with Washburne's earlier chapters, I did not, nor do I now, view myself as the sole motivator or leader engaged in educational reaffirmation or revolution in Winnetka. To know Winnetka is to know that virtually every member of the professional staff is a leader at something, sometime. The diversity and depth of convictions prevailing among these teachers is monumental! And, it seems to me that diversity begets diversity. For as dominant faculty figures of determined and dramatic coloring pass the retirement point, there seem to spring to their places relative newcomers, with equal competencies, vigor and diversity. In such a setting the superintendent is well advised to find the mechanism for channeling and articulating such power, balancing the diversity, and sharing the leadership. Such a mechanism is the Planning and Advisory Committee, described earlier.

Thus, in nearly all instances, when the first singular pronoun is used in these pages, the Superintendent of Schools is speaking with the voice of considered faculty consensus. Such consensus does not imply that the thousands of major and minor decisions reached over these recent years concerning the instructional program have been tossed up for faculty ayes and nays. Rather, the broad issues of reaffirmation or change have been the object of deep and lengthy discourse in the deliberations of the Planning and Advisory Committee of the Faculty. Subsequent specific decisions have been the responsibility of specific faculty committees, some of which have been at work for six or more years. All such decisions have been shared by the superintendent, and have been subject to ultimate endorsement by the Board of Education. (The place of lay advisory committees will be treated later.)

The Beginning of Curriculum Revision

In any case, the winter of 1956–57 found the Planning and Advisory Committee and the superintendent doing some heavy soul-searching. Beyond the reaffirmation of unique fundamental procedures, there was evidence of a need for a much more formal and concrete curriculum design, and a need for establishing a much higher academic expectation than had prevailed in grade level content at all grades. The ancient materials of instruction (locally prepared workbooks or textbooks) were out of stock in many instances, and were the object sometimes of frantic mimeographing and stapling, as teachers and pupils ran out of content.

I admit that as visitors or letters of inquiry called for samples of this or that document, or inquired about what exciting things we were doing with reading, or spelling or mathematics, I had to reply that the documents "were under revision" . . . or "we are not quite ready to send out our spelling program." It was at this point that we selected commercial textbooks for a number of subjects and grades, to augment or replace our local materials at least during a period of regrouping and stock-taking.

My annual report to the Board of Education at the end of 1956–57 included this passage:

> A clear weakness of the present program is a lack of any systematic and prescribed curriculum objectives, year-by-year, and grade-by-grade, with suggested techniques for fulfillment. While this resource might not have been necessary in the strong, stabilized faculty of some years ago, the need for concrete and specific direction of the teacher new to Winnetka is clear. Further, the role of the Board of Education and the community in the evaluation and adoption of curriculum guides must have greater attention.
>
> *   *   *
>
> But the development of course-of-study guides is not the real substance of a vigorous program of instruction. Indeed, the guides can be no more than a collection of words unless there is a unity and enthusiasm within the faculty, growing out of the stimulus and pattern afforded by involvement in creating the course of study. There must be an acceptance of the curriculum by the teachers, and a true sense of membership and vested interest in it if teachers are to fulfill the objectives established. The teachers must find foundation and broad direction and consistency in the guides, and must be free to rise above the guides and carry their children above and beyond the mechanical framework wherever their initiative, their wisdom, and the needs and desires of children may take them.
>
> The curriculum work contemplated here should be looked upon not as something new or revolutionary, but as a continuing force, which, in 1957 and. 1958, is formalizing and reaffirming that which is known to be the best in our present practice, and searching for ways to improve and replace that which we find weak.

The Planning and Advisory Committee reached a vigorous consensus in the winter of 1956–57, concluding that a large-scale curriculum revision was called for in virtually all academic fields, Kindergarten through Junior High School. (In Winnetka, as in much of Illinois, the high schools are separate institutions, organized on a township basis. In our case, Winnetka is one of the five communities sending its pupils to New Trier Township High School.) While a committee had been at work on a social studies curriculum prior to 1956, its product at the

Photo 3: In any dynamic school system, curriculum revision is a constant process. Faculty committees have overhauled all academic curricula in recent years, and written local, self-instructional text materials in mathematics, spelling, grammar. Much of this overhauling occurs during summer months.

time was inconclusive and fragmentary. No recent work had been done in mathematics, language arts, or science. Indeed, the science curriculum had been a subordinate appendage of the social studies, receiving passing and often inspired patches of attention from the teachers who enjoyed science, but receiving only the attention that its subordinate status implied from those who were unsure. Many teachers were unsure in science.

(Notwithstanding my dissatisfaction with the science program as I saw it in 1956, it must be stated that under C.W.'s leadership there had been certain unique science education ideas at work in Winnetka. They focussed largely at Grades IV and V. At Grade IV, in conjunction with the social studies period of early man, a good measure of geology and astronomy had been developed. At Grade V a daring offering in sex education as an element of physiology had flourished. In our current work we have built upon and extended these features.)

Organization for Curriculum Improvement

We are a small faculty, counting only a few over a hundred. With the many other in-service committee tasks to be done in accompaniment to the splashings of a new superintendent, there was good reason to avoid overloading the faculty with several new curriculum committee assignments. I thought that a major mathematics effort, along with a revival of the social studies committee, would be about all that we could tolerate. This would have meant two major curriculum committees on the job at the same time, with all work confined to after-school hours, weekends and holidays. The science advocates, learning that we were ready to divorce science from the social studies curriculum, insisted that they, too, were ready to start work. This left only the language arts. The already overworked faculty could not be expected to confront this, too. And indeed if the new superintendent had suggested it, there would have been a firm resistance. It was here that James Mann, gentle and beloved principal of many years, at a crucial meeting of the Planning and Advisory Committee, said, "As far as I can see, we are going all out for curriculum construction for the next few years. We might as well take on the language arts, too." Consensus.

And so it was, that, as in any good school system, the teachers of

Winnetka evaluated themselves in the fall of 1956, found themselves to be short of what they wanted to be, and returned to the theatre of inquiry, innovation and productivity that many of them had known so well some years before. For seven years now, nearly every teacher has been deeply and personally engaged in one or another compartment of curriculum development. The products, never really finished, are now in a form to be used—by ourselves and the many others who call for them. But the value has not been in the product. The value, as Washburne knew in 1920, was the personal, hip-deep involvement of all concerned in the affairs of educational creativity.

Guidelines for Curriculum Construction

At the start of the curriculum renaissance, the Planning and Advisory Committee published instructions of a general nature to all who were engaged in curriculum development, and as the several specific committees were organized that winter, specific instructions, *i.e.*, in the science curriculum, were published in turn. For the student of curriculum development, the following memorandum may be useful. It is the broad guide drafted by the superintendent, refined and sharpened by the Planning and Advisory Committee, endorsed by the Board of Education, and conveyed to the faculty as instruction for curriculum development, in general.

CURRICULUM CONSTRUCTION, GENERAL

The following principles, as developed by the Planning Committee, shall apply to all curriculum development in the Winnetka Schools:

1. The curriculum shall be expressed through course-of-study guides in each major field of learning. The course-of-study guide shall place major importance upon the freedom and the initiative of the teacher in the learning situation. The guide shall be considered a floor upon which the program is built, common to all teachers. All teachers shall be expected to fulfill the expectations of the guide, allowing for pupil differences. However, the guide shall not suggest a ceiling, nor should it suggest uniformity—or rigidity.

2. A course-of-study guide shall define the broad objectives of its program, the specific objectives by grade, and will suggest by example and extensive reference the means by which objectives can be realized.

3. The curriculum guide in any one field of learning must rest within a broad philosophical framework common to all. However, in achieving this common framework, there should be recognition of individual differences in the teaching talents which teachers truly possess; *e.g.*, one teacher may be very skillful in achieving learning through the creative approaches; another may inspire enthusiasm for learning by more direct methods.

4. The general format of the guide shall be common to all subject areas. The following arrangements shall be followed in all course-of-study guides. (Language Arts, Science, etc.)

    a. Title page, including names of committee.
    b. Table of contents, including appendices, tables, diagrams.
    c. Foreword, including committee history, dates, general arrangement for curriculum development, such as consultants, workshops, etc.
    d. Introduction by superintendent or other, designed to communicate the purposes of the guide to the faculty and the public.
    e. Overview of specific curriculum, itemizing broad content by grade levels.
    f. Statement of general objectives, including philosophical patterns in which the guide takes form.
    g. Brief summation of important research upon which guide is based; emphases which should govern use of the guide.
    h. Grade content and suggested techniques. This portion of the guide shall be so organized as to be complete by each grade level:

        (1) Specific objectives of the grade.
        (2) Outline of basic content to be accomplished by pupil, arranged sequentially for the grade.
        (3) Briefly stated techniques, keyed to content outline, suggesting methods of accomplishing specific objectives.

(4) Sample development of a unit should be included for each grade level.

(5) List of suggested teaching aids, including films, supplementary reading and materials, demonstration devices, pamphlets, field trips, reference materials, etc.

(6) Textbooks approved for use in program, with annotated summary of text, describing its major values as related to objectives.

(7) Enrichment activities. Suggestions for creative experiences relating to the program by grade level and age of children. Particular attention to individualized enrichment opportunities for the gifted child.

(8) Plans for teacher testing and other devices for evaluating pupil progress.

(The foregoing outline shall apply to each grade, Kindergarten through VIII, so that each teacher, particularly a new teacher, may absorb the scope of the grade for which he is responsible without attempting immediately to digest the full document.)

    i. Design for system-wide evaluation of pupil progress.
    j. Bibliography by grades, as well as references to professional works by grades.

5. Following initial research and the development of initial findings by the curriculum committee, opportunities will be provided for orderly evaluation, criticism and suggestion from the full faculty.

6. At a stage in the development of the curriculum guide, after committee judgments and beliefs have taken form, arrangements will be made for participation of lay citizens in the deliberations and final decisions of the faculty committee.

7. When the final document has been completed, it will be submitted to the Board of Education for formal adoption.

8. Upon adoption of the guide by the Board of Education, the committee is discharged. However, two or more members of the

committee should be considered available periodically for recall, to assist in evaluation, revision or reorganization of the guide in subsequent committee organization.

9. Authority of Committee.

While the curriculum committee will extend itself to gain constructive criticism and suggestions from the full faculty in arriving at its final program, the ultimate decisions as to what shall be taught and when rest with the committee in making their recommendation for formal adoption to the Board of Education. Upon adoption by the Board of Education, the program shall be uniformly implemented by all concerned within the limits of flexibility declared in the course-of-study guide.

Clarification of Responsibility

As a final observation, I would call attention to the concluding paragraph of the foregoing memorandum. One of the obstacles to forward movement in curriculum development, or any other worthy in-service task, is the uncertainty of authority for decisions . . . or, conversely, the ill-founded notion that under academic freedom there is an authority vested in all teachers in any faculty to cast their vote on any subject, notwithstanding the competence, relevance and qualifications of the member toward the issue at hand. Discursiveness, frustration, and inconclusive debate have been an ailment of many faculties. It was true of this one also.

A year after the publication of the above memorandum, an address by the superintendent to the faculty included the following reminder:

A curriculum committee, broadly representative of the full faculty, spends upwards of three or four years of intensive study, debate, and deliberation over what children shall learn. They are obliged to make a great many decisions. These decisions, in tentative form, are put before the full faculty from time to time, or before grade group meetings for criticism and comment. Suggestions and recommendations for change are returned to the committee for further debate and consideration. But the right of decision—short of the Board of Education—rests with that committee. The final responsibility for adoption rests with the Board of Education, who, as society's agents, determines what the schools shall teach. The Board of Education is heavily dependent upon the findings and recommendations of the professional staff; hence the responsibilities of the committee are of a very high order.

Summary

The distinguishing characteristics of education in Winnetka which came to prominence in the 1920's remain vital and effective today. Some of these characteristics are concrete and finite, easily viewed and appraised. Some are subtle and abstract, dealing with the spirit, devotion and commitment of the faculty and the community.

But, building upon the proposition that deep personal involvement in the planning and designing of a program by all who are to execute it is essential to high success, there was a need for broad and deep re-examination and evaluation of what had been. There was also a need to survey and exploit important research performed by others, assess and exploit new techniques, confront new social and academic needs. We called what we were doing "curriculum revision." By whatever name, it was a deep and searching overhaul of all that we were teaching.

In the fall of 1958 the superintendent spoke to the faculty, after two years of intensive work, with much more work yet to be done. This passage, perhaps better than a new statement would do, sums up the situation as it stood then:

Winnetka was an ordinary growing suburban town with an ordinary school system in the first two decades of this century. Then came the decade of the 20's with extraordinary devotion in the schools to research and development, including the risks and the frustrations; then came the 30's which were the flowering and fulfillment of the decade of discovery. The early French voyageurs who traveled the canoe route through the border lakes north of Minnesota 300 years ago paused systematically in the paddling, at certain fairly exact intervals, for what they called "the pipe." They rested on the paddles during the time it took to smoke a pipeful. Then they were off again. Part of the 40's and part of the 50's have been, in a sense, a pipe in these schools. We have rested on our paddles. Now, before anyone gets his hackles up, let me say that I am not referring to the essential daily tasks of good teaching and good education. I am referring to the leading edge of discovery and invention, for the good of education, U.S.A. And, let me say further that the French voyageurs would never have survived their journeys if they had not had their periodic pipes.

During our pipe, other schools, operating on a different cycle, also have found their place on the leading edge. They may have passed us by. They also may have gone down some blind alleys from which we can profit.

But, before we can truly stand secure on the leading edge, we must have a firm foothold in what we are now teaching. It is for this reason that intensive and unified curriculum work must be performed now, to give a secure foundation from which to thrust out to unknown territory. The uncertainties, the changes, the blank spots that have accumulated in the past twenty years with evolving staff, evolving administration, and changing times must be resolved; we must

have a concrete and specific course of study in all academic fields before we
can safely and with confidence move forward. We must, in other words, know
where we are before we attempt to discern where we are going, and before
we can truly turn our attention again to fundamental innovation and action
research.

If my judgment is true, there is a readiness in us for the return to the leading edge. There is a zest for discovery; there is a surging to put Winnetka once
again away out front. I think this is true not only in the faculty, but in the
community. If this readiness, this energy, this zest for the fray, is to be fruitfully
released, we must move quickly and surely to complete the foundation work in
basic curriculum design.

Reading this passage now, it was more exhortatory than it needed
to be. By 1958 the Winnetka Schools were once again yeasting and via-
ble. Virtually every teacher was deeply committed to some phase of
curriculum development, either as a committee member, or as the object of an experimental trial of new materials or techniques, or a member of important committees in categories other than curriculum. Study
of relevant current literature, assembly and review of current textbooks
and other instructional materials, preparation of drafts of curriculum
passages were performed on evenings, weekends and holidays. Two and
sometimes four committee meetings a week were scheduled for many
teachers, and the school calendar was blocked out from 4:00 P.M. to 6:00
P.M., Mondays through Thursdays. We were in the third year of what
eventually proved to be a six-year span of intensive curriculum construction.

The wistful backward glances had disappeared. The staff was on
the move again, creating *its own* design, and no longer coloring the line
drawings of others. There was fatigue; there was vigorous and sometimes stormy debate. But solid professional people were once again
thrusting against the status quo, and in this there was great satisfaction.

CHAPTER NINETEEN

Yesterday's Heresy

Is Today's Dogma

It is obviously vital to examine goals. We cannot
proceed in any orderly way to build, staff, and finance a
school until we agree on the job we want the school to do.

In discussing school goals, it seems to me that three
errors are often made. First, there is the temptation to think
that a school program which is good for one's own community must be good for all communities. Regional differences,
economic differences, differences in the desires of the people—all these things and many others make it impossible
to make many dogmatic generalities which apply to all
communities.

—JAMES R. KILLIAN, JR.
CHAIRMAN, Massachusetts
Institute of Technology

The preceding chapter described the processes by
which the Winnetka faculty re-examined its past
and gave new and affirmative life to certain local

historic teaching concepts, re-examined its present and future, and decided to make some major changes in what children should learn. As the four curriculum committees, each consisting of 15-20 teachers (Social Studies, Mathematics, Science and Language Arts) set about their respective tasks, there still appeared to be a partial vacuum in the center of our intellectual and professional activity. Questions such as the following dogged the early deliberations of the working committees: Are we still concerned with the whole child as we bend our energies toward more intensive academic goals? Are moral and spiritual values a responsibility of the schools? Do we identify the gifted child, as such, or rely on our theory of individual progression? How can we reduce pressures on children? How shall we find time for creativity if so much more academic learning is prescribed? Some of the catch phrases of the progressive education movement were still in vogue among some Winnetka teachers. Most of their ideas were sound, but their catch phrases in the late 1950's had a hollow ring, and they were beginning to realize it.

Toward Agreement on the Basic Purposes of Education

Understandably, there had never been, as far as I could discover, a "statement of philosophy" written about the Winnetka Schools, even though such expressions, at least on paper, were common in most school systems. There was, of course, C. W.'s classic work, A *Living Philosophy of Education*, which was something considerably more than a statement of philosophy. My own beliefs concerning the dignity and individuality and freedom of teachers had always made a system-wide "statement of philosophy" repugnant to me. I had studiously avoided attempting to draft such a philosophy during my first three years in Winnetka, believing that words mean different things to different people, especially when probing the abstract. It was more important that the faculty know me, know my administrative behavior under various circumstances (for good or bad) and know what I meant when I used words like freedom, creativity, democracy, initiative, values and experimentation before trying to utilize such terms in a grandiose statement. For such a statement, writer unknown, has little reliability for the reader.

Yet as Saylor and Alexander point out:

> Curriculum decisions are philosophical decisions—they represent a choice of values. . . . Thus, tradition comes to be established and practices come to be institutionalized. It is only as venturesome souls point out defects in the established procedure in terms of accomplishments, new conditions, or new ends to be sought, and propose new courses of action . . . that the traditional practices are changed. Again, these better procedures become tradition.[1]

I would add another point to the arguments of Saylor and Alexander. As major decisions are made concerning teaching and learning, it is essential that those who are to implement these decisions have a large part in their formulation if high success is to be realized. It was not enough that the professional staff of Winnetka in the late 1950's had inherited a distinguished educational system. For no matter how good it was, it was, generally speaking, not *theirs*. It had been conceived by others years earlier. Therefore, those things which were to be preserved had to be reconstituted from the start, making them our own, internalizing them, developing a spirit of vestedness about them. . . . And those things which were to be changed were, obviously, to be newly created solutions conceived by those who would carry out the ultimate tasks. I am certain that these conditions applied to the superintendent of schools, as well as to the teachers.

The vacuum at the center seemed to call for a declaration of goals to which the full professional staff would give broad endorsement. This is slightly different from an expression of educational philosophy. While each individual teacher has the right to establish and live by his own educational philosophy, and should not be coerced into wearing a prescribed pedagogical mantle, it is another matter to adapt that philosophy to a more or less unified expression of goals.

Thus, while the curriculum committees proceeded slowly and with great labor to reconsider the courses of study, there was launched a parallel and concurrent study of what we called *Beliefs and Objectives of the Winnetka Schools*. At the start, the Planning and Advisory Committee called upon Marion Carswell, then the senior-member-of-the-firm, to search out from the past all key expressions of educational goals that had, over several decades, been declared. Miss Carswell, in her

---

[1] Saylor, J. Galen and William M. Alexander, *Curriculum Planning*, Holt, Rinehart and Winston, Inc., New York City, 1954, p. 82.

close-to-retirement years, compiled several pages of significant notes, drawing upon much of Washburne's writing, and the expressions of the intervening superintendents, as well as more recent items of my own. Starting with this as a backlog, we weighed and culled the current writings of respected educational thinkers nationally, as interpreters of society's expectations for its schools. And most actively, we drew upon our own experience, intuition and knowledge of our community until a tightly packed portfolio of educational aspiration and vision was at hand.

A Slow Process, Involving All Concerned

These things were happening in the fall and winter of 1958. I mention the date for the student of school administration, whose perspective toward timetables of educational evolution may find some useful check points. The timetables run slowly, even in small faculties, when the members take the trouble to conduct themselves as responsible professional people. This is another way of saying that the creation and digestion of worthy education goals is a slow process if it is to be enduring.

In the winter of 1958–59 the Planning and Advisory Committee conveyed a four-page memorandum to the faculty summarizing in somewhat telegraphic form the collection of old and new educational ideals which had been compiled, asking that the full faculty give thought to the subject, as we continued to work toward a central statement of purpose for our schools. This was a way of alerting the faculty to the fact that a major statement was in the making, and that all concerned were welcome to offer contributions.

By the following fall we had compressed our thinking into 12 fundamental propositions, as a starting point. They were conveyed to the faculty for study and reaction along with a memorandum from the Superintendent of Schools which read in part:

> It is my belief that far too many school systems have developed "statements of philosophy" which qualify admirably as literary efforts, but bear little resemblance to the policies, practices and performance of the teachers, pupils and administrators concerned. The drafting of an acceptable philosophical

declaration is a fairly small matter, calling for no more effort than the lifting of passages from any number of authoritative works in the field, provided all one is seeking is an abstract, idealistic statement, unrelated to the immediate circumstances of teachers and children and unmindful of the personal convictions of faculty members. . . . On the other hand, however, it seems timely to state simply, and with a good ear for reality, the broad objectives which the Winnetka Schools should pursue . . . as foundations for the concurrent development of specific curricula.

The memorandum went on to schedule a number of workshops, building meetings and study sessions spread throughout the year for purposes of full faculty debate and involvement in the draft statement. It was expected that a year would be enough to gain consensus. Actually, the statement was not concluded and adopted by the Board of Education until the summer of 1961—a three-year project.

The 1959 memorandum concluded with this note to the faculty:

A word of caution is offered here. The statement of objectives which we propose to develop here can be subject to vigorous dispute among conscientious professional people. It has been my experience that any attempt to find universal acceptance of a philosophical statement in all its subtleties and nuances either circumscribes itself with qualifying hedges, or emasculates itself through such colorless, arid and "acceptable" phrases that it offers no real message of importance. It is our hope to avoid this pitfall through thoughtful consensus on the large issues; it is our hope that we can avoid the fatiguing task of trying to separate the fly specks from the pepper.

Thus, at a fairly low-paced tempo the faculty weighed and debated upon the question of what our schools should be. During this period the Superintendent of Schools kept the Board of Education advised of developments, periodically submitted tentative statements to the Board and the faculty for refinement or modification. In the summer of 1961, after three years of deliberations, a sub-committee of the faculty met with the superintendent and collated all faculty recommendations and suggestions that had accrued from individual building meetings and study groups. All teachers had had a copy of a semi-final draft for several months. Finally, the faculty sub-committee gave its endorsement, the Board of Education adopted the statement, and, at least to the degree that an expression of educational goals can be committed to writing, Winnetka had a statement of Beliefs and Objectives. That fall, 1961, the Board of Education published it in brochure form, as its annual report to the community. The statement follows:

BELIEFS AND OBJECTIVES
OF THE WINNETKA SCHOOLS

This statement is the result of an intensive study by the faculty during 1959–61, followed by further study and endorsement by the Board of Education. It seeks to express the ideals and the hopes which underlie the total program of the Winnetka Schools.

Beliefs

The Winnetka Schools enjoy a unique position as the instrument of a highly favored community clearly committed to educational excellence. Unhampered by excessive population growth and its attendant problems, endowed with strong financial support, and encouraged by active and devoted school patrons, these schools have served and should continue to serve as an educational laboratory for the pursuit and discovery of ever better ways to teach and to learn. They should, further, participate actively in the determination and demonstration of the schools' place in America, as society seeks to deploy appropriate responsibilities among the home, the community and other institutions.

We place very high emphasis upon the individual pupil, endeavoring to provide a learning environment which will call forth his own determination to fulfill his capacities intellectually, physically, socially and spiritually. Fulfillment of the individual in his several parts must take account of the wide spectrum of differences in abilities.

But preoccupation with the individual is not enough. The schools as instruments of society must be concerned with the enhancement and preservation of our ideals and values as a corporate people, as we seek to produce a better society in each succeeding generation. Self-government, free world leadership, increasingly complex corporate and political organizations . . . yes, survival in these unsteady times calls for an enlarged measure of training and commitment toward active membership by individuals in the social order we call America. Thus the group and its subtle obligations and processes becomes a matrix for learning in school. However, individuality, creativity and equality of opportunity have made us a great people. These fundamentals of our culture should be built upon—not submerged—as we enlarge our concerns for groups. The wise and perceptive teacher will balance our ideals concerning the hearts and minds of individuals with our teachings concerning institutions of men, and will see to it that freedom, initiative, creativity, and the right to be different are not subordinated to our concerns for organizations and groups.

The goals of education in the United States, once we depart from the individual himself, have been essentially nationalistic. We have sought to equip men and women for effective citizenship and vocation through individual fulfillment in the service of the nation and its parts. We may now be entering a time that will call upon us to rise above the provincial implications of the improvement of the immediate social order in America. Our successful pursuit of material and social advantages as a nation have placed us, whether we like it or not, at the head of all free nations. While still struggling to achieve the democratic ideal at home, we are thrust into the role of reluctant champion of half a world much less ready than we for democracy. Heretofore we have cherished our freedom, guarded our treasures, exalted our heroes and our traditions, uplifted our people through science, industry and education, all in a generally self-serving context as a nation. Now we find ourselves exporting the ideas of freedom, generously sharing our treasure, helping others to find their own heroic history, and attempting to give others our science, our industry and our education. All this seems to imply that our free enterprise, including under its broad mantle public education as we know it, is reaching a point of maturity where materialism is not necessarily the measure of success or happiness. Our values seem to be moving to a higher level than those equated in goods or dollars. We are heavily motivated toward survival, it is true, as we share our strength with many nations. But, beyond survival, we seem to be accepting the realities and responsibilities of a community of free peoples, living no more than a day's travel apart. This condition, not yet wholly confronted, has much meaning for education in the years immediately ahead.

Coming full circle, and returning from the world to the community, we see the schools as instruments of society, as well as influencers of society. Consistent with the law, the policies and practices of the schools must be declared by the people they serve, through the elected Board of Education. Yet, the increasingly complex art and science of teaching calls for great faith in the professional staff who declare, by recommendation to the Board of Education, those issues and alternatives among which educational choices must be made. Correspondingly, as representatives of the community and society, the Board of Education must create and maintain the mechanisms through which informed and concerned citizens may make known their expectations for the schools, and, as opportunities arise, participate directly in the orderly development of recommendations for Board of Education consideration.

Thus, we contemplate the setting for the child of the 1960's who shall be a mature member of the society of 2000. It has been said, "Give me the child until he is seven, and he is mine thereafter." We may, in our clumsier and nobler way, say, "Let this child flourish under the privileges and disciplines of responsible freedom through childhood, and he will abide in no other way."

In summary, the objectives which follow should be viewed in the light of these foregoing beliefs ... our deep commitment to the individual in all his parts; our acceptance of our obligation to give primary emphasis to intellectual excellence; our concern for preserving the American ideal with its basic doctrines of free enterprise and equal opportunity for all; and, lately, but no less vigorously, our acceptance of the selfless disciplines and obligations of the brotherhood of man under God, as long revealed by the Judeo-Christian ethic.

Objectives

Within the context of the Beliefs declared above, we seek for all Winnetka children a learning environment which will foster the following broad objectives, which in turn should find their place in the more specific curricula of the schools.

1. *Give Primary and Unremitting Devotion to Intellectual Growth*

    While the schools have no monopoly on the measures through which children grow intellectually, they are the one universal and systematic institution organized for sequential intellectual development of pupils. While other institutions take responsibility for the social, emotional, spiritual and physical growth of the child, the school shares these responsibilities. But for systematic intellectual growth, consistent with the developmental theories of psychology, the schools accept prime responsibility.

Intellectual growth means much more than an increasing competence in the academic content of the curriculum. We must endeavor to stimulate in the child a love for learning, an attitude of inquiry, a passion for truth and beauty, a questioning mind. The learning of right answers is not enough ... beyond answers alone we must help children ask right questions, and discover their answers through creative thinking, reasoning, judging, and understanding. We must help children know that learning is its own reward, uncluttered by momentary symbolic rewards for accomplishments or penalties for failures.

Learning can best flourish when teachers, supported by adequate materials, create a climate in which children are genuinely desirous of learning. It will flourish when children become, through the teacher's stimulation, self-motivated, knowing that learning is necessary and important, and why they are engaged upon it. And it behooves us to be sure that it *is* necessary and important. Conclusions, values, solutions to problems are not taught ... they are learned, created, possessed internally by the child, having been excited by the teacher, and having been led by the teacher to the place where the answers might be found.

We recall Kahlil Gibran in *The Prophet:*

The teacher who walks in the shadow of the temple, among his followers, gives not of his wisdom but rather his faith and his lovingness. If he is indeed wise he does not bid you enter the house of his wisdom but rather leads you to the threshold of your own mind.

Example: The goal record device which establishes the grade-by-grade academic expectations is the individual pupil's accounting system for knowing what is expected of him, and knowing what he has satisfactorily completed. He is encouraged to advance through the content at as swift a pace as the teacher feels he is capable of undertaking. He is expected to possess mastery, or 100 per cent fulfillment of the prescribed goals, for example, in spelling, as established sequentially by grade. No marks or other symbols attach to the goals achieved. He is presumed to know what learnings are expected of him, and where he stands in the fulfillment of these expectations.

2. *Teach the Basic Skills Thoroughly*

We seek for each child a mastery of the tools of learning as essential to the more abstract learning and thinking which follows. To read well, and with appropriate pace and comprehension, to express himself effectively and fluently in speech and writing, to perform with precision the fundamental mathematical processes, and to have a command of the scientific process of thought are reasonable expectations for nearly every child by the conclusion of grade eight.

While much learning takes place by incidental or indirect processes both in and out of school, the arrangements for the mastery of the basic skills must be systematic, orderly, and well planned. The curricular design must provide step-by-step content requirements consistent with mental age and maturity of the child and must be sufficiently flexible to release and challenge the swift learner and be within the grasp of success for the slow learner. Teaching techniques and materials should be adapted to this condition.

We hold that *understanding* the skill being performed and the *reason* for its process are elements of skill learning that we must seek for each child. His learning will accordingly be swifter and more enduring. Practice, drill, reteaching and periodic testing, including diagnostic testing, are essential to consistent accomplishment in the basic skills. However, mere memorization, mere word calling, and mere reckoning of numerical solutions are not evidence of mastery.

Finally, as skills are taught, they must be put to use. The unused fact or word or competence with numbers is soon lost. The curriculum, through imaginative devices for creative and practical *planned* activity by pupils, should take heavy account of this condition.

Example: The curriculum in mathematics includes pupil textbooks developed by this faculty, providing sequential learnings, or simple programmed learnings. Each child is required to progress through the text, periodically performing prescribed tests which seek to determine his *understanding* as well as his manipulation of mathematical ideas. He does not proceed to higher expectations until he wholly grasps the stage-by-stage progression of content.

3. *Consider the Child a Total Human Being*

As stated above, the intellectual growth of children is a primary obligation of the schools. Yet, children are possessed of other parts than the mind. We know that intellectual fulfillment cannot be attained separately from social growth, emotional growth and physical growth. A balanced educational program takes account of the realities of the child as a member of the group, accepted or rejected, aggressive or shy, a leader at times, and then a follower. Most of man's adult effectiveness rests upon his relationship with others, as well as upon his intellectual and intuitive powers. The classroom and the school are social groups. The opportunities for direct and indirect social learnings are limitless.

Emotional growth of children leaves much still to be discovered. We know that mental health is highly important to effective academic progress. We know that significant numbers of children are severely handicapped in intellectual fulfillment for reason of emotional obstacles. Success, security and affection are essential elements of the learning environment, and for that matter for the environment of all humans.

Physical growth, treated more fully in Item 7, must be recalled here as an aspect of human development running concurrently with and having direct bearing upon intellectual growth.

Children are possessed of widely varying degrees of development in these several categories. Likewise, they are possessed of many varying aptitudes and attitudes, some evolving from school and some evolving from other origins. We know that the child is the focus of, and is superior to, all the influences to which he is exposed. The schools must take account of these conditions, accepting each child at the point of maturity where he is, and proceed individually from that point forward.

In establishing this objective we hold that apart from academic learning the child should be trained in the skills of social intercourse appropriate to his maturity, and he should develop good mental and physical health. This is not to say that bland togetherness or eternal social and emotional compatibility need be sought as an ideal. We expect children to rise above group convention when reason so prescribes, and to be emotionally upset and not the least bit happy when conditions prompt unhappiness. We declare that the school is a good place for guided experience and exposures in the non-academic affairs of humans, behaving naturally, and that to overlook these learning situations is to lose extraordinary opportunities for fulfilling children.

Example: High emphasis upon school-home communication helps to implement this objective. The check list for parent-teacher conferences provides for exchange of information and advice concerning the child's social and emotional characteristics. As needed, the resources of the psychologist and counselor are used to augment the knowledge about the child and to interpret the knowledge to parents.

4. *In Cooperation with the Home and Other Social Institutions, Help Children Develop Attitudes, Habits, Values, Appreciations and Understandings Essential to a Constructive Adult Life as an Articulate, Contributing Member of Our Society*

Toward realizing this objective, we must provide the setting and the stimulus for the child to learn the truths about the world in which he lives . . . the bad as well as the good . . . the grays as well as the blacks and whites. He must learn that choices must be made among realistic alternatives, and that these choices are based upon values and convictions which he possesses through learning and rational deliberation. He must acquire the self-discipline and habits of scientific thought and intellectual pursuit of truth, based upon earnest inquiry. The skills of inquiry and debate call for scholarly application to the weighing of alternatives; these processes are wares of the school.

The child must learn the obligations and practices of a citizen in a democracy. He must learn that one of his obligations is constant vigilance toward the preservation of the enduring self-evident values of freedom, and to participate actively in freedom's processes and disciplines, both in the community and the larger society. Truthful and realistic involvement in controversial issues and the mechanisms of self-government are essential in the classrooms and the schools if these values are to be nourished and internalized by young people. To speak of freedom and to parrot the ideologies of democracy are not enough. Democracy, its attitudes, habits and values, is a way of life, a believing, a deep and abiding concern. It calls for the involvement of the heart as well as the mind.

Clearly these young people must be accustomed to the processes of change. For their world will continue swiftly to change. We, as adults, cannot equip them with sure knowledge of what the changes will be, but we will endow them well if we fit them for truly intelligent expectation of change.

The satisfying fruits of hard work, the truths of brotherhood, the enduring commitment to the dignity and worth of all humans, the knowledge of history, both past and present, and a sense of communion and intimacy with the peoples of the world and their ways of life are clear and present goals of these schools. They are the subtle overtones and shadows that we call *values*. They put flesh on the bones of the basic skills.

Example: At the upper grades, the social studies curriculum establishes specified readings and discussions surrounding the Constitution, the Bill of Rights and other
literature of freedom. Current events, including exposure
to the imperfections of democracy at home, as well as
totalitarian practices abroad, are drawn upon to illuminate
the realities of freedom. It is intended that internalized
values deriving from this kind of learning will become a
part of the pupil's evolving nature. Coercion or external
indoctrination are alien to this objective; rather we seek a
deeper and more fundamental nourishment of personal
convictions.

5. *Discover and Respond to the Special Talents and Needs of
all Children*

These schools are heavily committed to the reality of
individual differences. Placing high emphasis upon the con-
sulting resources of the school psychologist, teachers must
seek constantly the ways in which individual pupils can
release their powers and competencies. Not only in the field
of academic learning, but in art, music, construction, drama,
leadership, social responsibilities, speaking, writing, mechanical aptitudes, and in many other ways children can find
fulfillment. We want children with extreme needs, such as
in the case of the very swift learners, and the talented, or
those with physical or mental handicaps, to find maximum
opportunities for success. We want them to know and
understand beauty and creativity, and have a beginning
understanding of the human spirit.

Example: As a part of the Northern Suburban Special
Education District, the Winnetka Schools identify children
with limitations or handicaps, and provide special instructional services and facilities for them. Exceptional needs
include sight-saving, hard-of-hearing, educationally mentally
handicapped, trainable mentally handicapped, orthopedic,
brain damaged, and deaf.

6. *Develop the Habits of Rational Thinking and Problem-Solving*

Children should learn that there are very few absolutes. Most of the ideas and "truths" of our civilization are subject to condition, qualification and opinion. A variety of textbooks and other resources, an honest confrontation of controversial issues appropriate to the maturity of the child, a weighing of evidence, and the removal of emotion and prejudice advance the pursuit of this objective. This is not to say that teachers should be neutral. They should be free to share their own convictions, revealing other persuasions with equal interest.

The processes of scientific thinking are called forth here: observation and reporting of data, collection and testing of facts, declaring and testing of hypotheses. The terms *always, never, none* and *all* are alien to this objective.

Children should not be discouraged from questioning authority in an atmosphere of respectful, scholarly debate. This leads to the development of convictions ... convictions duly arrived at, and possessed by children. Once a conviction is reached students must realize that they must accept the consequences of their convictions.

Example: The science curriculum places high stress on the scientific process—the declaring of a hypothesis, the trial of alternatives, the observation of results, and the accurate reporting of conclusions. Starting at about Grade IV this process becomes a systematic part of science learning. Not limited to the science curriculum, critical thinking is encouraged among all children at all times.

7. *Foster Physical and Mental Health*

The attitudes and skills relating to physical education, physiology, including appropriate sex education, health education and safety education are essential to desirable total growth. Vigorous physical activity appropriate to the maturity of the child is essential for the development of strong

bodies. The playing field and the gym offer worthy laboratories for the discrete learnings of cooperation, fair play and
honor, leadership and the role of the follower.

Mental health in the schools, mentioned earlier, leaves
many unknowns at this stage of educational history. We
know that the entire atmosphere of the school, including
the mental health of the adults in it, has much to do with
the mental health of children. We know that mental health
implies a personal sense of well-being, essential to effective
academic learning. It derives from a child's mastery of his
environment and his own emotions, appropriate to his
maturity. Teachers foster good mental health through
genuine affection for and acceptance of the child, through
creating an atmosphere of clearly defined limits and expectations, and through insuring frequent realistic success
at the child's level.

Example: Our design for instruction places the pupil
largely in competition with himself. Teachers individualize
the meaning of "success" knowing that each child must, at
least occasionally, succeed. What is success for one child
may be a very low order of work for another. A written
composition developed with care and hard labor by a child
with limited powers is recognized as "successful" by the
teacher's endorsement and comment, whereas a similar
piece of work written by a child with high ability and
creativity would be rejected as unworthy.

8. *Provide a Setting which Stimulates Social and Aesthetic
Development.*

Appreciations, attitudes, self-discipline, abstract values,
discrimination between good and evil, beauty and ugliness—
are functions of the spirit as well as the mind. One does not,
for instance, "learn" the values of liberty by merely hearing
about them or reading about them. He is moved by experience and curriculum arrangements to *understand and feel
and internalize* these values as emotional as well as intellectual processes. One does not learn self-discipline by being
coercively controlled at all times. Pupils must learn to make

choices between right and wrong, accepting the consequences for wrong-doing.

SOCIAL DEVELOPMENT

Our schools should provide many controlled and supervised experiences for children which lead to the *discovery by them* of values concerning people. Teachers can do much to clear the way and design the arrangements in which social skills are realistically called forth. Within the context of this objective are included the following elements of social growth: acceptance of responsibility, critical thinking, self-discipline, respect for others, the dignity of the human spirit, acceptance of rightful authority, and the processes of effective group action. Student government, consistent with maturity, as a laboratory of democracy, is a fruitful setting for learning of the obligations of freedom. Consistency, clearly defined standards, and demonstrated respect for authority by teachers are reliable tools. Emulation of teachers by children in the context of this objective is a powerful force.

AESTHETIC DEVELOPMENT

Beauty and order, not unlike social values, are elements of education which cannot be "taught." They are learned. The child is led, through rich experiences and exposures, to internalize his appreciation for beauty and to know the worth of order. These forces, like freedom, are intangible functions of the spirit of civilized man.

Art, music, literature, drama, speech, creative writing and craft work are the more obvious channels for the cultivation of aesthetic values. Yet beauty and order may be found in all parts of a child's environment, not least of all in human relations. The unfolding mysteries of science, or mathematical phenomena, are indeed possessed of beauty and order.

Children should begin to cultivate good taste, discrimination and recognition of aesthetic worth. They should begin to discriminate between the truly fine and the shoddy.

They should be encouraged and warmly supported in their own acts of creativity in all the arts, and should be held to worthy standards, compatible with their competence and maturity.

Example: At all levels of maturity children are involved in self-government activities which closely parallel adult patterns of citizenship. Student council, safety committee, Junior Red Cross are realistic arrangements for learning the processes and procedures of social organization. Errors and misjudgments by children are sometimes permitted by the faculty to progress to their unhappy conclusions for the advantage of the learners.

9. *Develop a Respect for Hard Work and an Acceptance of Responsibility for Its Completion*

Our way of life in this country is swiftly removing the natural obstacles to existence that made our fathers strong and resourceful. As a society Americans do not on the whole have to struggle to survive. Hard work in our cultural and advertising idiom is something to be deplored and avoided through service devices and machines. This places upon the teacher an increasing responsibility to offset the diminishing necessity for physical labor by the enhancement of intellectual labor. For labor we must.

Further, it is clear that the schools possess an opportunity to provide outlets for the manual and creative potential in children through providing programs and materials for realistic physical work with tools and other media. This is compatible with the do-it-yourself trend in modern living.

Expecting and accepting the highest degree of intellectual excellence that the child is capable of performing should be basic in the teacher's philosophy. So, too, is it the teacher's responsibility to direct a child that he may learn the joy and satisfaction of performing the most menial task to the best of his ability. The condition of mental health described earlier, having to do with *realistic success*, is closely related to this objective. The child is not truly successful when he knows he has fulfilled his teacher's expectations without extending himself to the fullest.

Example: Pupil projects, as in science, social studies, language arts and other fields, developed by small groups or individuals are encouraged for creative learnings. High expectations and standards, especially for the exceptionally able children, are established. Honors Quality recognition at Junior High level in the form of an HQ stamp provides for the teacher and child a symbol of coveted excellence, attainable in any category of school work.

10. *Give High Prominence to Moral and Spiritual Values*

Perhaps at no time in our history has it been so vital for Americans to have a transcending sense of purpose beyond survival and materialism. The home and the church bear the primary responsibility for instilling in youth the moral and spiritual values which undergird our culture. However, the schools, through their uniquely universal relationships to the lives of all people, have an obligation to declare and enhance the moral and spiritual precepts common to western civilization. Without a foundation philosophy giving consistency and meaning to our thoughts and actions, we are without purpose or direction.

We are a people largely committed to a belief in an Almighty. Our founding fathers and subsequent governments have made this clear. The foundation ethic of our Judeo-Christian culture is love. The separation of church from state does not demand a separation of God from schools.

Accidents of denominationalism may occur; infringement of the agnostic's rights may be questioned. As in many compartments of education, the schools and the teachers must take a position best calculated to serve all people. The teaching of moral and spiritual values, consistent with the broad, non-denominational truths of our pluralistic culture, is inescapable.

Example: Appropriate to the child's maturity and the curriculum, we teach about religion, avoiding sectarian emphases; our literature and art abound in relevant spiritual expressions. As occasions arise we teach compassion and respect toward our inter-faith likenesses and differences. The responsibilities of brotherhood find abundant opportunities for realization at all levels: fund raising, clothing drives, UNICEF projects, International Understandings Club are typical.

* * *

It will be noted in subsequent chapters that during this period of Winnetka's school history a very large emphasis was given to the active involvement of lay citizen advisory committees in the affairs of education. One might expect that lay citizens would have been called into the development of the Beliefs and Objectives. This was not the case. While there is logic and value in sharing nearly everything of a planning nature with community representatives, it was felt that this task was so very fundamental to the clearly established legal responsibilities of the Board of Education and the professional vision and integrity of the faculty, that to delegate even an advisory role to others would have been in bad taste.

Thus, the faculty, speaking from a position of professional aspiration and conviction, and the Board of Education, speaking from the position of the society being served by the schools, undertook an exciting contract of partnership for the good of children. The president of the Board of Education in that fall of 1961 [2] conveyed the annual report to the community with a letter which read in part as follows:

> In establishing a statement of goals we do not assert that in all instances these goals are fulfilled, for indeed "man's reach does exceed his grasp." But as a blueprint against which we may judge ourselves, and be judged by you, the Board of Education and the professional staff convey this document for your thoughtful scrutiny.

Summary

In the late 1950's the Winnetka faculty took upon itself the task of constructing a new and fresh statement of the underlying purposes

---

[2] C. Bouton McDougal, attorney and businessman, and devoted champion of good education, was president of the Winnetka Board of Education at this time.

of education. Developed over a three-year period, the statement of educational objectives could be abbreviated as follows:

1. Give primary and unremitting devotion to intellectual growth.
2. Teach the basic skills thoroughly.
3. Consider the child a total human being.
4. In cooperation with the home and other social institutions, help children develop attitudes, habits, values, appreciations and understandings essential to a constructive adult life as an articulate, contributing member of our society.
5. Discover and respond to the special talents and needs of all children.
6. Develop the habits of rational thinking and problem-solving.
7. Foster physical and mental health.
8. Provide a setting which stimulates social and aesthetic development.
9. Develop a respect for hard work and an acceptance of responsibility for its completion.
10. Give high prominence to moral and spiritual values.

Clearly committed to renewed service to education at large, through research and innovation, the Winnetka faculty needed such a statement to serve not only its own purposes as a foundation for curriculum development, but an instrument for local public understanding in a time of change and forward movement. The document found wide and affirmative response in the community.

CHAPTER TWENTY

Mathematics

in Winnetka

Mathematics today as a science or discipline is an entirely different subject from what it was even a generation ago.

—Commission on
Mathematics
College Entrance Examining Board

As we examine Winnetka today, comparing it, so to speak, in the mirror of the 1920–1940 period, the academic curriculum has now been systematized in its four major parts. These parts consist of mathematics, the social studies, science and the language arts. Of the four components, mathematics will be treated first, for a number of reasons. Being more nearly finite or absolute in its nature, the study of numbers lends itself more readily to quantitative comparison. Further, of all subject matter being taught, there is at this time more excitement and constructive disorder in our teaching of mathematics in the Winnetka Schools than in the other curricula.

One may wonder in the first place why we speak of mathematics in the elementary schools, rather than arithmetic. It is because we are dealing with mathematics in our evolving curriculum, K-8, as distinguished from arithmetic as a component of mathematics. Actually, our formal curriculum at this moment is only beginning to encompass a few highlights and shadows of the "new mathematics," particularly in the higher and lower grades. Elementary concepts of algebra, inequalities, equalities, unknowns, number properties, and varied number bases are becoming familiar terms in our primary grades as we experiment in the classrooms with these mathematical processes. Additional information on our experimental ideas in mathematics will follow later in this chapter.

Recalling certain key characteristics of the early Winnetka design, the teaching of arithmetic was particularly suited to individualization. Again, this derived from the finite nature of numbers. Self-instruction and self-correction, and speed tests for mastery, were exceptionally compatible with arithmetic learnings. It is further recalled that locally developed workbooks or textbooks had been found essential to the technique of individual progression.

In 1956 and 1957 the faculty confronted with much concern the issue of whether to attempt to suspend arithmetic teaching from the locally developed materials and adopt commercial textbooks, to continue to use the original local materials, or to face the problem of constructing new locally developed materials compatible with the swiftly growing body of knowledge concerning mathematics education. The original materials, in the construction of which C.W., with several key Winnetka teachers, had made revolutionary strides, were in short supply and were obsolete in problem content. For example, the fourth grade texts in arithmetic problems offered haircuts in our $2 economy of 1958 at 75 cents; carfare to Evanston was three cents, against 40-cent reality. These, of course, were minor disparities, insofar as their instructional usefulness was concerned, but they dated the materials revealingly, often to the amusement and ridicule of children.

Reaffirmation of the Process;
Re-evaluation of the Content

The fact that the Winnetka materials were in short supply, and were dated by their problem references, was not the basic source of concern. After much deliberation, we had reaffirmed the *process* of individualization, and reaffirmed the self-instruction *techniques*. But we had serious doubts about the *placement of content* within the design. Broadly speaking, the Winnetka design had veered consciously in the direction of deferring certain learnings from conventional placement in a given grade to placement in higher grades. This was not only true in arithmetic but in other fields. I respected Washburne's philosophy on this subject, and I endeavored to accept it, upon the advice of able teachers. Yet, my own convictions pressed me in the opposite direction. To make an oversimple generalization, Washburne believed that greater learning efficiency would derive from deferring learnings until they could be more easily and quickly grasped by children. To carry the over-simplication a further step, I believed that children should be expected to learn subject matter—in this case arithmetic concepts—at the earliest possible age, allowing for extreme differences in readiness and potential. I saw no point in having a child wait until fourth grade to learn long division if he could *learn* it and *understand* it, and find satisfaction in the process at third grade or second grade. One might find a parallel in the repertory of our elementary school orchestras. While they might render *Dixie* with spirit and precision, they found greater challenge, and quite adequate success, with some of Bach's fugues. The children and teachers understandably preferred Bach once *Dixie* was behind them, imperfect as the Bach rendition might be.

Indeed, I am sure it was C.W.'s theory that a child in Grade II could, conceivably, progress individually to the content of Grade IV while sitting in Grade II. Yet, the fact that grade content was established at given grade levels, with goal cards and instructional materials designed accordingly, tended to make that content the expectation of the grade, in spite of the theoretical vertical mobility of the Winnetka design. Human beings, both children and teachers, tend to want to know what is expected. If the expectations are fulfilled, even though easily and promptly, they tend to say, "That's done." Washburne would be the first to deny this, and claim that in his design the work is never done.

The difference between theory and the reality of teaching 25 variant children still persuades me that even the best teachers are pressed when individual progression reaches a classroom span for the extreme children of a year behind or a year ahead of the prescribed grade content. In other words, a third-grade class can be individualized over a spread of Grade II content through Grade IV content, with hard work by the teacher; if the spread goes beyond the three-year-span, the instruction becomes so diffuse as to be thin.

When I assert that the grade content in arithmetic, as I found it in Winnetka in the late 1950's, was not sufficiently challenging to children, I realize that I am flying in the face of Washburne's research with the Committee of Seven.[1] I am not the first to question the findings of this committee, nor do I possess current formal research to refute their findings. There are explanations, however, for setting aside the grade-placement evidence which C.W. described earlier.

One explanation was offered with considerable insight by James Mann, veteran Winnetka principal, who had worked closely with C.W. If the Committee of Seven found certain things to be true in the 1920's, defining the mental age at which children most effectively learn certain arithmetic concepts, it is not surprising that we now believe they can learn these same things at an earlier age, was Mann's notion. "I have had a feeling all along," wrote Mann, "that one of the reasons we are ready for a redistribution downward of arithmetic content is that we are reaping the rewards of better teaching following the emphasis on *concept* teaching." We have better-trained teachers, we have made much progress in the teaching of arithmetic through *meaning* and *understanding* as distinct from tricks. It followed that children *should* be learning more in 1959 than they did when the Committee of Seven did its research.

There were other, less rational reasons for the change, but they undoubtedly influenced our thinking in the faculty in the late 1950's. For example, a teacher joined our Winnetka staff having taught successfully in the middle grades of a Cleveland suburb. She is a first-rate teacher. She had not been here long when she observed, "These children are actually brighter on the whole than those I had in Ohio, yet our curriculum only calls for them to be doing work in fourth grade arith-

---

[1] See Chapter Two, p. 32.

metic that third graders were doing well there. May I not go on with my full fourth grade group into the fifth grade goals?"

The theoretical answer is "Yes, by all means, proceed as rapidly as the children can go, provided you are certain of their full understanding of the work, and are not merely getting right answers." But, in effect, we had to say, "This would mean each of the fifth-grade teachers next year will have eight or ten of your pupils who will be starting at sixth grade level, and this will be very difficult for them to confront in trying to organize classes. You had better stick to the prescribed curriculum until we can get it changed."

Now C.W. would say, "What in blazes is wrong with the fifth-grade teachers? Of course, they should carry on, wherever they find their pupils; I don't care if it's eighth grade!" But, I repeat, Washburne had been long gone and not everybody understood his plan as well as he, and many new teachers were simply not sufficiently skilled to execute it well when faced with 25 different children, performing at 25 different levels.

My own judgment during this period was influenced, I am sure, by such incidents as the following:

I had been on the job about six months when I had a long distance telephone call from a large eastern city. The caller was a mother who had recently moved from Winnetka to the city. She said, "I am in the office of the Superintendent of Schools of _____. We have been trying to enroll the two boys at grades three and five. I am calling at my expense to ask the Superintendent to tell you in person what he just told me." There was a pause, some uneasy noises, and then the Superintendent: "Yes, Mrs. _____ asked me to tell you that whenever we get children transferring from Winnetka we put them back a year in our schools because they are behind in their arithmetic."

It is easy to get angry at such a situation. One can write a long letter to the superintendent explaining in detail that there is no such thing as being "behind in arithmetic in Winnetka" . . . that I would bank on the child's success at any grade to which he had been recommended by his Winnetka principal . . . that we believed the child possessed compensating learnings in other fields that would show themselves in his new placement. One could also get angry at the stupidity of a school administrator who would permit himself such generalizations about children or school systems.

But that was not really the point. I had not come to Winnetka to defend it in long distance telephone calls—or in argumentative exchanges of correspondence. My job was to keep a superior school system superior, and if the world of mathematics was changing, this would be one of the things that would have to change in Winnetka.

Increasing the Learning Expectations

Most of our teachers were ready for upgrading the content of the curriculum. But the task was not that simple. We had committed ourselves to preserving the basic processes and techniques. The question of grade-placement of content immediately raised the question of instructional materials. It was not simply a matter of pushing the Grade V individualized text to Grade IV, or the Grade IV text to Grade III. We found that some of the original content of Grade IV should go to Grade II, some to Grade III, and some should remain in Grade IV. A number of teachers, some fairly new to Winnetka, and some veterans, declared that they would try to use commercial textbooks for a period of two or three years, adapting them to individualized instruction if such were possible. This relieved the immediate and crucial issue of what to do about reproducing and republishing the old materials. Thus in the fall of 1958, at Grades IV, V and VI, where the materials problem was most severe, we adopted commercial texts, with some misgiving, for an interim period, until we could gather our thoughts on what would be the best long-term solutions to the teaching of mathematics in Winnetka. Commercial texts were then in general use in Grades VII and VIII.

Winnetka Materials

A brief word of history is relevant here. If high emphasis appears to be attached to the place of instructional materials in Winnetka, it is because, in order to understand instruction within the Winnetka design, one must understand the very high reliance on individualized workbooks or textbooks.

The earliest locally developed workbooks in Winnetka were written by Carleton Washburne with the assistance of several teachers, and were published in 1925. They were entitled *Washburne Individual Arithmetics*, and were published by World Book Company. I believe the books, consisting of 12 parts, were designed to carry the pupils from Grade I through Grade VIII content. Very properly, consistent with the Winnetka theory, the books did not carry grade level labels. The concept that in recent years has been called popularly "the ungraded primary school" was truly in effect in Washburne's arithmetic materials, the content, rather than the child, being ungraded.

These books were the essential instruments of individualized arithmetic teaching and learning. The child at about grade one or two would read such a passage as this extract from the Winnetka material, probably to himself:

Suppose you want to add	18 $\underline{7}$
8 and 7 are 15; so you write the 5 part of the 15 like this:	18 $\underline{7}$ 5
Then you add the 1 part of 15 to the 1 part of 18. 1 and 1 are 2. You	18 $\underline{7}$
put 2 in front of the 5, like this:	25

While the foregoing illustration of self-instructional material would bring violent protest from the modern mathematics advocates of place value in the 1960's, who would call this technique a "gimmick for answers without understanding," the fact is that many thousands of children prospered under the design and gained good foundations for subsequent mathematics learnings (if not understandings) as testified by high school and college success.

Yet, as we continue to examine history further, it is evident that in the early 1940's the faculty was ready to set aside this 1925 material, and replace it with new, fresh workbooks, undoubtedly responsive to what was then the best available research in the field. Washburne, Charlotte Carlson, Laura Dawson, Frederick Reed and Esther Wetzel worked on major revisions of Winnetka arithmetic materials, which were published in the early 1940's. These remained in use until the interim adoption of commercial texts was made in 1958. The 1943 materials remained in active use by many teachers, along with commercial materials.

This revision of the early 1940's was a great work, continuing the

tradition of excellence and high faculty involvement that had characterized Winnetka. Yet, what I believe to be a major flaw in the program
must have begun to make itself felt at this time. The concept of individual progression assumed that the child could proceed steadily into
the learning expectations of higher grades. Let us say that a swift-learning
child at Grade IV in January had reached a fifth-grade level of proficiency in arithmetic and by the end of the year was starting sixth grade
work. The following year at Grade V this child quickly completes the
sixth grade expectations; moves on into seventh grade work; finally, at
Grade VI the child completes the expectations of Grades VII and VIII.
The design was unclear as to what mathematics learnings remained for
this child in junior high school, with two years to go, and his arithmetic
"finished."

A further misfortune befell the design at this time. Carleton Washburne entered military service while the new (1943) instructional materials were still under development. Materials for Grades VII and VIII
had not been written. When I arrived in 1956 the upper grades, including Grade VI, were using commercial materials more or less exclusively.
The self-instruction, self-correction, individual progression concept, accordingly, had become diluted at the upper grades, resulting in good
solid instruction of a more conventional order, utilizing conventional
materials.

Before concluding this note of history, mention should be made of
the Winnetka Press, which was an essential aspect of the locally developed materials. As Winnetka's reputation for innovation and creative
teaching spread, there were such demands for materials that the ordinary
resources of a small school system were inadequate to handle the edit-
ing, printing, publication and distribution of the outpourings of the
faculty. Under C.W.'s leadership, a quasi-private corporation was
created to produce and distribute the materials. They were sold at a
small profit throughout the United States and abroad, and were distributed at cost to the Winnetka Schools.

The Press, suffering from the adversities of World War II, and
more particularly from the loss of C.W.'s leadership, gradually diminished in influence and service until 1952, when its small remaining
money was turned over to the Board of Education, and its status dissolved. We find ourselves in 1963 with massive production tasks and
no Winnetka Press to handle the work load; it is easy to see the logic

that led to the creation of the Press. Some instrument not unlike the Press probably lies in our immediate future. We now call our limited operation the Materials Center, from which we try to respond to many requests for samples.

Local Materials Indispensable

This historical overview of *Winnetka materials* has been offered to underscore the vital significance of such materials to the effective implementation of what was called the Winnetka Plan. I came slowly to understand and accept the indispensability of local materials as distinguished from commercial texts for the individualized teaching of some subjects. (Winnetka uses many commercial texts in all fields, some as primary resources, some as supplementary resources.)

By the fall of 1959 we had been struggling for two years, first to make do with old dog-eared and outdated workbooks, then to install, at least temporarily, commercial textbooks, and all the while we were endeavoring to increase substantially the grade level expectations for learning. At this time I received a very earnest message from one of Winnetka's master teachers. It is revealing of the concern and devotion which existed in the faculty during this period of mathematical upheaval.

> ...We on the arithmetic curriculum commitee are charged with laying a floor, interim though it may be, on which future creative new curriculum design can rest. I am concerned about what will happen to our pupils in the "interim."
>
> Discovery is arithmetic; arithmetic has not been learned unless meanings have been discovered and applied by the child in the thought process.
>
> Discovery may happen accidentally, or it may happen through a planned sequence of experiences: (1) lecture demonstration, (2) directed group experiences, and (3) individual discovery by each pupil, including individual practice of skills, individual application to life situations, self-evaluation, and the development of an attitude of pride and pleasure in learning.
>
> There are ample resources, both in teacher competence and instructional materials for the first two essentials. But if we abandon the *individual discovery* component, we lose much that is good in our admittedly inadequate present program.
>
> A new teacher (and there will be many joining us), unacquainted with the concepts of self-teaching and pupil responsibility, will surely rely almost wholly on lecture-demonstration and group experience. The philosophy that has made Winnetka unique will gradually disappear. I urge with all my heart that we turn our energies to the creation of vigorous, well-constructed, modern materials for self-instruction. It is only through such instruments that children will incorporate arithmetic learnings into their very bone marrow.

If I had not already come very close to forming my own judgment about the essentiality of locally developed workbooks and textbooks, this earnest message, knowing the author, was a clincher.

The New Content

Coincidentally with the overturning of the arithmetic curriculum in Winnetka, the late fifties had brought into sharp consideration the term *modern mathematics*. No one in our faculty at the time, least of all the Superintendent of Schools, was competent to lead us toward an understanding and appreciation of the surging changes occurring in the world of numbers. The College Entrance Examining Board, reflecting the views of mathematics scholars, declared in 1958:

> New developments have been extensive; new concepts have been revolutionary. The sheer bulk of mathematical development is staggering.
> ... In order that the ... curricula meet the needs of mathematics itself, and of its applications, there must be a change. A new program, oriented to the needs of the second half of the twentieth century, and based on a dynamic conception of mathematics is required.[2]

Influenced by such passages, as well as the increased revolutionary activity in good high school and college mathematics programs nationally, we knew that if modern mathematics was truly as revolutionary as the experts declared, it had to find its headwaters in the kindergarten. This also meant that a full generation of teachers who were wholly innocent of modern mathematics, and were quite willing, by and large, to remain that way, stood between the pupils and the goals of the new mathematicians.

New Leadership in Mathematics

It was clear that we needed a person on our faculty who was, first of all, deeply concerned with young children and the learning process, but who at the same time was indeed a mathematics scholar of the highest order. Unlikely as it may seem, after a two-year search starting in 1958 we found exactly the person we had envisioned. Miss Lola June May joined the Winnetka faculty in the fall of 1960 following a distinguished record in elementary, high school, and university mathematics teaching. These schools have not been the same since. Lola May's influ-

---

[2] Extracts from *Program for College Preparatory Mathematics*, Report of the Commission on Mathematics, College Entrance Examination Board, reprinted by permission.

ence, leadership and scholarship heavily mark the accounting which follows in the remainder of this chapter.

Before Miss May joined us, there had been earnest, dogged—discursive, yes—but positive forward movement by the faculty. In the summer of 1959, under the leadership of Lucille Murray, the brilliant young principal who had succeeded Frederick Reed at Greeley School, the Arithmetic Curriculum Committee published its interim guide. The introduction included this passage:

> We found much of our current grade level content placement based on the research of the thirties,[3] which recommended delaying the placement of content until the child was believed to have attained the mental age at which the concepts involved could most easily be mastered. . . . In the judgment of many of our group, there is much merit in the basic idea which inspired this research, but the placement suggested does not always seem to fit our modern children as we know them. Weighing all factors together the Committee agreed to recommend addition of content. . . .

C.W. will doubtless challenge our departure from the exhaustive and impressive research findings of the Committee of Seven, without adequate further research to support our conclusions. Our case rests on the intuitive feelings of teachers, and upon the demonstrated success of children. Indeed, the changes in grade placement which will be recorded below may be only a small beginning. We are proceeding on the assumption that we have yet to discover a great deal about how much a child can learn and *wholly understand* at an early age or, for that matter, at any age, fruitfully, happily, and compatibly with the burgeoning knowledge of the late 20th century.

In 1939 the findings of the Committee of Seven had been published, and undoubtedly had a heavy influence on the grade placement of arithmetic concepts in Winnetka. A search of the records has revealed a number of goal record cards from the earlier years, for comparison with the current goal record card. Grade III seems to have been the grade for which the cards have been preserved, hence these are compared, using a typical year (in this case, 1948). (The goal record cards were constantly under revision during Washburne's time and thereafter, as would be expected.)

The following table seeks to relate the 1948 grade level content of the third grade arithmetic curriculum with the third grade content today, following extensive faculty study and deliberation.

---

[3] By the Committee of Seven.

COMPARISON OF GRADE III ARITHMETIC GOAL RECORD ITEMS

1948 AND 1962: WINNETKA PUBLIC SCHOOLS

*(Read the table from the top to bottom for sequence of
learning expectations during the school year)*

1948	1962
1. Review test (numbers to 10)	Review test (numbers to 18)
2. Roman numbers to XII	Roman numbers to L
3. Learn meanings of numbers, 11-20	Review meanings of numbers to 200 (From Grade II)
4. Review addition facts	Review addition and subtraction, 2-place numbers
5. Review subtraction facts	Learn relationship of multiplication and addition, products to 20
6. Review easy multiplication facts	Learn division facts to 20
7. Learn simple addition to 20	Learn addition, 2-digit numbers, no carrying
8. Learn single-column addition to 20	Learn subtraction, 2-digit numbers, no regrouping
9. Learn meaning of numbers to 100	Learn changing of money, with decimals to $1.00 (addition and subtraction)
10. Simple addition to 100	Learn addition, 2-digit numbers with carrying
11. Learn to use easy fractions	Learn use of simple fractions: $\frac{1}{2}$, $\frac{1}{3}$, $\frac{1}{4}$, $\frac{1}{6}$, $\frac{1}{8}$
12. ———	Learn addition, 3-digit numbers, 3 addends
13. ———	Learn subtraction, 2-digit numbers with regrouping
14. ———	Learn multiplication facts, 3's, 4's, 5's
15. ———	Learn multiplication, 3-digit numbers
16. ———	Learn division facts, using 2's, 3's, 4's, 5's
17. ———	Learn simple division

(The following *additional expectations*, not formally noted on the goal cards are prescribed in the curriculum as additional elements of grade three expectations):
Preview place values through thousands
Preview meaning of zero
Preview ounces, pounds, pecks, bushels
Develop readiness for uneven division
Preview estimating sums and differences
Preview money problems with multiplication and division of decimals

(Minor liberties have been taken in the arrangement and terminology of this table to facilitate comparison. The actual 1962 goal card for Grade III may be examined with all other goal cards in the Appendix.)

This table is not offered in ostentatious self-righteousness to make unhappy comparisons between the past and the present. It is a piece of evidence submitted to demonstrate the proposition that in the late fifties and early sixties the Winnetka faculty had moved substantially toward a higher academic content expectation in elementary mathematics. Similar comparisons at other grade levels and in other subjects would reveal similar results.

But quite apart from grade level content *per se*, the world of numbers was found to be changing in its very nature—or, better stated, the world of numbers as it is viewed by mathematicians was slowly coming into focus as an instrument of elementary education quite different from what had been taught for many generations. A report published by a citizens' advisory committee of the Westport, Connecticut, Public Schools in 1959 stated:

> The traditional, rigidly compartmented curriculum (in mathematics) has cracked apart. Anyone who attempts to study the current mathematics curriculum finds he is studying a transient situation.

And so it was in Winnetka. Dr. Henry Ford had joined our staff as principal of the Skokie Junior High School, bringing to our faculty strong resources from his immediate past experience as professor of mathematics education at Hofstra College. He effectively shared the leadership in the Arithmetic Curriculum Committee, in addition to his many other duties, affording us the advantage of a fresh and objective spirit.

In the spring of 1960 the faculty mathematics curriculum committee, after two years of earnest experimentation with commercial textbooks at the middle grades, summarized their feelings on this subject:

> A commercial text, or a collection of texts, written for *group instruction* is virtually impossible to adapt to individual mastery and *independent progression*. A number of us would like to work this summer on materials we know we need, that we think will be useful for children.

With the encouragement of the Planning and Advisory Committee, five teachers were invited to undertake the task of writing new materials for the middle grades to displace the commercial materials and preserve individualized instruction while we continued to explore modern elementary mathematics.

Our own local problems of philosophy, materials, and grade place-

ment were made no more simple by the stirring reports coming out of
the School Mathematics Study Group at Yale University; the University
of Maryland Mathematics Project; the University of Illinois Committee
on School Mathematics. *The New York Times* in a thoughtful review
of the revolution in mathematics education in 1959 observed an experimental program in Syracuse:

> The program, which begins at grade four, starts teaching algebra at the
> beginning, as this subject is considered the basis for arithmetic.
> It has been found that relatively low I.Q. pupils could handle . . . mathe-
> matics . . . and the more talented elementary grade pupils were progressing
> through levels reserved for high school seniors.[4]

The "New" Mathematics

Lola May joined our staff in this time of systematic confusion, as
Mathematics Consultant. She had been actively involved in the School
Mathematics Study Group materials at New Trier High School. We arranged early for her to visit with and evaluate the celebrated experimental work of Dr. Max Beberman at the University of Illinois. A
brilliant mathematician in her own right, she brought to our faculty
a tremendous excitement about how children might learn and enjoy
mathematics. She made no pretenses about possessing expert knowledge
of child growth and development, but she listened painstakingly and
intently to those who did know. More important, she possessed a deep
affection for children and a wholesome and obvious respect for their
intellect. She was determined to destroy the legend that mathematics
was mysterious or fearsome for teachers as well as children.

Her first task was to solidify the interim curriculum which had been
adopted just prior to her arrival, and to further the development of
instructional materials to support it. The several teachers on the
materials-writing committee noted earlier had performed a monumental
task in creating new, fresh, challenging workbooks and textbooks in
Grades III, IV, and V in the summer of 1960. Miss Helen Danforth,
star Winnetka teacher, had carried the chief burden of this leadership
in close collaboration with Donald Cawelti, Assistant Superintendent.
Mr. Cawelti, who had for many years served as principal of the Junior
High School, carried in his multi-phased portfolio the subtitle, Director

---

[4] *The New York Times,* July 26, 1959. Reprinted by permission.

of Research. Whether "interim" or not, and, acknowledging their adherence to traditional mathematics as distinguished from modern mathematics, the new materials were a source of high satisfaction and pride in the faculty.

As an example of the kind of productivity of which this remarkable staff is capable, the following locally developed instructional materials were finalized and published in the summer of 1960, as Winnetka rededicated itself to the proposition that true individualization of instruction calls for individualized materials, prepared locally by the teachers who are to use them:

GRADE III

Winnetka Functional Arithmetic, Book III, Part I, 127 pages (roughly a half year's work for typical pupils)
Winnetka Functional Arithmetic, Book III, Part II, 113 pages
Test Book III, Part I, 31 pages
Test Book III, Part II, 22 pages

GRADE IV

Winnetka Functional Arithmetic, Book IV, Part I, 171 pages
Winnetka Functional Arithmetic, Book IV, Part II, 200 pages
Test Book IV, 55 pages
Teachers' Manual and Key, Book IV, 47 pages

GRADE V

Winnetka Functional Arithmetic, Book V, Part I, 193 pages
Winnetka Functional Arithmetic, Book V, Part II, 182 pages
Test Book V, 18 pages
Teachers' Key, Test Book V, 10 pages

Teachers of the middle grades, including new teachers, quickly and affirmatively put the new materials to work, relegating the commercial texts to the function of supplementary or supporting materials.

The following year, working nights and weekends, Miss May, with a nucleus of new math neophites in the faculty, rewrote the local textbooks and tests for Grade V, adapting them to the terminology of modern mathematics. She then wrote completely new materials in the new mathematics context for Grade VI. At Grades VII and VIII we adopted the materials published by the School Mathematics Study Group. This gave us a completely fresh set of mathematics texts for Grades III through VIII, with V through VIII cast tentatively in the modern mathematics context.

Apart from the writing of texts and tests, however, we are now engaged in system-wide exploration of wholly new approaches to the world of numbers. For example, the Cuisenaire Rods may be found in primary grades, as children begin to understand the commutative law without necessarily knowing the name of it. Passing beyond the rods, our Mathematics Consultant is developing her own learning theory for young children, based on the venerable number line. It is likely that more will be heard of this technique in the near future.

Trial and Error

Up to this time we have not prescribed specific and formal curricular goals in the new mathematics, or established goal card items that necessarily reflect the new math *per se*. This step must await further trial and study, and further in-service education of teachers in the theories and practices of modern mathematics. But our investigations, starting in Grade I, and moving to Grade II in 1962, give promise of exciting changes to come. If the reader will examine the mathematics goal card for Grade II, 1962, in the Appendix, he will find such items as the following, which reflect our tentative and enlarging beliefs about what children can learn within the modern mathematics approach: an understanding of zero, place value, difference between numerals and numbers, identification and definition of simple geometric figures, mathematical application of the compass, knowledge of line segments, infinity, perpendiculars, and the algebraic implications of open sentences for the notation of word problems.

We have not yet carried these goals formally into the grades above first and second, pending further assessment of our hypotheses.

After a year of trial and exploration in the Winnetka Schools, our Mathematics Consultant made these observations in her annual report:

> We, as well as the rest of the country, have stood still for a long time and have trained teachers on the assumption that (on the teaching of arithmetic) we stand still forever. Teachers have been trained to teach a certain thing a certain way, and now both the "things" and the "way" must be changed....

...The trend of modern mathematics requires that we design our curriculum to cause children to discover the properties of numbers, learn to think out processes, and gain a genuine understanding of the structure of mathematics prior to Grade VIII.

Miss May spent much of her time that first year sitting in primary grade classrooms, talking with primary grade teachers, and teaching revolutionary mathematical ideas to primary grade children. Her report continues with an accounting of her immediate experience with children:

The number line is a remarkable device for teaching and learning. Each kindergarten should have one for those who are ready to cope with it. In Grade I it starts pupils on their way in addition and subtraction. I also used it in Grade I for multiplication and division. It works with fractions for Grade II children; it also introduces the commutative property of numbers, which we call the "order property" for second graders.

Geometry should also start at kindergarten. The open sentence, or simple algebraic ideas, work successfully in grades one and two:

$$\square + 4 = 8$$

or

$$\square + \triangle = 8$$

or

$$(\square + 2) - 5 = 14$$

Figure 6

We begin to understand *sets* in the primary grades, but more of this seems likely to be expected at the middle grades. Inequalities as well as equality can be taught at Grade I. Geometry, some call it informal geometry, is readily grasped by first and second graders. To first graders we can teach line segment, triangle, quadrilateral and pentagon. We deal with the geometric term "point."

Third graders discover the three angles of a triangle. They learn the names of various angles. They learn about simple closed curves. They can work at circles, bisect lines, and line segments. Solid geometry seems to fit at Grade IV, where we start the understandings with regular solids and cylinders. We use protractors here....

A Look Ahead in Primary Grades Mathematics

The report concludes with a forecast of an elementary mathematics curriculum content which may reasonably be expected in the next few years. The report covers kindergarten through Grade VIII. For relevance to the earlier table describing the Grade III comparison between 1948 expectations and those of the present, Miss May's prediction for future Grade III mathematics goals has been selected for this illustration:

1. Review of commutative and association properties of numbers (from Grade II).
2. Understanding of numbers to 1000; know place, order and sequence.
3. Counting by 1's, 2's, 3's, 4's, 5's, 10's, 20's etc. up to 1,000, starting with any number, using sequence.
4. Odd and even aspects of numbers.
5. Master addition and subtraction facts
       Addition by columns and endings
       Subtraction by additive method.
6. Multiplication with a product to 100.
7. Division with a dividend to 100.
8. Place value of numbers 1 to 100,000; understanding the sequence, 1 to 100.
9. Commutative and associative properties of addition and multiplication.
10. Introduce distributive property of numbers
       Example: $7 \times 15 = (7 \times 10) + (7 \times 5)$.
11. Combination of processes, using set of fractions as well as set of whole numbers.
12. Use of parentheses in mathematics.
13. Open sentences, combining all four processes.
14. Geometry; no formulae, only reasoning.
       Lines
       Figures
       Perimeters
       Areas
15. Denominate numbers.
       Linear units
       Time units
       Weight units
       Money units
       Square measure
16. Word problems illustrating the four processes; two-step problems involving different processes.
17. The use of number bases other than 10 for many third graders.

The foregoing table is not intended to record what we are now doing at Grade III in Winnetka. It projects what we may be doing, in whole or in part, based upon experimental work now current. The Grade III example is typical of the inquiry we are pursuing. Similar changes are being explored at all grade levels.

One very obvious need for a faculty contemplating the transition from traditional elementary arithmetic to modern mathematics is in-service education of all teachers having anything to do with numbers. Foot-dragging and hostility to the new mathematics may be expected so long as the idea casts a threatening shadow of mystery over otherwise competent teachers. Accordingly, in the winter of 1961-62 Miss May conducted an intensive 15-week seminar, intended to open the way for a few teachers to re-learn their arithmetic in the new context and possibly affect others by contagion. The offering was optional, scheduled for two hours of late afternoon class work each week. We expected a few, perhaps 10 to 15 hardy adventurers, to respond. Over half the faculty, some 56 teachers, enrolled and flourished in the offering. Teachers of shop, home-making and social studies took to the seminar, along with regular elementary classroom teachers, and junior high teachers of departmental mathematics. The spirit of discovery, so warmly prescribed for children, became the mood of the seminar. Gradual affirmation and acceptance of the new mathematics followed. Further seminars are now being suggested by those who missed the first one or want more. (We attached the equivalent of two semester hours of graduate-level credit to the offering, as related to our salary schedule.)

By this time many parents in the community were becoming puzzled, uneasy, and startled, in roughly that order, as seven-year-olds began to speak knowingly of the binary system and the commutative property. Miss May met with many parent groups to inform them and put them at ease. She was finally persuaded to write a pamphlet [5] on the subject for parents and teachers, which was transformed from a mimeographed intramural message to a successful trade publication in the fall of 1962.

Speed and Mastery

A final note should be added to clarify certain terms which characterize the basic Winnetka design for mathematics instruction, as it

[5] May, Lola J., *Major Concepts of Elementary Modern Mathematics*, John Colburn Associates, Wilmette, Ill., 1962, 60 pp.

has been preserved broadly through the years, in spite of changes in content. There are no scores or marks in mathematics. The child is expected to *master* a given concept; this means theoretically 100 per cent accuracy, within a specified time limit, for each child, before he proceeds to the next concept listed chronologically on the goal card. Mastery is determined by the individual teacher administering the timed test, following practice tests which the child administers to himself. The child may present himself for mastery testing whenever he and the teacher agree he is ready. Our curriculum interprets speed and mastery as follows:

> Speed practice tests—responses to number combinations and processes within given time limits—locate and pinpoint specific difficulties of the individual child. The speed with which the child responds depends upon his mastery of the basic number facts. The speed of a written response also depends upon the physical process of writing, and upon emotional factors. Minimum speed standards have been established for each topic in each grade. These standards are sufficiently low so that nearly all children can, with practice, reach them without sacrificing 100 percent accuracy. In a few cases the teacher working with the atypical child may set an individual goal for the child, allowing some liberalization in speed and accuracy before he takes the final goal test. One hundred percent accuracy should be sought for nearly all children. Teachers should keep clearly in mind throughout all the work that speed is secondary to accuracy.
>
> When the child has demonstrated through self-administered, timed practice tests that he is ready for the timed final test for mastery, the teacher should administer the test. If 100 percent accuracy within the reasonable time limits is not achieved, he should return to further drill or the practice tests, and then undertake the final test again in a different form. Upon satisfactory evidence of mastery, in the judgment of the teacher, the child should proceed to the next goal.

Conclusion

The Winnetka design for the teaching and learning of elementary mathematics for many years included several unique characteristics. Prominent among these were the following: self-instruction and self-correction by means of locally developed drill and testing materials; individual progression through content at the child's rate; use of the goal card to account for individual progress; practice tests; sequential final tests for mastery under speed conditions; wide variation in pace and accomplishment of children within a given class; deferral of grade placement of certain content to later years, as distinguished from conventional placement; and high emphasis upon *relevance* and *utility* of the mathematics learnings.

With the exception of grade placement of content, and the emphasis upon immediate utility, these historic processes have been earnestly re-evaluated, alternates have been tentatively explored and set aside, and the *design* by and large has been reaffirmed and endorsed for the present and future. The wisdom of the Winnetka faculty of the 1920's is only now coming into full appreciation as knowing experts of 1963, throughout the nation, give high importance to self-instruction, individual progression by means of programmed learning, and the importance of *meaningful* mathematical ideas in learning. The Winnetka self-instruction materials were, in a very real sense, unsophisticated teaching machines or programmed learning devices.

The only major departure from the early design exists in grade level content. Rather than seek deferral of learning, we seek acceleration of learning, when the content can clearly lead to intellectual satisfaction, success and mastery by most of the children of a given grade. Accordingly, an interim course of study has been put into effect prescribing a significantly larger expectation or content at all grade levels. New instructional materials have been created by the faculty and adopted by the Board of Education in compatibility with the new and enlarged goals. (*See* the Appendix.)

A departure, in degree only, from the earlier design rests in our hypothesis that the *discovery* of mathematical propositions by children is, in and of itself, a worthy educational attainment, even though the concept discovered may not have immediate utility in the child's life. We obviously rely heavily on the motivation implicit in utility, but we do not hold this as a basic or absolute criterion of our design. For example, a child in Grade II may begin to comprehend "infinity" without having a ready application for it in his daily life. Year by year he will develop further in the spiral that Bruner calls "structure," moving from his momentarily concrete vision of infinity as an endless line to the more abstract digestion of the proposition.

The interim curriculum and its corresponding materials are gradually being displaced as we enter our third year of exploring the significance of modern mathematics as a relevant instrument for elementary

education. Trial and error in this context are now current. Much remains
to be done in testing and validating our hypotheses about what mathematical concepts young children can and should learn. Even more
remains to be done to assist teachers in reconstructing their own beliefs
and habits in the world of numbers. As is likely in any faculty of proud
and able people, there is little immediate agreement; but there is a high
zest for discovering better ways to teach and learn.

CHAPTER TWENTY-ONE

More Curriculum

Evolution

While the schools have no monopoly on the measures through which children grow intellectually, they are the one universal and systematic institution organized for sequential intellectual development of pupils.

—From Objective Number One
Beliefs and Objectives of the Winnetka Schools, 1961

The preceding chapter developed in considerable detail the evolution of our curriculum in the field of mathematics. Broadly speaking, the same kind of changes took place in the design of the other academic learnings during the 1956-63 period: Social Studies, Science and the Language Arts. These academic fields will be reviewed in their evolutionary context in this chapter, without attempting as much specific accounting as was afforded in the case of mathematics.

Perhaps the most useful message of this chapter, for the student of education, is the *process* of curriculum change. No claim is made for the uniqueness or superiority of our process. I record it as a case study in the workings of a faculty committed to excellence, and willing to accept the consequences.

As noted in an earlier chapter, one of the peculiar conditions I found in Winnetka in 1956 was the absence of anything that could honestly be called a curriculum guide in any field. The locally prepared material (some of it upwards of 20 years old); the goal cards; and the splendid folk-lore of teacher-to-teacher osmosis *was* the curriculum. In many ways this could have been defended. To begin with, it had worked. Further, one might argue that teacher creativity and spontaneity were more likely to flower under the unstructured design of "non-curriculum" than would be the case in a more conventional curricular organization.

But it must be remembered that each passing year found the instructional materials more yellowed with age and irrelevance, the goal cards more patched with the printer's expediency, and the awesome staff of veteran ranks thinning. In the fall of 1956 we set about curriculum development on all four fronts. The decision was reached by the newly reorganized Planning and Advisory Committee in one of its earlier acts of high responsibility.

Curriculum Construction, General

The decision to undertake curriculum development on all fronts (Social Studies, Mathematics, Science and Language Arts) was an audacious one. For a less able and dedicated faculty it could have been a serious error. Yet the setting in that fall of 1956 reconstructs itself clearly in my mind, as the Planning and Advisory Committee deliberated the question.

A small group of teachers had, prior to my joining the faculty, launched an earnest effort toward a course-of-study guide in the Social Studies under the very able leadership of Charlotte Carlson, veteran, though still young, Winnetka teacher, who had been one of C.W.'s promising protégés. This work in Social Studies was clearly under way.

The science leadership, resting in the competent and scholarly hands of Dr. Donald A. Boyer, was restive in the continued subordination of Science as a wing of the Social Studies (as was quite common nationally at the time). It was clear that we were ready to move toward major curriculum design in science. At the same time, the faculty had revealed an impatience and uncertainty with the arithmetic design. And, as for language arts, this broad, shadowy, vital field was probably the least organized and systematized of the lot.

It was early winter in 1956 when the Planning and Advisory Committee contemplated the "all fronts" question. It will be recalled that James Mann, elementary principal, had urged in the Planning Committee that we go all the way in committing ourselves to an overhaul of the full curriculum. Jim's unostentatious observation was one of those historic "little" items in the life of an institution that, unpredictably, becomes an enduring benchmark. If I, in my newly-arrived and suspect authority, had offered the suggestion, it would have fallen on the faculty like a bleak condemnation. That Jim, a cautious and beloved veteran of many Winnetka years, said it was the trigger of its acceptance. The Planning and Advisory Committee responded in concert behind the idea. The faculty, shaken at first, rallied in agreement. We undertook a complete upheaval of the curriculum, which only now, in 1963, has begun to level off in a systematic design. Six years of heavy work followed the Planning and Advisory Committee action—after-school hours, week-ends, vacations and often in classrooms—as innovations were tried and adopted.

Exchange of Faith, Again

To give system and order to the work of the curriculum committees of teachers which were beginning to form, the Planning and Advisory Committee developed a broad statement on the philosophy and design of curriculum, which was distributed to the professional staff. This statement is reproduced in Chapter Eighteen. It was the purpose of this statement to free the staff for creative change, yet to preserve the well-deserved pride and integrity that prevailed in the status quo. In other words, we sought forward movement, with unity and consistency in the processes of curriculum construction, without condemning those who felt there was no better way. Those with eyes only "in the backs of their heads" were few. Some did remarkable turn-abouts, contributing heavily to forward movement as they came to understand it.

Some of the social scientists and other scholars who observe and contribute wisely to our profession of education have much to say about the theory of curriculum. They say, "There must be a taxonomy . . . a classification . . . an arrangement of goals before there can be an arrangement of learnings." I understand these friends from the universities. Yet, we did not establish the broad, system-wide goals in concrete terms until we had been at work on curriculum for three years. There was a definite reason for this. I was still, that first year, just getting to know the faculty, and they me. Any statement of goals in education depends very heavily upon the semantic subtleties that reveal their meanings only through a knowledge of the *persons* concerned. One superintendent of schools can speak with vigor and conviction on "creativity," for example, and mean something quite different from another superintendent down the road who speaks with equal vigor and conviction on the same subject. By knowing the person, we come to know what he means.

Thus, we reversed the order of goals and curriculum, insofar as the historic chronology of a formal statement of objectives is concerned. But the goals and the underlying philosophy of our schools came to be *implicit in the process,* as we worked together during the late 1950's. Without at first taking the ultimate step of putting our system-wide philosophical goals on paper, a spirit of consensus began to permeate the several curriculum committees. One might almost say that an unspoken, unrecorded, unstructured statement of goals as a foundation for the specifics of curriculum development has advantages unknown to the advocates of taxonomy. The corporate body of the faculty, in applying itself to the *process* of curriculum construction, involuntarily and without self-consciousness, began to work within certain *implicit* philosophical goals. Vague though they might have been in the minds of diverse workers, they were no more vague than they would have been if we had endeavored to declare the fine points of pedagogical aspiration in the abstract, before applying ourselves to the *process.*

A Philosophy Is a Process More Than a Product

The shadowy forms of broad, system-wide goals or objectives during those years of curriculum upheaval included at least the following: a reaffirmation of Winnetka's role as experimenter, innovator and contributor to education at large; a realization that the school's unique function is that of fostering intellectual growth; a reaffirmation of concern for the social-emotional-physical child, with the acknowledgment that for some years education had pressed this theme so loudly that our listeners had began to wonder at the place of intellect in schools; and through it all there came a sharpening focus on the place of the school as a moral force, no longer willing to be neutral, sterile or silent in the controversial affairs of international politics, brotherhood, values, attitudes. We began to search for a design in which the schools could exercise a larger role in helping children develop convictions about freedom and responsibility without risking coercion or indoctrination, or emotional exhortation. We reaffirmed our high devotion to the individualization of instruction, for which Winnetka had long been known; we reaffirmed certain mechanical features of curriculum, such as the individualized goal card, the need for locally developed instructional materials, the high emphasis on the parent conference, as distinguished from grades or marks. We renewed our concern with creativity.

In any case, whether or not the cart came before the horse, curriculum construction went forward. When the time came in 1959–60 to declare our *Beliefs and Objectives*, the task was made much easier. We could relate our ideals to the concrete expectations of the curriculum we were building. We could move from the specific to the general, knowing what the words that we were using meant within the staff.

The broad guide for curriculum development, which the Planning and Advisory Committee adopted in 1956, has been a useful instrument. It has served as a frequent checkpoint for those engaged in the curriculum building task, and it has, upon looking back at it over five years, held up fairly well, as such instruments go. (*See* Chapter Eighteen.)

Directions to Curriculum Committees

As curriculum committees of the faculty were launched, one by one during the winter of 1956–57, each member was given a copy of the general directions for curriculum development. Committee chairmen met with the Planning and Advisory Committee to gain a sense of the central spirit behind our curriculum movement. Further, as a more specific set of instructions to each committee, the Planning and Advisory Committee submitted a memorandum describing in fairly concrete terms the task to be performed by that particular committee. As an example of the instructions to the curriculum committee, the following memorandum is offered, again for possible relevance to those who use this chapter as a case study in the practices of curriculum construction.

MEMORANDUM

TO: Science Committee
FROM: Planning Committee

Reference is made to the general curriculum guide instructions furnished herewith.

The Science Committee is requested to develop a program for science instruction in the Winnetka Schools, such program to encompass Kindergarten through Grade VIII. The committee is requested to consider and act upon the following:

A. *Background and Philosophy*

1. Evaluation of present program as designed with the Social Studies program; identification of weaknesses and strengths.
2. The development of the scientific process in children as a means of thinking and acting.
3. Review of important research in science teaching over past several years toward utilizing important developments in this field.

B. *Content*

1. Determine the minimum scientific concepts and understandings to be taught at each grade level. Offer stimulation and suggestions for imaginative exploration beyond the minimum, with extensive concrete examples for the unsure teacher.
2. Arrange the sequence of the content by grade levels developmentally, one concept growing out of another, consistent with the age, maturity, and needs of children. This would suggest, for example, if magnets are

taught at Grade I, they should not automatically be omitted at Grade VI if they serve a need at Grade VI.

3. Design a plan providing at all levels for the release and guidance of scientifically talented children well beyond the minimum grade level content.

4. Determine whether standard texts shall be used, and, if so, what texts, and at what grade levels. Consider use of rich science reference libraries by grade levels or rooms as an alternate to basic texts.

5. Determine essential instructional materials and plant facilities by grade level, as related to content. Include audio-visual materials, charts, models, particularly those which shall be considered uniform for all, as distinguished from optional.

6. Develop within the format of the course-of-study guide such charts, sketches and diagrams as are appropriate to dramatize and make clear the scientific concepts called for. Insure consistency in techniques among teachers on basic procedures.

7. Design plan for testing and evaluating pupil progress.

C. *Corollary Administrative Issues to Be Resolved*

1. Consider the development of a goal card consistent with the minimum curricular requirements, allowing for unusual growth by exceptional pupils.

2. Encourage a posture for subsequent educational experimentation, particularly as to content and methods by grade, and time-allocations for the accomplishment of objectives.

3. Evaluate Winnetka instructional and testing materials in science, their revision, or their replacement as supplementary teaching materials.

4. Articulate with New Trier High School curriculum, with special attention to guidance of selected pupils toward advanced work.

Funds for the support of this program can be provided as needed by the committee in consultation with the Superintendent. At such time as the committee is prepared to invite laymen to join, the Superintendent will assist in developing lay membership.

At such time as the committee is prepared to present its program, a series of faculty workshops will be arranged.

A document similar in format to the "science instructions" above, but, of course, differing widely in content, was originated in the Planning Committee for each of the several curriculum committees.

Committees were formed through the volunteer process, except for the post of chairman. Chairmen, in some cases, were obvious choices, such as in the instance of Dr. Boyer, our school-wide consultant in Science. When less obvious choices were at hand, the Planning and Advisory Committee deliberated at length over the most likely member of the administrative or teaching staff for the job. When an indi-

vidual had been named by consensus in the Planning and Advisory
Committee I visited him, described the job in all its dire proportions
and invited him to take it on, in addition to other duties. It is a remarkable credit to this faculty that no person declined such an invitation. It is further remarkable that as the call went out for volunteers,
every committee had more respondents than it needed to fill its ranks.
By the end of a year of organization, virtually every member of the
academic faculty was engaged in one curriculum committee—a few in
two. Even beginning teachers, not yet ready to make major contributions to curriculum evolution, found places as observers and pick-and-
shovel research workers in the curriculum overhaul. It is perhaps too
obvious to mention that curriculum construction of the kind in which
we found ourselves is far and away the most positive and fruitful in-
service education program that could be conceived for a faculty.

Committees varied in number of members from 10 in the Science
Committee (about one teacher per grade level) to as many as 27 in
the Language Arts Committee, where numerous sub-committees in related fields were required. As some members retired or left our schools,
other newcomers, and swiftly growing young teachers, took their places.
The work went on for six years, culminating in 1962 in a tentative
plateau, from which further evolution will undoubtedly spring.

No attempt will be made to record the details of these curricula.
A brief sketch of each is offered to afford the reader an idea of the
scope and nature of the courses of study.

Social Studies

The Social Studies Committee, having been the first to get started,
was the first to reach a terminal point. (Interestingly, while there had
been some reluctance in the faculty about getting at curriculum revision, the present spirit of change and "unfinished business" prevents me
from saying the work has been "concluded." "Terminal point" means
that the document was adopted by the Board of Education and published.)

Our Social Studies Guide is a 300-page document, following the
format prescribed in the memorandum on Curriculum Construction,
General. Its objectives, conceived in prolonged and studious labor by
the faculty committee, and subsequently by a lay advisory committee,
follow:

BROAD OBJECTIVES OF THE
SOCIAL STUDIES CURRICULUM

Many books have been written, with more to follow, describing the objectives of a modern social studies curriculum. As man's knowledge of man increases and becomes more complex, there is a tendency to broaden social studies goals and verbalize glowing objectives which may or may not bear fruit in the classroom.

The committee has chosen to state its broad objectives as simply as possible, with the expectation that they shall be understood, accepted and fulfilled.

The specific objectives of the various grade levels are extensions of the broad objectives.

This curriculum, functioning in cooperation with home, church, and other community institutions, seeks to establish in all pupils, over the span of years between kindergarten and grade eight:

1. An understanding of and a practicing adherence to the democratic way of life, with its responsibilities as well as its privileges.
2. A foundation in historical, political, economic, sociological and geographic facts and principles upon which to develop the skills and attitudes of competent citizenship.
3. An understanding of the American system of free enterprise.
4. A respect for the dignity and rights of every individual, including the individual's right to differ.
5. A concern for the welfare of others, consistent with the Judeo-Christian principles of brotherhood in our culture.
6. The continuing development of personal moral and spiritual convictions.
7. An introduction to the principal social, economic, religious, political, and geographic conditions and orders under which man has lived.
8. An understanding of the changes produced in cultures of the world due to technological developments.
9. An appreciation of the interrelatedness and the interdependence of the peoples of the world, notwithstanding dissimilarities of cultures and their ways of life.
10. A continuing sense of responsibility to community, state, nation and world, and toward building a better society.
11. Knowledge and skill in the processes of human relations among individuals and among groups, with emphasis upon orderly change.
12. Knowledge and skill in securing, sifting, evaluating, organizing, and presenting information in all the social science fields, and culminating in readiness and desire for future study at more advanced levels.
13. Respect for authority based on an understanding of its necessity to an orderly society.

One possibly unique feature of our guide is the treatment of AREAS OF STUDY, *vis-à-vis* UNDERSTANDINGS. Throughout our guide the outline of areas of study form the left-hand column on the page, while opposite the *learning* is what we call the *understanding* or the abiding concept which we expect children to derive from the specific content. For example, at grade six, where we treat ancient history through the Middle Ages, the curriculum format looks like this:

Areas of Study	Understandings
C. Beginnings of Western Civilization in Greece	
1. Geography of the land	Greek civilization was built upon the
2. Greek City States	remains of older civilizations.
a. Athens	
b. Sparta	
3. Greek Democracy	Important advances in art, architecture
a. Socrates	and sciences were made among the
b. Plato	peoples of Greece.
c. Aristotle	
4. Alexander and spread of Greek culture	Greek advances in democracy and individuality became a very important
a. Hellenistic age	factor of Western Civilization and
b. Education	modern democracy.
c. Libraries—museums	
d. Alexandria	
5. Contributions of the Greeks	
a. First democratic government	
b. Great thinkers and writers	
c. Olympic games	
d. Fine sculpture	
e. Architectural form	
f. Poetry and drama	
g. Advances in science	
h. Schools, libraries and museums	
D. Spread of Western Civilization by Rome	The Roman ability to organize in the fields of law, government, and engi-
1. Geography and culture of the land	neering spread and maintained civilization throughout the entire Mediter-
2. Roman Empire	ranean region for centuries.
a. Beginning of Rome	
b. Roman Republic	
c. Soldier citizens of Rome	
d. Roman heroes	Christianity was born and spread through-
e. Roman law	out the entire Mediterranean World
f. Roman conquests extended Roman laws	during the period of the Roman Empire.
g. Roman roads	
h. Rome and Carthage	
i. The two Caesars	
j. Religion of the Romans	
3. Contributions of Roman Empire	
a. Government	
b. Travel and trade	
c. Spread of art, literature and sciences	

While all children may not achieve mastery in detail in the various *areas of study* at their grade level, it is our assumption that the *understandings* will become a part of each growing youngster as he internalizes the broad truths of civilized man and his world.

Reduced to bare bones, the chronology of our Social Studies Curriculum is as follows:

Kgn.:	Human Relations, Cooperation, Adjustment to Living Together in School
Grade I:	Life in Homes, School, Community
Grade II:	Community: Organization, Services, Geography
Grade III:	Early America: The Indian, The Explorer, The Pioneer. Introduction to American History.
Grade IV:	Our Earth and Ways of Life on It: Introduction to Pre-History, Geography; High Emphasis on Study Skills including Map-Reading.
Grade V:	Life in the United States: American History from the Period of Exploration Through the 18th Century.
Grade VI:	Past and Present of Europe and Asia: World History from Beginnings of Civilization through the Renaissance; Comparative Religions; Comparative Government.
Grade VII:	Interrelatedness of Countries of the World: World Geography, Introduction to Economics, Political Science, Emphasis on Western Hemisphere. Limited Introduction to Far East; Soviet Union.
Grade VIII:	Struggle to Establish and Maintain American Way of Life: United States History from the Revolution; Citizenship, Government, Economics; Responsibilities Under Freedom; Attitudes and Convictions in Support of a Democracy.

It will be recalled that C.W. gave high prominence to the group-and-creative-ativities element of the Winnetka Schools as he guided them. This element remains strong today, though in a different context from that recalled by Washburne. Before passing on from the Social Studies, mention should be made of the Creative Activities teacher as an important role relating especially, but not exclusively, to the Social Studies. Each elementary school has on its faculty a teacher known today as the Creative Activities teacher.[1] Not assigned to any specific class, this teacher is especially competent in art, drama, construction, field trips, and various other areas of creative instruction. She is a close-at-hand resource for the classroom teacher as children move comfortably from the concrete academic learning to the creative activity. Most often the creative activity *grows out of* the academic learning, as the classroom teacher, the creative activities teacher and the children conceive and develop cooperatively an exciting and *relevant* experience that gives reality to the abstract . . . that gives meaning to the curricular goal. As noted above, the social studies lend themselves particulary to this arrangement of learning. For example, the Grade III Social Studies curriculum gives high emphasis to early American history, with its migration, hardships, and patterns of life among the pioneers. Following a period of study of home life among pioneer families, the children in Grade III might, under the guidance of the classroom teacher and the creative activities teacher, decide to make reproductions of pioneer tools and implements. This means research, a field trip to the Chicago Historical Society, visits to an antique shop, the collection of artifacts from home. It means measurements, scale drawings, selection of construction materials and budgeting of time.

Here the Creative Activities teacher becomes the facilitator, the guide, the mistress of the wood-working shop, the artist, the procurer of materials, the field trip coordinator, the behind-the-scenes stage manager for the classroom teacher, who might otherwise, with considerable justification, decide that just too many other things had to be done, and the labor entailed merely in gathering raw materials was beyond her limits of time.

Not the least of the Creative Activities is dramatic play in the lower grades, gradually taking more sophisticated form in creative dramatics in the middle and upper grades. Children, working with the classroom teacher and the special teacher, select a theme in history, or a passage in literature or biography that has relevance to the curriculum, and develop a creative drama to communicate the theme. No lines are formally memorized; characters are defined and projected; roles may be passed from one child to another from day to day. Scenery, properties

---

[1] Group and Creative Activities teacher, Socialized Activities teacher are earlier terms meaning the same thing.

and stage management may be called into the scope of the activity if it goes that far. On the other hand, creative dramatics can be quite a sufficient end in itself for the players without an audience. It is a splendid activity for motivating and digesting worthwhile formal learning.

Suffice it to say that *relevant* enrichment of learning through Creative Activities in the Social Studies (not to mention other fields) holds a high place in the current Winnetka design. For a third grader to reproduce in wood a pioneer farmer's axe, or a mother's wool carding instrument, or a yoke for the carrying of water buckets, gives meaning and value, and high motivation for the prescribed learnings. History becomes relevant; time and space take on emerging meaning for 9-year-olds; appreciation for the American way of life possesses concreteness and conviction, beyond the rote of catch phrases.

Science

When we reached our decision to disengage the Science curriculum from its context as an arm of the Social Studies, we were, in effect, giving this subject equal prominence with mathematics, the language arts and the social studies at all grade levels. The conventional pattern in many schools of the United States has treated "nature study" as its science in the grades, with little real attention to science in its broader implications and disciplines before grade seven. To the extent that we have departed from this pattern, we feel a significant contribution is being made to education at large. By good fortune, our work in the Science curriculum had been going on for two years when Russia's *Sputnik* gave public endorsement and momentum to the field of elementary Science. Our staff members in Science and our curriculum guide have been in steady demand from other schools nationally for the past few years for workshops, seminars and in-service guidance. Our aspiration that we may afford a useful advantage to education beyond Winnetka is being fulfilled in some degree in this field.

The Winnetka curriculum in Science, like all proper curricula, is not "concluded." It has reached a point of momentary stabilization, with clearly defined goals and procedures for Grades Kindergarten through VIII. The guide consists of 210 pages, organized by grade levels in what we call a *conical spiral* arrangement of content. Not necessarily unique with us, we believe we have made good use of the spiral concept. The term to us means a repeated sequence of scientific learnings, beginning at Kindergarten, and proceeding through the Junior High School, with increased depth of treatment at specified grade levels as the child matures (or as the cone enlarges). For example, the idea of *force* as a scientific concept begins to catch the interest and perception of the kindergarten child as he discovers the behavior of a magnetic toy or object. At Grade I or II, he makes further observations with infinite experiences with *force*. By Grade IV he is discovering magnetic fields and the elements of electricity, and by Grade VII he is able to create an electrical mechanism deriving from magnetic principles, as only one of many experiences with *force*. We imply, of course, that the spiral may continue through high school and college and beyond, as increased sophistication in the magnet provides infinite further challenges.

The magnet, as one element of the "great idea" of *force*, is only one simple example of the *conical spiral* curriculum. Many scientific concepts are arranged in systematic sequence, not only for the concepts themselves, but, perhaps of greater importance, for the habits of thought, and the processes of scientific inquiry which they stimulate.

Several basic propositions undergirded our development of science education in Winnetka in the late 1950's. By coincidence, international events gave hearty support to our work at that time, as Americans discovered that Russian scientists appeared to have outdistanced ours in some fields. In any case, intensification of the elementary and junior high Science curriculum, particularly as it related to the identification and motivation of potential science scholars, became a popular front, and remains so at this writing.

But other equally important propositions motivated our work, too.

1. We were heavily influenced by Sir Charles P. Snow's powerful book, *The Two Cultures*.[2] Snow, with heavy documentation and persuasive vision, declared that Western civilization was bisecting itself astride the literary-artistic culture and the scientific culture —and in so doing, destroying itself. We were determined to equip children and adolescents for living constructively within a whole culture that included the humanities *and* science.

---

[2] Cambridge University Press, 1959.

2. We were determined to rise above the constricted circumstances of conventional elementary science education, as it had evolved in America. Holding to the "faculty psychology" theory of learning, science education had limited itself to the "how-and-what" pablum of the early 1900's, rationalizing its position on the notion that pre-adolescent children could not reason. Ample evidence [3] persuaded us that children at all ages can reason, and we felt that the Science curriculum should derive from this assumption.

3. We acknowledged that the dynamic and swift-changing world of science demanded a larger and more constant scholarship than most general classroom teachers could possibly provide. In other words, we began to view science as a fluid and swiftly growing body of knowledge which non-scientist classroom teachers could not be expected to command. Yet we depended in large part below Grade VII (where we departmentalize) upon the general classroom teacher for science instruction in the self-contained classroom. This condition led us to organize, define and staff the role of Science Consultant as a constant and informed resource to the general classroom teacher. More will be said of this role.

4. We believed that at whatever grade level, the child's approach to science should no longer be one of hearing "about" or reading "about" or being reassured "about" a scientific proposition. We decided that the abundant indifference to science among many competent junior high and senior high school pupils was the sorry fruit of this deadly setting. We determined to provide the arrangements for children to *discover* scientific concepts, simple or complex; respond with natural curiosity to the phenomena of science; and by inquiry, observation and reason derive a *discovered* explanation. We felt there was a *structure* to science that was relevant to the maturity of all children, and that the earlier we could acquaint them with this *structure*, the more exciting and intuitive and self-motivated would be their learning.

Our science guide endeavors to fulfill the foregoing propositions. Its broad objectives, derived in concert with a committee of lay citizens appointed by the Board of Education, are as follows:

---

[3] Underhill, Orren E., *The Origins and Development of Elementary School Science*, Scott, Foresman & Co., N.Y., 1941.

1. To cultivate in each child scientific attitudes and the use of the scientific method: through nurturing curiosity, through developing habits of searching for facts and evidence on which to base conclusions or observations, and through expressing observations and conclusions clearly and accurately.

2. To help each child understand and accept the disciplines of science learning for two ends. On the one hand, he should acquire a broad knowledge of the nature of the world, compatible with the liberal arts tradition; and on the other, he should receive a foundation for utilitarian application of science principles in constructive living, in the practice of health and safety prinicples, and in the conservation of resources.

3. To provide an organized and psychologically sound progression of science experiences that continuously redevelop over broad periods of several years the main areas of natural science.

4. To create a science-learning environment sufficiently flexible to accommodate the wide-ranging interests and the broad spectrum of abilities to be found in each class: individual projects, subgroups of children organized around common interests, and special attention to slow and to swift learners.

5. To identify and stimulate those children possessing high interest and aptitude for further science learnings, guiding them toward vocational career consideration; and to encourage *all* children toward enriched adult avocational interests and activities.

6. To reveal to children the inter-relatedness of all learning, giving prominence to the articulation of science learnings with those of mathematics, the language arts and the social sciences.

7. To excite each child with the comprehension of beauty and order in the universe, and to acquaint him with the ever-swiftening change in man's command of science.

8. To instill in children an appreciation for the dignity of the human being, and to emphasize man's obligation to turn the sciences to ends which will serve all mankind constructively.

Recalling the conical spiral arrangement for sequential learning, the following major scientific concepts comprise the scope of the curriculum, Kindergarten through Grade VIII. We call them the *Great Ideas of Science:*

1. Properties of Matter
2. Matter, Space and Time
3. Phenomena of Earth and Universe
4. Physical and Chemical Environment of Life
5. Variety in Living Things
6. Characteristics of Life Processes

Each of these *great ideas* is unfolded, grade by grade, in a context appropriate to the maturity and experience of the child. As an example, let us examine Item 2 above, Matter, Space and Time. This *great idea* breaks down into the following abbreviated outline:

a. *Force:* distinguished from *energy*
    Kinds of forces (many examples and demonstrations)
b. *Energy:* forms
    Mechanical, etc.; through radiation
c. *Physical space,* size, time
    Quantitative measurements (metric)
    Timed energy or power
    Transformation of energy

This brief outline of one of the major concepts is then distributed in the spiral to the grade level content of several grades. In Grade IV, for example, the concept of *force* takes the following form for specific pupil learnings:

Changing Earth (Notice the articulation with Social Studies prehistory learnings)
    Four concepts are developed by pupils, demonstrating the effect of force and energy in the evolution of the earth's form (erosion, sedimentation, etc.)
    Two concepts in heat energy forms (volcanic action, etc.)
        (Note the introduction to geology as an element of science, illuminated as *heat* and *force* concepts cut across the spectrum of other scientific fields)
    Loss of heat; resulting earth forms: uplifts, mountains
    Forces of gravity, energy; effect on highlands

Solar System (Note introduction to Astronomy)
    Sun as source of energy (many concepts developed by pupils)

Radiation
Variety of forces
Variety of energy forms

Water (Carry over earlier learnings in weather from Grade III)
Deriving energy from sun (three concepts)
Distributes energy constructively and destructively

These notes, lifted in abbreviated form from the Science curriculum of Grade IV, are intended to elucidate the conical spiral notion described above.

Even as brief a sketch as this concerning science education in Winnetka would be incomplete if we were to omit reference to the sex education content which has long held an important place in our science teaching. At Grade V, along with the conventional instruction in physiology (under the *great idea* of Characteristics of Life Processes), the Science curriculum includes a unit on human growth and reproduction. The timeliness of this topic has been demonstrated consistently, as young people begin to become aware of sex differences. The reproductive system, along with the respiratory, digestive, circulatory systems and other scientific explanations of the functioning of man and animals characterize this program. Nomenclature and vocabulary are objectively and scientifically introduced. The use of small animals in the classroom for observation and care by children at this time is highly relevant. We believe that much of the secretive sniggering and vulgarity, of which 10-year-olds are monumentally capable, are reduced to a minimum through this instruction. Knocking cautiously on my imitation wood desk-top, I credit the absence of lavatory murals in our schools to this program.

At Grade VII the general science program required for all children for at least one semester includes a unit on sex education which normally requires about two weeks of instruction. At this level we separate boys and girls during this unit, assigning men teachers to the boys' classes and women teachers to the girls'. Consistent with the spiral design of the Science curriculum, the subject is examined more fully, still resting largely on the physiology theme, as distinguished from the emotional or moral.

Yet, clearly, the social behavior aspects of sex education inevitably are treated, as discussion and exchange between pupils and teacher evolve. Donald Boyer, Science Consultant, after many years of experience with the Junior High program, has developed a very effective short book on sex education for the early adolescent; we use it as a text for the Grade VII unit.[4]

Parents have accepted this program with warmth and understanding. We do not presume to interpose the schools between children and parents in this sensitive subject. We tell parents about the program, urging them to build upon the schools' scientific teachings through the more personal and intimate conversations that can nourish and strengthen the bonds between parents and children.

The Language Arts

The Winnetka curriculum in the Language Arts is the product of a five-year faculty study, reaching publication in the fall of 1961. Immediately following the publication of the first draft, the Board of Education appointed a lay advisory committee of citizens to work with the faculty committee in a thorough evaluation and critical examination of the document. Numerous clarifications, adjustments and a few basic modifications resulted from the joint study by faculty and laymen. The work of the lay-faculty committee took about nine months, following publication of the first draft. Upon agreement in the lay-faculty committee, the document was forwarded with a statement of endorsement to the Board of Education. The Board, following further study and adjustment formally adopted the curriculum. (The curricula in the Social Studies and Science also have undergone productive and mutually satisfying evaluation by faculty-citizens committees in the same manner as above. Mathematics will follow after further trial and adaptation of new content by teachers.)

The present course of study in the Language Arts, consisting of three volumes, totals some 700 pages. The three volumes are as follows:

Volume I
Listening
Speaking and Drama
Reading
Composition

---

[4] Boyer, Donald A., *For Youth to Know*, Laidlaw Brothers, River Forest, Ill., 48 pp.

Handwriting
Grammar and Usage

Volume II
Spelling (Including word lists)

Volume III
The Library: Its Literature and Poetry
Techniques for Research and Reference
Annotated Reading Lists Suggested by Grade Levels
Suggested Literature for Reluctant Readers

While, again, no claim is made that our work in the Language Arts is necessarily unique, there are a number of features of the program that may, in the context of case-study be useful for others. Let us examine this curriculum in the sequence of its table of contents described above:

Listening: We make a rather large point of the fact that hearing is quite different from listening. Starting at Kindergarten, and continuing with increasing sophistication to Grade VIII, we treat *listening* as a skill to be learned. Often taken for granted, listening is probably the most common and universal instrument for formal and informal learning by children and adults, notwithstanding the importance of the textbook. Our faculty, in conceiving this element of the Language Arts curriculum, drew upon the research of others, notably at college and university level, which revealed grave inefficiency in the performance of the untrained, unskilled listener.

We drill children in listening habits, giving prominence to accuracy, perception of the mood of the speaker, critical evaluation of the speaker's message and implications, and efficiency in deduction and summarization of the message. Modest experiments in the techniques of listening are being carried on by some of our middle grade teachers. We have much to learn about this skill and its teaching techniques.

Speaking: Again, starting at Kindergarten, and continuing through all grades, we place high emphasis upon speech, as (along with listening) the primary instrument of civilized communication. Our attention to speech falls into two broad categories: (1) equipping all children with the facility and skills for effective speech as a means of communication, and (2) corrective speech, not only for the severely handicapped, who require specialized instruction, but for those with minor speech flaws, which may be readily rectified by the classroom teacher. Dramatic play in the kindergarten–primary grades; creative drama in the middle grades; and more formal drama and literary readings in the upper grades provide media for this learning. Of high prominence, as noted earlier, is the creative drama setting, say at Grade IV, where a group of children conceive a worthy story, or derive it from the literature, and then, without formal memorization or preparation, enact the tale by role-playing and spontaneous dialogue, either with or without an external audience. The Creative Activities teacher often fortifies this element of the Language Arts. The familiar show-and-tell of the primary grades is, of course, a steady device for the induction of children into effective speech skills and serenity in communication when standing before others.

Reading: Our reading program extends to all levels, encompassing not only the basic skills of speed and comprehension, but discrimination, critical appraisal, appreciation of literature, adaptation of reading rate to content and purpose, and a beginning exposure to semantics. We are probably unorthodox in our practice of avoiding a given reading "system" or commercial publisher. We are sometimes erroneously described as being opposed to commercial reading materials. On the contrary, we utilize many responsible and effective commercial materials, giving teachers considerable freedom in their choice, for example, of primers and early readers. We hold that no single publisher is necessarily the "best" or final authority in reading, yet all the prominent publishers are included in our resources of reading materials.

In developing our own design for the teaching of reading, our curriculum committee built into the guide the best techniques they could lift from the commercial teachers' manuals, plus the findings of current research scholars in the field. We start an exposure to phonetic analysis, for example, in the kindergarten, and continue it through Grade VIII. However, allowing a solid place for phonics in our instruction, particularly at Grade III and beyond, we give primary emphasis to visual, rather than auditory skills for those children (comprising the majority) who prosper under a comprehensive approach to reading. A grade by grade chart of our sequences in reading instruction follows for those who would pursue the matter in detail.

GRADE LEVEL OBJECTIVES FOR READING

Winnetka Public Schools, Winnetka, Illinois

	GRADES 1 AND 2

I. READINESS	1. Provide classroom atmosphere and activities to stimulate interest in reading.
	   a. Toys, puzzles, pictures, nature materials, games.
	   b. Language activities, painting, drawing, observations, writing.
	2. Develop a desire to read.
	3. Develop the ability to listen.
	4. Develop the ability to think and speak clearly.
	5. Develop visual and auditory acuity.
	6. Direct attention to left-to-right and top-to-bottom of reading format.
	7. Develop a meaningful vocabulary, including a background of experiences.
	8. Take into account mental factors; physical, social and emotional development.

II. INTERESTS AND TASTES	1. Provide attractive and interesting materials: books, pictures and magazines. 2. Develop ability to see relationship between present interests and written material and ability to seek appropriate material. 3. Develop recognition of the need for reading. 4. Develop selectivity and appreciation of prose and poetry. 5. Develop good library habits.
III. WORD RECOGNITION	1. Develop association between the printed symbol and the object, experience and/or idea. 2. Develop appropriate phonics and structural analysis skills for this level. (*See* PHONICS SECTION)
IV. COMPREHENSION	1. Continue to provide a background of experience and information. 2. Begin development of elements of a sentence, including punctuation. 3. Develop ability to grasp general idea of selection. 4. Develop ability to pick out specific facts or details. 5. Develop ability to read and follow directions. 6. Develop ability to understand a sequence of ideas and to predict outcomes. 7. Develop ability to derive literal and interpretative meanings. 8. Develop ability to read aloud with understanding and expression. 9. Develop concepts relating to the common areas of living and learning: science, social studies, etc.

	GRADES 1 AND 2 (*cont.*)
IV. COMPREHENSION	10. Develop specific vocabulary for content areas. 11. Develop understanding of pictures and charts.
V. EFFECTIVE USE OF READING MATERIALS	1. Develop understanding that books have different types of content: imaginative, informative, humorous, and factual. 2. Develop understanding in child of role as active participant in reading—empathy with story. 3. Develop understanding of reading for enjoyment. 4. Develop skill in gaining information from reading. 5. Develop skill in oral reading to share information or interpret material. 6. Develop skill in silent reading. 7. Develop good reading habits and attitudes. 8. Introduce the concept of alphabetizing. 9. Develop awareness of various types of reading materials: books, magazines, newspapers, bulletins, etc.

VI.
EVALUATION
	1. Formal evaluation by standardized tests.
	2. Formal test available to teachers:
	    a. Basic Sight Word Lists.
	    b. Gray Oral Test.
	    c. Winnetka Phonics Tests.
	3. Informal evaluation:
	    a. Teacher's day-by-day observation, conferences.
	    b. Teacher-made tests of vocabulary and comprehension.
	    c. Actual work done by children—reports, etc.
	    d. Weekly Reader Tests, workbook.
	4. Referrals for special help. (*See* ACADEMIC CLINIC SECTION)

	GRADE 3
I. **READINESS**	1. Continue and expand 1st and 2nd grade Readiness. 2. Continue development of reading skills and techniques. 3. Expand and develop key words, concepts, and functional vocabulary.
II. **INTERESTS** **AND TASTES**	1. Continue and expand 1st and 2nd grade Interests and Tastes. 2. Develop selectivity in reading. 3. Develop an appreciation of the past. 4. Develop awareness of current events and world understandings.
III. **WORD** **RECOGNITION**	1. Continue and expand 1st and 2nd grade Word Recognition Skills. 2. Continue and expand word attack skills. (*See* PHONICS SECTION)
IV. **COMPREHENSION**	1. Continue and expand 1st and 2nd grade Comprehension. 2. Develop ability to recognize a story or plot structure. 3. Analyze inner drives and emotions of story characters. 4. Identify and evaluate character traits. 5. Develop perception of relationships, time, place, cause-effect. 6. Recognize use of punctuation for meanings: period, comma, question mark, exclamation mark.
V. **EFFECTIVE USE** **OF READING** **MATERIALS**	1. Continue and expand 1st and 2nd grade Effective Use of Materials. 2. Develop reading as a means of finding answers to specific questions. 3. Develop reading as an aid to personal development. 4. Develop reading as a contributing factor to solution of group problems. 5. Increase emphasis on silent reading.

VI.
EVALUATION
	1. Formal evaluation by standardized tests.
	2. Informal evaluation—continue as in 1st and 2nd grade, adapting to level.
	    a. Tests—from such materials as *Weekly Reader*, *News-Time*, etc.
	    b. Self-evaluation of progress.
	    c. Group evaluation.
	3. Referrals for special help. (*See* ACADEMIC CLINIC SECTION)

	GRADE 4
I. READINESS	1. Continue and expand 3rd grade Readiness.

II.
 	
INTERESTS
AND TASTES
	1. Continue and expand 3rd grade Interests and Tastes.
	2. Widen and strengthen informational backgrounds.
	3. Analyze literary value of selection, with particular use in mind, e.g. drama.
	4. Appreciate aesthetic value, techniques.
	    a. Description and characterization.
	    b. Portrayal of moods (use of adjs.).
	    c. Develop thought, action, climax.

III. WORD RECOGNITION	1. Continue and expand 3rd Grade Word Recognition Skills. 2. Continue and expand word attack skills. (*See* PHONICS SECTION)
IV. COMPREHENSION	1. Continue and expand 3rd grade Comprehension. 2. Develop ability to see relationships among words in a sentence and sentences in a paragraph. 3. Discover and discuss commonly used figures of speech. 4. Interpret emotive expressions. 5. Develop ability to arrive at conclusions or generalizations. 6. Continue study of punctuation, adding quotation marks. 7. Develop ability to discover meaning of words from context.
V. EFFECTIVE USE OF READING MATERIALS	1. Continue and expand 3rd grade Effective Use of Materials. 2. Develop skill in adjusting speed to materials, and needs. 3. Develop skill in skimming for general import in locating information. 4. Introduce use of dictionary. 5. Develop skill in use of graphic materials, charts, tables, and maps. 6. Begin to develop speed in reading.
VI. EVALUATION	1. Formal evaluation by standardized tests. 2. Informal evaluation—continue as in 3rd grade, adapting to grade level. 3. Referrals for special help. (*See* ACADEMIC CLINIC SECTION)

	GRADE 5
I. **READINESS**	1. Continue and expand 4th grade Readiness. 2. Capitalize on children's increasing awareness of the world around them.
II. **INTERESTS** **AND TASTES**	1. Continue and expand 4th grade Interests and Tastes. 2. Draw upon examples of fine prose and poetry for class discussion.

III.
WORD
RECOGNITION
	1. Continue and expand 4th grade Word Recognition Skills.
	2. Continue and expand word attack skills.
	    a. Phonics and structural analysis. (*See* PHONICS SECTION)
	    b. Derivatives of words.

IV.
COMPREHENSION
	1. Continue and expand 4th grade Comprehension.
	2. Develop ability to organize main ideas and dependent ideas.
	3. Develop interpretations of figurative, idiomatic and picturesque language.
	4. Develop ability to make inferences and sense implications.
	5. Build meanings—single words, phrases, clauses, etc.
	6. Increase awareness of semantics—
	    a. Relationship of language to growth and experience.
	    b. Multiple meanings of words.
	    c. Change in meanings with time and place.
	    d. Emotional aspects of language.

V. **EFFECTIVE USE** **OF READING** **MATERIALS**	1. Continue and expand 4th grade Effective Use of Materials. 2. Further adaptation of speeds and skills to content areas. 3. Develop skill in note-taking, summarizing and simple outlining. 4. Develop skill for locating information: table of contents, footnotes, and glossary; card catalog, encyclopedia and reference books; use of dictionary. (*See* LIBRARY SECTION, Guide III) 5. Develop an increasing awareness of need for reliability on reference sources.

VI.
EVALUATION
	1. Formal evaluation by standardized tests.
	2. Informal evaluation—
	    a. Continue as in 4th grade, adapting to grade level.
	    b. Test of library and reference skills.
	3. Referrals for special help. (*See* ACADEMIC CLINIC SECTION)

	GRADE 6
I. READINESS	1. Continue and expand 5th grade Readiness.
II. INTERESTS AND TASTES	1. Continue and expand 5th grade Interests and Tastes. 2. Relate Language Arts experiences to music, theatre, fine art, dance, as well as literature.

III.
 	
WORD
RECOGNITION
	1. Continue and expand 5th grade Word Recognition Skills.
	2. Continue and expand word attack skills.
	    a. Phonics and structural analysis. (*See* PHONICS SECTION)
	    b. Recognize foreign origin of words.

IV. COMPREHENSION	1. Continue and expand 5th grade Comprehension. 2. Develop recognition and use of simple outlines and topic sentences as aids to understanding. 3. Develop ability to read critically to appraise relative values. 4. Develop knowledge of shades of meanings of words. 5. Continue strong vocabulary emphasis.
V. EFFECTIVE USE OF READING MATERIALS	1. Continue and expand 5th grade Effective Use of Materials. 2. Develop increasing independence in choosing books for specific purposes. 3. Develop expanding interests in literature, history, and science. 4. Begin the use of multiple and comparative sources for reference.
VI. EVALUATION	1. Formal evaluation by standardized tests. 2. Informal evaluation— a. Continue as in 5th grade, adapting to grade level. 3. Referrals for special help. (*See* ACADEMIC CLINIC SECTION)

	GRADE 7
I. READINESS	1. Continue and expand 6th grade Readiness. 2. Develop increased awareness of world relationships and problems. 3. Encourage appetite for rich literature, in quantity.
II. INTERESTS AND TASTES	1. Continue and expand 6th grade Interests and Tastes. 2. Expand widely in fields of personal interests. 3. Develop understanding of the short story essentials as a type of literature. 4. Develop increased understanding of poetry and dramatic materials.
III. WORD RECOGNITION	1. Continue and expand 6th grade Word Recognition Skills. 2. Increased expansion of recognition vocabulary. (*See* PHONICS SECTION)

IV.
COMPREHENSION
	1. Continue and expand 6th grade Comprehension.
	2. Develop ability to sense structure and design.
	3. Develop awareness of transitions in thoughts.
	4. Develop balance of speed and comprehension to increased demands of curriculum.
	5. Develop greater understanding of types of literature—
	    a. Fiction
	    b. Biography
	    c. Poetry
	    d. Simple Essay
	6. Develop increased skill in interpreting figures of speech.

V.
EFFECTIVE USE
OF READING
MATERIALS
	1. Continue and expand 6th grade Effective Use of Materials.
	2. Develop skill in use of complex maps, graphs, charts, etc. (*See* ARITHMETIC AND SCIENCE GUIDES)
	3. Increase skill in adapting reading methods to needs: skimming, study reading, oral, etc.
	4. Learn to analyze newspaper reading—
	    a. Editorials c. Propaganda
	    b. Cartoons d. Editorial policy and point of view
	5. Develop interest in good magazines: information, hobbies, and references.

VI.
EVALUATION
	1. Formal evaluation by standardized tests.
	2. Informal evaluation—
	    a. Continue as in 6th grade, adapting to grade level.
	    b. Tests published by S.R.A., *Reader's Digest*, etc.
	3. Referrals for special help. (*See* ACADEMIC CLINIC SECTION)

	GRADE 8
I. READINESS	1. Continue and expand 7th grade Readiness. 2. Relate reading speed and comprehension to the reality of swiftly expanding academic expectations in all fields.
II. INTERESTS AND TASTES	1. Continue and expand 7th grade Interests and Tastes. 2. Increase the understanding of the novel as a type of literature. 3. Develop greater appreciation of various dialects and speech patterns. 4. Interpret point of view, attitudes and feelings of author.
III. WORD RECOGNITION	1. Continue and expand 7th grade Word Recognition skills. (*See* PHONICS SECTION)
IV. COMPREHENSION	1. Continue and expand 7th grade Comprehension. 2. Develop increased skill in weighing multiple sources of information. 3. Develop increased skill in interpreting relationships: character to character; incident to incident; and character to incident. 4. Recognize and interpret symbolism and allusions.

V.
 	
EFFECTIVE USE
OF READING
MATERIALS
	1. Continue and expand 7th grade Effective Use of Materials.
	2. Increase skill in drawing on all types of reading—
	   a. Skimming to locate or survey.
	   b. Intensive for specific detail.
	   c. Interpretive to express feeling.

VI. EVALUATION	1. Formal evaluation by standardized tests. 2. Informal evaluation— a. Continue as in 7th grade, adapting to grade level. 3. Referrals for special help. (*See* ACADEMIC CLINIC SECTION)

300

Composition: We hold, not uniquely, that children learn to write well only by writing. Starting in Grade IV we expect from each child a piece of responsible written work weekly, consistent with his maturity and experience. The work may be an expository statement, a letter, a book review, a piece of creative writing, or any other form deemed suitable by the teacher.

We endeavor to classify the written work of pupils into two categories: those items written for the child's own enjoyment, often encouraging flights of fancy and poetic adventure, which are reviewed by the teacher, but not corrected for mechanics; and those items which are appropriate for communication to others, in which case the teacher exercises sharp evaluation and expectations for precision and correctness. In all cases of written work, teachers are expected to comment in considerable detail upon the child's effectiveness, encouraging, pointing out strengths and weaknesses, commending or taking to task—but in any event revealing prompt and critical appraisal of the writer's current performance.

We have a system-wide "standard for written work" giving consistency and uniformity to the format for all grade levels. We also have a system-wide code for teachers' corrective notations.

Handwriting: Somewhat unique in this field also, Winnetka has for many years deferred the adoption of cursive writing to a point in the child's growth considerably later than the conventional Grade III. While a number of the curricular practices in Winnetka had, over the years, pursued the *deferral of learning* idea, many of these deferrals, such as in mathematics, science, grammar, and usage have been modified and even reversed in our current curriculum revision. However, in the case of handwriting, we have examined the evidence, and maintained the pattern of deferral in the interest of teaching economy.

Our children become fairly competent and skillful in the use of manuscript writing by Grade III. When most children in the United States "convert" to cursive writing starting at this point, and continue their "conversion" for a labored, time-consuming, and often illegible three- or four-year period, we refine the manuscript hand, encouraging speed and legibility until Grade VI. (We provide experience in *reading* cursive writing starting at Grade IV.) At Grade VI, when the child's coordination, confidence, and skill in the manuscript hand is quite steady, we provide an intensive course under a handwriting specialist of the departmentalized Junior High School, in the transition to cursive writing. The course lasts for about seven weeks, with daily 40-minute classes. At the conclusion of the course the child has learned cursive writing without the labored, time-consuming, and frustrating struggle that often characterizes middle-grade penmanship. We believe (but cannot prove) that most children respond with greater confidence, eagerness, and creativity to their writing tasks during the Grade IV to VI period when drawing upon the familiar manuscript form, than would be the case with the still unsure cursive hand. At Grade VI, when maturity and increased muscular coordination have come about, penmanship skill in the cursive hand is quickly accomplished. Children and parents then decide which hand the child shall employ for the future. Boys tend to favor the cursive hand in their choices, and girls the manuscript. Our objective is a swift, legible hand. More often than not, the manuscript hand meets this objective more effectively than the cursive hand.

By the end of the eighth grade, virtually all children have become proficient at typing, with at least one semester of intensive typing instruction. Nearly all major composition papers, by the end of Grade VIII, are submitted typewritten, with this skill prevailing in high school and post-high school writing.

Grammar and Usage: This term, for us, embraces all of the mechanics of correct expression, including punctuation, paragraphing, form, sentence structure, the parts of speech, and rhetoric. In this category, our present curriculum has departed widely from the former Winnetka pattern. Our current developments suggest considerably broader and deeper learning expectations at all grades. For a time, the Winnetka Schools deferred the teaching of formal grammar to Grade VIII, with the belief (not greatly different from that affecting handwriting) that the mechanics of our language could be rather quickly and efficiently mastered in a short while at Grade VIII, avoiding the inefficient and time-consuming struggle at an earlier age. Evidence has unfolded over the years, indicating that the heavy expectations for grammar and usage at Grade VIII, accumulated by "deferral," were so demanding that (a) they were not wholly mastered in the year, and (b) much other important work in the Grade VIII language arts, such as creative writing and literature, had to be curtailed. Accordingly, we have spread the teaching of grammar and usage over all the upper grades, starting at Grade III.

An interesting overview of the history of the Language Arts curriculum may be gained by examining the goal cards at select points over the past 20 years, at Grade IV, for example. (*Turn to pages 304-305.*) The left column records the goals at the time of Winnetka's earlier historic peak; the middle column reveals the expectations just prior to the present curriculum revision; the right-hand column records the expectations of the current curriculum as first installed in 1961.

The selected extract of the goal record card offers two uses to the reader. It reveals the increased academic expectation that has unfolded over the past 20 years, not only in Winnetka, but in education generally. Secondly, it affords the reader a closer view of just what a goal record card is. Recalling earlier chapters, it has been stated that the goal record card or some equivalent instrument is absolutely essential to the orderliness of truly individualized instruction. Viewing the example cited in its full context, there would be a space following each item in which the teacher records the date the child demonstrates a mastery of the item, through a test, and returns the card to the child for his safekeeping. Group work does not imply mastery at the grade level where it occurs, necessarily, but introduces the goal in anticipation of mastery at a later level. The tests are uniform, system-wide, and are available to the pupil at any time that he and his teacher feel he is ready to demonstrate his proficiency. The teacher keeps a master record of all goal card postings, revealing patterns of strength and weakness throughout the class, and within individuals. Admitting the continuing nature of our curriculum revision, we have not, as of 1963, completed all language arts mastery tests in all content in all grades. These are among the current "things to do."

Before leaving the fourth grade goal card example, it must be noted that the extract I have cited is only one of several parts of the fourth grade card (or for that matter, for any grade card). The other parts, without listing their content, include columns of content items and date spaces for Social Studies, Science, Mathematics, Individual Reading Record (titles), Handwriting, Spelling, and Compositions. (The full spectrum of goal record cards is offered in the Appendix.)

The reader is again reminded that the "fourth grade" appellation

COMPARISON OF WINNETKA GOAL CARDS
IN GRAMMAR AND USAGE [5]

Grade IV—Select Years, 1944–1961

GRAMMAR AND USAGE GOALS GRADE IV—1944	GRAMMAR AND USAGE GOALS GRADE IV—1956	GRAMMAR AND USAGE GOALS GRADE IV—1961
1. The Sentence (review)	1. The Sentence (review)	Punctuation
2. Capitals (review)	2. Capitals:	1. Capital letters
3. Capitals:	Book titles	Persons, places,
Names of people	Special names	nationalities
4. Capitals:	3. Capitals:	Personal titles
Cities	Names of people	Book, poem, story
States	4. Capitals:	titles
Countries	Cities	Lines of poetry
5. Capitals:	States	Heading, greeting,
Mountains	Countries	closing of corre-
Oceans	5. Capitals:	spondence
etc.	Mountains	2. Periods: (Review
6. Letters (corresp.)	Rivers	Sentences)
7. Envelopes	Oceans	Declarative sen-
8. Review, Sentences &	Lakes	tences
Capitals	etc.	After abbreviations
	6. Abbreviations	and initials
	7. Commas	3. Question marks (Re-
	8. Letters	view Sentences)
	9. Envelopes	Interrogative sen-
	10. Review, Sentences &	tences
	Capitals	4. Exclamation point
		(Review Sentences)
		Exclamatory sen-
		tences
		Interjection
		5. Commas
		Heading, greeting,
		closing in corre-
		spondence
		6. Apostrophe
		Contractions
		GROUP WORK
		Parts of Speech
		7. Nouns
		Number, gender, as
		subject
		8. Verbs
		Action and being,
		as predicate
		Punctuation (cont'd.)
		9. Capitals for abbrevia-
		tion, proper nouns
		10. Capitals for familiar
		names, direct address
		11. Commas, words in
		series

[5] We define all the skills relating to the correct mechanics of expression as Grammar and Usage.

COMPARISON OF WINNETKA GOAL CARDS
IN GRAMMAR AND USAGE (*Continued*)
Grade IV—Select Years, 1944–1961

GRAMMAR AND USAGE GOALS GRADE IV—1944	GRAMMAR AND USAGE GOALS GRADE IV—1956	GRAMMAR AND USAGE GOALS GRADE IV—1961

		Punctuation (cont'd.)
		12. Commas, proper names
		13. Apostrophe, possessives
		14. Hyphen, to divide words
		
		Use of Dictionary
		15. Alphabetical order
		16. Accent marks
		17. Diacritical marks
		18. Syllables
		19. Guide words
		20. Definitions
		
		Preview (when other goals are accomplished)
		
		Parts of Speech
		21. Nouns: proper, common, possessive
		22. Adjectives: recognition; modifiers of nouns and pronouns
		23. Pronouns: recognition, number, gender, used as subject
		
		Punctuation
		24. Capital letter:
		    In quotation
		    Particular documents,
		    Historic events
		    Outlining
		25. Periods:
		    Imperative sentences
		    Outlining
		26. Commas
		    Yes and no in conversation
		    In business letter form
		27. Colon
		    Salutation in business letter
		    Between hour and minute
		28. Quotation marks

Note: The goals in grammar and usage were modified further in 1962, without major change in content. (*See* Language Arts Goal Record Card 4 in Appendix.)

attaching to this goal card is only relevant to the expectations for the typical fourth grade child in a given subject area. By the nature of our definition of individualization, some children sitting in Grade IV may still be wrestling with the "Grade III" goal card as late as mid-term, while a few at the other extreme may, by late winter, proceed into the further challenges of the Grade V card in one or more subject areas.

Spelling

We believe we have developed a revolutionary and very promising approach to the teaching of spelling. Its uniqueness rests upon the familiar Winnetka term, *individualization*. Several of our ablest teachers, long at ease with individual progression, self-instruction, self-correction and ungraded content in arithmetic, wondered why individualization in spelling could not be equally fruitful for the teacher and learner. Conventional spelling instruction in groups seems to assume that all children possess the same competencies, interests and needs in spelling. Yet any teacher will quickly agree that this is far from the truth. Some children, "natural spellers" perhaps, find no satisfaction or stimulus in turning out correctly spelled word lists that are so easy for them as to call forth ridicule. Correspondingly, for the child who must labor at his spelling, little is gained by constant failure at words beyond his competence, readily mastered by many of his classmates.

Accordingly, under the vigorous and creative leadership of Lucille Murray, novice principal of Greeley School in 1960 and erstwhile master Winnetka teacher of the middle grades, a new design for spelling instruction has become a part of our language arts curriculum in all grades. Basically, the design revolves about a skeleton of 10 *levels* of spelling competence or spelling difficulty combined with frequency of usage. The levels are not related to grades or age, but solely to the pupil's spelling competence. Starting at the middle of Grade II, the teacher determines by survey tests the *level* at which the child already possesses mastery. Starting at Level I, which contains 60 words, the teacher administers tests in blocks of 20 words. Typical words in this list include *father, going, house,* etc., compatible with research as to *usage* by the child. The child who demonstrates mastery of the words proceeds at once to Level II, and so on, until he reaches a level where he fails one or more words in the 20-word test. The lists are graduated in terms of *frequency of use,* as well as difficulty. We have drawn on the research of Botel in this field.

This process we call *initial placement.* Thereafter a child studies *his own word list at his own level,* the words increasing in difficulty and quantity as the levels increase. At Level V, for example, there are 200 words; at Level IX, 600, or 30 lists of 20 words each. Before declaring himself ready for a *test for mastery* at a given level, a child must undertake a *pre-test* at that level, working in partnership with a designated child of like ability (or, perhaps, unlike ability when the teacher sees an opportunity for constructive unmatched pairing). The following extract from the Teacher's Manual is revealing of the process:

> When every word on his list has been *pre-tested* and every word missed studied according to the plan, the child may sign up in a place designated by the teacher as qualified to take the *final test* on that list.
>
> A good speller may be able to handle several *basic lists* (within a level) a week, plus some additional words and still have adequate time to write and to engage in other valuable spelling activity. He will have very few words requiring further study following each *pre-testing.* The teacher can readily determine those who are able to move at a fast rate with accuracy and understanding. She will need to expect much higher level spelling and word analysis performance from these fast-moving children in all written areas, and much purposeful writing. . . .
>
> The average-to-poor speller may need to ask his partner to re-test him after careful, independent study of each word missed on his pre-test before applying for the final test. . . .
>
> The poor speller may need to take five or six words at a time from his list of twenty. He may require longer than a week to make his list of twenty.

When a number of children have declared their readiness for the final test, the teacher groups them, if appropriate, and administers the final test for the level by dictation to those requesting it. If the child performs at 100 per cent accuracy, he proceeds to the next level. If not, he restudies the level of his current placement, and subsequently again requests the test for mastery. It is clear that a child in Grade III may be working at a spelling level typical of most fifth graders. Correspondingly, there will be fifth graders performing no better than the typical third grader. Our present evidence, while still limited to two years of trial, suggests that virtually all children shall have attained mastery of the 10 levels by Grade VI. As a child completes Level X, he proceeds into other selected spelling lists, derived from the usual classic resources such as Fitzgerald's *Master Demon List of 222 Words; Words Most*

Frequently Misspelled by Adults; and *500 Uncommon Words Most Frequently Misspelled.* We have added to these collections words accumulated by Helen Danforth, master fourth grade teacher in Winnetka, as *Spelling Requested by Children When Writing Stories and Reports, Grade IV.* We are also compiling lists of words deriving from specialized learnings in other subject areas such as Mathematics (circumference, parallelogram, multiplier), Science, and the Social Studies as well.

Clearly, we have drawn heavily upon the historic Winnetka philosophy in designing this procedure for spelling instruction. Indeed, as C.W. reads this exposition, he may well find a nostalgic satisfaction that will soften his dismay at some of our departures in other areas from the design he fathered 40 years ago.

The Library

To attempt to give adequate prominence to our library program within the dimensions of a chapter subhead is not only unrealistic, but profane. We give very high priority to the library and the librarians. Starting at kindergarten level and proceeding through all grades, children are enticed by our librarians (two at elementary level, two at junior high) to enjoy the many fruits on their shelves. (I have offended one of our Methodist patrons by referring to the "fine wines in our library cellars.")

Our curriculum in the Language Arts establishes a Library Guide as a separate publication (Language Arts, Part III). This guide defines the processes and practices of library usage through the child's early developmental years, and into an expected mastery of library techniques and procedures for research by Grade VIII. Consistent with our high devotion to the individual, we believe that library materials should be provided in a wide spectrum of subjects, and a deep arrangement of ascending intellectual fulfillment.

Starting at the kindergarten level our librarian makes the library a joyous and satisfying place, with story-telling periods and opportunities for "take-outs." Continuing through the grades, the children always know the library is open, whether or not our librarians are present, and they know they are always welcome. By Grade III they know how to use the card file and how to charge out a book to themselves. By fourth grade, group "readers" are not readily discernible in the classroom; instead children are reading "on their own" for the most part, under benevolent and sometimes persuasive guidance from the teacher. Typically, a child reads a book about every two weeks above Grade III, reporting on it either in writing, speech, or through some other creative medium such as a display or map or diorama.

At Junior High level, an intensive six-week period of daily library instruction is prescribed for all sixth graders, under the direct teaching of the head librarian. This is a part of the sixth grade survey offering. As children progress in their various junior high learnings, it is not uncommon for the librarian to resort to inter-library loan arrangements from nearby Northwestern University to satisfy an able and well-motivated seventh or eighth grader whose appetite and demands exceed our collection or the collection in the high school.

The bulk of the Library Guide consists of recommended reading lists in annotated form, classified by age or grade levels. This guide is furnished to all children, and to all parents who request it. It is the thoughtful compilation of the best literature, old and new, that our teachers and librarians have discovered for children. It is not a *required* reading list. It is an attractive menu for savoring and selecting. It helps parents in the acquisition of home libraries. It articulates with our local public library. It is kept current with periodic revisions to include important new works.

If my enthusiasm for our library program shows, I plead guilty. We are blessed with professional librarians whose art and science are uncommonly matched by their dedication to children and the joys of their learning. Our statistics concerning books per child, shelf-feet per school, and other exacting criteria significantly surpass those standards recently pronounced by the American Library Association. Notwithstanding my Yankee frugality in the deployment of public funds, I can think of no more prudent investment in education than the unhesitating support of library expenditures.

Our Language Arts Curriculum, first thing of its kind in Winnetka, is now in its second year of trial. Culminating five years of heavy faculty labor under the wise, gentle and intuitive leadership of fourth grade teacher Helen Vann, faculty committee chairman, this work promises to produce useful testimony for others who would teach children the skillful and eloquent use of our language and its literature.

Summary

As we hold the mirror of the 1920's and 1930's to Winnetka's instructional program in 1963, we see many basic elements of solid continuity, reaffirmation and reactivation. Those underlying essentials of Washburne's Winnetka design which have stood the test of time, survived a changing faculty and administration, and remained standing amid the ashes of Progressive Education, are as vital today in Winnetka (and, unfortunately, nearly as unique) as they were 40 years ago. They may be quickly cited, as revealed in examples of this chapter: a constant and never-quite-victorious struggle for true individualization for the fulfillment of every child; corresponding tools for individualization, including the goal record card, locally developed instructional materials, including tests for mastery; self-instruction through widely diversified media as distinguished from basal texts; high prominence of the library and individualized reading; acknowledgment of widely varying extremes of competence among children of any grade, in any subject area, irrespective of such grouping as may be attempted; rejection of grades or scores as measures of pupil progress, and as false motivators, with reliance, instead, upon specific and candid personal evaluation of pupil performance by the teacher; the expectation of 100 per cent mastery by all pupils in those subjects of a relatively finite nature such as mathematics, grammar, and spelling which lend themselves to exact quantitative measurement.

While holding to these foregoing historic and fundamental characteristics of education in Winnetka, we have during the past seven years made significant changes in the specifics of the learning expectations. As in the case of Mathematics, we have introduced a whole new body of learnings in Science, starting at kindergarten. In the Language Arts we have introduced the formal structure of English and its disciplines much earlier than was true in the 1930–1940 design.

In short, while earnestly reaffirming much of the central message of historic Winnetka, we have reversed one theory that C.W. held dear, the *deferral of learning*. While Washburne would be reluctant to use the term or even to acknowledge it as a theory held dear, he would take satisfaction in the writings of that other giant of the education of the 1920's, Marietta Pierce Johnson, who said, "The prolonging of childhood is the hope of the race—the longer the time from birth to maturity, the higher the organism." [6] In Winnetka, today, we would agree that the prolongation of youth is right and good, but we do not necessarily inhibit the youthful heart and mind when we afford it such nourishment as it seems willing and eager to digest. Nor do we agree that Mrs. Johnson's "hope of the race" is endangered by scholarship.

------

[6] Johnson, Marietta, *Youth in a World of Men,* 1929.

■

CHAPTER TWENTY-TWO

Current Events

in Winnetka

■
■

A superior school today may be an inferior school a decade from now—unless bold, imaginative steps to improve *quality* are taken.

—J. Lloyd Trump,
Images of the Future,
The Ford Foundation

Most of the preceding chapters which deal with Winnetka today have endeavored to reveal *implicitly* the spirit of evolution and innovation that characterizes our instructional program. This chapter seeks to give an explicit accounting of numerous additional activities that seem to possess a degree of originality or inquiry. They are treated briefly, necessarily, for purposes of identification only, with the invitation to interested observers to ask for more. While no attempt is made here to include all the items loosely called experimental, now current in Winnetka, I have selected those topics most often the object of inquiry from correspondents or visitors. Most of the items reported here are new, at least to us; a few, while still unique, have been in effect for many years. All are justified under the title of our book, and are offered, not as suggested models or as success stories, but as a part of our account of the Winnetka Schools. Most of our current investigations are on-going, incomplete, inconclusive and subjective. They are exciting, often frustrating, and from some of them we may derive a rich discovery for ourselves and others.

We accept experimentation and action research as a necessary and normal part of our function. In 1961, the Annual Report of the Board of Education drew upon a statement developed earlier by the faculty:

> ... These schools have served and should continue to serve as an educational laboratory for the pursuit and discovery of ever better ways to teach and to learn. They should, further, participate actively in the determination and demonstration of the school's place in America, as society seeks to deploy appropriate responsibilities among the home, the community, and other institutions.

Significantly, the Winnetka Caucus platform, annual blueprint for the municipal governing bodies, giving voice to the wishes of the people, declared in the late fall of 1961:

> Schools. We approve the educational policies in effect. We urge the Winnetka Board of Education and the Winnetka school officials to continue such research in teaching techniques and other measures as are needed to preserve Winnetka's leadership in elementary education and to give our children the finest preparation for higher education.

What Should the Schools Teach?

Probably the most fundamental, yet the most intangible of the dynamic forces now current in Winnetka is our unspoken, unstructured search for the *role* of the schools in this teeming half-century. On the surface of this evolution, one may quickly perceive the rejection of Winnetka's earlier "deferral of formal learning" theory, as we investigate the feasibility of introducing certain propositions in algebra and geometry in the primary grades, and as we release Junior High children in the mysteries of atomic structure. English grammar, foreign language in the early grades, disciplined composition at all levels are further signs of this rejection.

Yet, beyond our hypothesis that some children can, given the opportunity, acquire knowledge and skills with efficiency much earlier than our conventions prescribe, there is a deeper and more subtle hypothesis in our present search. As a faculty we began this undeclared exploration in 1956–57, adapting our curriculum through our trials and errors as we went along. Perhaps we would not even cite this condition as a dynamic force in our present design if there had not been a corresponding force of extraordinary importance running, apparently parallel to our thinking, in the late 1950's.

In September, 1959, some 35 scholars in the natural and social sciences and in education gathered at Wood's Hole on Cape Cod. Sponsored by the National Academy of Sciences, this gathering was prompted by "the conviction that [the schools] were at the beginning of a period of new progress in, and concern for, creating curricula and ways of teaching . . ." In 1960 Jerome S. Bruner's monumental little volume, reporting the Wood's Hole meeting, put into words the very ideas with which we in Winnetka had been engaged:

> What may be emerging as a mark of our own generation is a widespread renewal of concern for the quality and intellectual aims of education, but without abandonment of the ideal that education should serve as a means of training well-balanced citizens for a democracy.
>
> *   *   *
>
> The teaching and learning of *structure* rather than simply the mastery of facts and techniques is at the center of the problem. . . .
>
> *   *   *
>
> If earlier learning is to render later learning easier, it must do so by providing a *general picture*. . . .
>
> *   *   *
>
> . . . The foundations of any subject may be taught to anybody at any age in some form. . . .[1]

Bruner quotes at length from a Wood's Hole paper, prepared by Professor Bärbel Inhelder, psychologist of the Institut Rousseau, Geneva, in which she gave an account of her research with Swiss children, particularly in science and mathematics learnings:

---

[1] Extracts from Jerome S. Bruner, *The Process of Education*, Harvard University Press, Cambridge, 1960.

> Basic notions in these fields [geometry and physics] are perfectly accessible to children of seven to ten years of age, provided that they are divorced from their mathematical expression and studied through materials that the child can handle himself. . . . There is evidence to indicate that such vigorous and relevant early training has the effect of making later learning easier. Indeed the experiments in "learning set" seem to indicate just that—that one not only learns specifics, but in so doing learns how to learn.[2]

Whether we had been walking in the Wood's Hole footsteps in the late 1950's, without knowing it, I cannot say. In any event, when Professor Bruner's report was published in May of 1960, it gave articulation and relevance to the groping, inarticulate and unstructured hunches that we had been pursuing for four years. Typical of our explorations were the following: The spiral curriculum in the great ideas of science; the understandings of order and structure as distinguished from facts and figures in our social studies; the stimulation of intuition and the application of logic in our work with mathematics in the primary grades, and the hunch that *all* the number processes are best taught all of a piece to first graders (*see* Chapter Twenty); our insistence upon *much* disciplined speech and writing in the middle and upper grades.

Thus, it may be said that underlying all of the exploratory activity in the Winnetka Schools in the past few years is an earnest re-evaluation of what children can learn at various stages of their development, and what society may and may not expect of its schools. Indeed, we are proceeding on hunches, reinforced though we may be by Bruner and his scholars:

> Nor need we wait for all the research findings to be in before proceeding, for a skillful teacher can . . . teach what seems to be intuitively right for children of different ages, correcting as he goes.[3]

Turning from this obscure and evasive topic, let us examine some of the more substantive pieces of investigation in Winnetka's current classrooms, with apologies for their brevity of treatment.

The Academic Underachiever

Since the fall of 1959, we have been engaged in fairly intensive research on the child we call (acknowledging the semantic pitfalls)

---

[2] *Ibid.*, p. 43.
[3] *Op. cit.*, Bruner.

the *academic underachiever*. Our study is supported by a modest foundation grant, providing the half-time services of a project coordinator. Our definition for the academic underachiever is the child with high academic potential, with low or inconsistent school achievement. Identification of underachievers rests partly upon the psychological test, but, more importantly, upon teacher and peer evaluation, as well as self-selection. In the latter three categories we have found a significantly consistent pattern of identification.

Believing that underachievement is closely related to lack of motivation, we have concentrated our study on the child's self-concept. Hypothesizing that academic underachievement is in some way explained as a cultural phenomenon deriving from a gap between the child's activities and interests and those of the adult world, we have sought to bridge this gap by establishing a close and cordial intellectual partnership between the underachiever and a successful cooperating adult. Carrying the rationale a bit further, we believe that the increasing specialization and corresponding obscurity of adult vocation, particularly in the case of the father or grandfather, leaves the child with no clear appreciation for "what it takes to be a responsible, successful grownup."

For our adult partners we have selected a number of retired men and women, all over age 65, whose career histories and interests range from navigation to poultry raising, and from electronics to surgery. These senior citizens work voluntarily with a selected pair of academic underachievers (presently limited to Grades III, IV, and V) during a 45-minute period a week, in a conference room separated from the class. The "instruction" may have to do with the excavation of the Dead Sea scrolls, or how an electric coil functions, or the mathematics of bicycle wheels and gears. In any case, the regular classroom teacher manages to adapt the activities of the classroom so that, upon completing a session with the senior citizen, the pair of underachievers return to their classroom with a report, a demonstration, or a project for display, the purpose of which is to give the underachiever a new view of himself as an effective intellectual performer. The senior citizens and the teachers concerned are assigned, coached and scheduled by the coordinator. The coordinator also secures initial concurrence from the parents, and keeps the parents and teachers closely informed of progress.

While it is early to declare the outcomes of this investigation, we

Photo 4: Senior Citizens share their projects with program coordinator. "Seniors" serve as volunteers in working with the Academic Underachiever program.

have reason to be optimistic. The first two years of the project were limited to some 12 third grade children in a pilot study. Currently, we have formalized the study more systematically, with 36 children identified among 18 classrooms, and with a corresponding 36 matched underachievers serving as the control group. Our observations over the past two years of the pilot study indicate that something very good (we are not sure just what) happens to the child in this experiment. The 120 or 130 I.Q. youngster in many instances begins, after a year or so, to perform more closely in accordance with his potential. Perhaps he would have anyway. We will know more after another year or two. It is possible that we will have some worthwhile clues to the mysteries of the "slow starter" or the "late bloomer" who have for so long frustrated teachers and principals. (A not insignificant by-product of this activity is the wonderful spirit of purpose and fulfillment that our senior citizens seem to derive from their teaching. It is not uncommon for a senior to spend 8-10 hours preparing for his 45-minute "class." The pupil-teacher ratio is *luxurious!* All the senior citizens are volunteers.)

There is no special rank order to these items being reported in this chapter. If any sequence is discernible, it is coincidental. If any arrangement exists, it is prompted only by my effort to respond to the varying appetites of the reader.

Teaching about Communism in Public Schools

Following a year of study by a small faculty committee, culminating in a system-wide workshop, we are considering an extension of our social studies curriculum which will introduce elementary concepts of international communism as a subject to be learned in junior high school. We are well aware of the pitfalls attaching to this proposition, not the least of which is community understanding. Another major uncertainty lies in whether the prevailing mood of pupils, teachers, press media and government permit the subject to be examined rationally, unemotionally and free of indoctrination. Materials of instruction, suitable for the Junior High age group, leave much to be desired. Yet, a careful screening of journal articles, editorial comment and the publications of concerned national organizations appears to show promise.

In confronting the question of teaching about communism our Board of Education knew that community feelings could run high on the question, with the possibility of an unhappy "choosing of sides" in the public arena. Therefore, before taking a positive position on the subject, but encouraging continued faculty planning, they urged the superintendent to seek opportunities to open the question publicly. Over a period of several weeks I found occasions to speak to P.T.A.'s and other groups, describing what appeared to be a growing need for confrontation in the schools, and some of the possible solutions that the faculty had developed. At each of these meetings the audience was urged to express in a letter to the superintendent or the Board of Education any admonitions or apprehensions toward the proposition. Interestingly, and contrary to what some of the Board members had expected, very warm support (or silent acceptance) came from what might be classified as the conservative arm of the community. Those in education will appreciate that only a very few years ago, adventures in this direction would have been condemned as dangerously radical by the conservative community. In our case, strong opposition and concern was voiced by those who feared violation of civil rights, and who mistrusted the objectivity of the schools. Their concern was honest and reasonable on the whole, and we took careful note of admonitions against "thought control" and the teaching of hatred. As in all controversy concerned with education, it is clear that more good than bad comes from the clash of conflicting viewpoints, and the ultimate decisions are wiser and more enduring when they grow from the labored reconciliation of differences.

As we continue to weigh the question, and seek a sound solution in 1963, we continue to feel the obligation to face the task, rather than turn away from it, in the face of controversy. There are several reasons:

1. We feel that our prior and transcending task is the teaching of the processes and obligations of American freedom. American freedom (so easily taken for granted) seems to us to carry greater promise when illuminated factually and unemotionally in the shadow of totalitarianism.

2. Children *are* learning about communism, inescapably. Press, television, jokes and cartoons, adult conversation and, of course, the implications of military preparedness and anxiety surround

these children in and out of school. Their curbstone impressions of international communism tend to be superficial, erroneous, hate-producing and fearful. Rational classroom disclosure of facts appears to be an obligation of the schools.

3. Finally, as observed by one of our patron-correspondents (and incidentally a highly respected liberal leader of our community, who departed in this controversy from his companions): "When we realize that over half the world is under the domination of an alien and hostile political system, it is inescapable that our children, at all ages, must be taught to live intelligently with this condition. I respect the competence of the Winnetka Schools to perform this added dimension in their curriculum."

During the next year we will very likely complete our lay faculty study of this question, resulting in a supplement to the Social Studies curriculum, starting lightly at Grade V perhaps and proceeding through Junior High School. The approach will very probably be in the categories of history, geography and economics, with political and ideological dimensions treated at Grade VIII, if at all, following the study of the Constitution, Bill of Rights and the other great instruments of freedom.

The Role of the Consultant

As educational organization continues to change in the national scene, with Trump's variable class sizes and the team teaching concept currently under persuasive scrutiny, we are increasingly aware of the strategic importance of the highly specialized teacher, and his relationship to the "general" teacher. With the tremendous burgeoning of knowledge, particularly in technical-scientific fields, we are concerned about the futility of keeping general classroom teachers in the elementary grades current and competent in some of the subjects they must teach, notably science and mathematics. (Although we believe that our current research is relevant to all special teachers, quite apart from the current science-technology interest.)

For some years we have had an active *science consultant* in the Winnetka Schools. In the late 1950's we expanded this position from one to two individuals, each called science consultant, for deployment among four schools, affecting some 2,000 children. One individual was strong in the biological sciences, the other in the physical sciences. We were concerned (and still are) with the most efficient use of the consultant's time and energies. Admitting that highly trained and uniquely competent specialists in this field or any other (to include mathematics, music, art, reading, speech, drama, etc.) will never be available in abundance, we sought to determine the types of teaching activities by the consultant which produced the largest academic gain in children. In short, this has been a study of productivity.

We have spent two years, with the vigorous support of the University of Chicago staff members, pursuing this inquiry. We sought answers to these questions: Is the consultant, given a fixed number of hours per week, more effective as a person-to-person resource for the "generalist" classroom teacher? Is he more effective, given the same amount of time, displacing the classroom teacher—an itinerant, spreading himself among many classrooms for short periods? Is he more effective as the teacher of a large group, say two or three classrooms combined, for more frequent periods of instruction than would be possible in conventional class groups?

At the end of the first year, following pre-testing and post-testing, with a tightly structured and scheduled itinerary for the two consultants, we thought we had the answer. Situation One called for the consultant to provide direct counsel, support, motivation, teaching materials, suggestions, amplifications to the general classroom teacher in half of our Grades VI. In Situation Two, the consultant gave an equal amount of time afforded in Situation One to direct classroom teaching, superseding the classroom teacher once a week. The outcome, as Ginther of Chicago put it, was favorable to Situation One:

> The resulting F was 6.3 which, for the given degree of freedom yielded P between .05 and .01. Indeed, the hypothesis (that no significant difference would derive) had to be rejected. There seemed to be a significant difference in gain-scores between Situation One and Situation Two, with Situation One having the advantage.[4]

Not satisfied that we had eliminated the variance inherent in the differing competencies of the general classroom teachers, we replicated

---

[4] Ginther, John R., *Achievement in Sixth Grade Science Associated with Two Roles of Science Consultants*, Dembar Publications, Inc., Madison, Wis.

the exercise in the fall of 1960, with situations reversed. To our disappointment, we found no significant difference between the two situations. We are continuing to pursue what we believe is an important question in school organization in spite of the limited outcomes to date.

The project is by no means without profit thus far. John Fritz, companion to Ginther in this investigation, reports certain by-products of the inquiry as follows:

> In contrast to the findings of last year no significant differences were found in the achievement of students in the two situations. (Last year, student achievement favored the classes that were taught conventionally.) However, data dealing with the sensed competency of teachers as indicated on the pre- and post-teacher opinionnaires tended to follow the pattern observed in last year's results: The teachers in the conventional situation assessed themselves as slightly more competent at the end of the unit; the teachers for whom the science consultants taught one-third of their classes (the teachers observed and recorded specified activities on observation schedules on these occasions) perceived themselves as somewhat less competent at the end when compared to their self-assessment at the beginning of the project. Evidently, though the post-mean differences on the two scales of "familiarity" and "teaching" between the two groups of teachers were not statistically significant, the data of both years suggest that teachers in the conventional teaching structure tended to perceive themselves as relatively more competent at the end of the units in comparison to the teachers who enjoyed the presumed advantage of observing the consultants teach some of their classes directly. Despite this tendency in perceived sensed competence, post-achievement test results of the teachers favored neither group.
>
> If there is a tendency toward relatively lower self-appraisal of teaching competence in situations where classroom teachers share the burden of direct teaching with "master teachers," then schools, attempting to upgrade the quality of instruction through a wider sharing of the expert teacher in team teaching projects or through television, may have to reckon with the effect of such programs on the classroom teacher's perceptions of himself as a professionally competent individual. In such efforts, one of whose primary purposes is the generation of continued professional growth of the teacher, careful attention will have to be directed at the nature of the teacher's prevailing self-concept, personality differences that reflect themselves in the capacity to tolerate and exploit the discrepancy or gap between his present adequacy or "real" professional self and his projection of what he might or could become—his perception of the possible—and, perhaps more important, the measures of group and individual support and encouragement that schools may introduce in programs designed to foster the continued growth in professional competence of the teacher now in the classroom.[5]

[5] Fritz, John, *Faculty Memo*, Graduate School of Education, University of Chicago, June 15, 1961.

Personnel Policies, Including
Teacher Compensation

In the spring and summer of 1957, acting upon instructions from the Board of Education, a citizens' advisory committee on teachers' salaries worked for eight months to produce a design for professional compensation that was described at the time by *The New York Times* as "the first major breakthrough in teachers' salaries." Adopted with minor adjustments by the Board of Education, and ratified by a five to one ratio of referendum support in the community, this schedule has been perhaps the most significant of Winnetka's contributions to education at large in the current period. The 73-page report of the Advisory Committee, selling for fifty cents, went through four printings before we gave up and compressed its message into a few mimeographed pages for more convenient distribution. After six years our mail continues to indicate a high interest in this subject; the requests for public addresses and panel participation by our professional staff and Board members are frequent. Thus, we may assume that, at least to a degree, one of the criteria which the lay committee set for itself is being fulfilled:

> *To contribute an uplifting influence to the dignity and prestige of teaching in the United States.*
>
> Of course we will not guarantee that this schedule will have immediate and far-reaching consequence among teachers everywhere. We hope it will. We are firmly convinced that the significance of salaries in the $10,000 to $12,000 bracket for competent teachers as they near the peak of their teaching careers will far exceed the dollars involved.
>
> We have studied the record of teachers' salaries throughout the country over the past 50 years. We have examined the familiar statistics of salary comparisons with truck drivers, bartenders, baggage men . . . with teachers' salaries following behind. We have examined the progress of salaries in the other professions, again with teachers far behind. . . . One of the difficulties of establishing clear-cut data on comparisons over the years is that we question whether at any time in our history the teacher enjoyed a recognition in salary and social standing anywhere nearly consistent with his crucial place in our culture.
>
> About 1933-34 the average teacher's salary was approximately the same as the average employed person's salary in the United States. Since that date, in spite of steady and encouraging increases in teachers' salaries, the average salaries of all others have moved ahead faster.
>
> We believe that the people of this country do not deliberately choose to pay their teachers so little. We believe the present condition is a product of inertia and general lack of information. We believe that fundamental American

values regarding the place of the teacher must be illuminated. The average citizen and taxpayer would probably be startled to learn that he pays twice as much for liquor and tobacco as he does for education . . . or that he pays $1.75 for amusements against every dollar he pays for education.

American education is heavily subsidized by the teachers themselves— through underpayment. The typical Winnetka household pays a school tax of about $200-$400 a year. The typical Winnetka teacher makes a far greater contribution through failure to receive a salary commensurate with the value of his services. What is true here is true almost universally. Winnetka has long enjoyed a leading place in American education as well as in many other walks of life. Winnetka has a responsibility to assume leadership in the field of teacher salaries, to establish standards to which other communities may aspire. What Winnetka does, for good or bad, has implications far beyond the bounds of our Village. This your committee has kept in mind in formulating its conclusions.[6]

I offer this extract of the report to reveal the flavor and spirit that is attainable in the workings of lay advisory committees in education. Indeed, a Superintendent of Schools, or a teachers' organization, or even a Board of Education could not say these things without overtones of self-pity, self-service, or argumentation. When lay citizens speak this way the message is completely different.

Perhaps the most dramatic element of our salary policy, which attracted the most attention at the time, was the provision for classroom teachers to aspire to $12,000 salaries. Other communities have subsequently equalled or surpassed this figure. But there are more subtle and far-reaching implications of the design which I feel are more enduring and revolutionary, if less dramatic. One of the features of the citizens' report which has been widely misunderstood, and which continues to be a subject of keen interest among school administrators, is the treatment of merit rating. Here is one of the subtleties of the design which holds high promise for education. The citizens committee had conceived what they chose to call an *incentive schedule*, with opportunities for teachers *to elect to assume the responsibilities* leading to higher salary recognition. Further, they prescribed checks and balances for this process, including the *non-automatic increment*, and the requirement for *pre-approval* of teachers' contemplated in-service growth activities by the administration and a faculty committee before salary recognition could follow. Having created this design, these business

---

[6] Report of the Citizens' Advisory Committee on Teacher Salaries, Winnetka, Illinois, January, 1958 (out of print).

men and professional men took their stand on merit rating in its *conventional check-listing, quantitative, competitive form:*

> Superficially, the idea of merit rating is appealing. We are inclined to assume that since human beings differ in their competencies, they should be rewarded according to their worth. This would call for some device that measures the effectiveness of teaching, either subjectively or objectively. However, teaching is an art as well as a science. There is no known device which objectively measures teaching competency, even though this goal has been vigorously pursued by educators for many years.

> But quite apart from the lack of valid foundations for measuring teaching competency, your committee feels that the end purposes of education should be examined before assuming that merit rating has a place in education at this time. We found that education in Winnetka calls for a very high degree of cooperation and unity. We found that the pupil as the object of education is the product of many human influences, working in harmony and good faith.

> If it is our purpose, and we believe it is, to design compensation policies that will produce a better product, a better program, a better educational design for Winnetka, we do not believe this would be achieved by merit rating. We do not feel that good teachers, now giving all the energy they can offer to children, will somehow discover more energy under a merit system. Nor do we feel that teachers with less devotion and concern will necessarily struggle to do better for reasons of such limited financial differential as can be incorporated in a merit salary device. This is primarily a problem of the administrative and supervisory staff. We do not feel that the competitive implications of merit awards are consistent with the cooperative and mutually helpful practices which now characterize our faculty. We do not think the role of the Superintendent as a leader and stimulator and object of faith and good will would be enhanced if he were also the rater, the distributor of financial awards, the judge and jury, as well as counsel.

> There is frequently a predisposition in favor of merit rating in principle on the part of businessmen because of the generally prevailing business practice of seeking to compensate employes in terms of their relative worth. Even in business, however, where individual performance is much more susceptible to objective measurement and evaluation, merit rating in the strict sense can be applied to only a limited degree. Salary differentials between various jobs are primarily historical in character, or the result of competitive pressures, and only secondarily a consequence of rational determination. Salary differentials between individuals in the same job categories are often more a reflection of relative length of service than of measured differences in performance. This is not very different, although much less clear-cut, from general practice in education.

> Most businessmen who have had experience with formal systems of rating employees on the elements comprising their jobs will testify to the artificiality and restricted value of such procedures, recognizing that in the end chief reliance is likely to be placed on judgments that are largely subjective. The classic industrial example of reward according to merit is found in systems of incentive compensation, where employees are paid on the basis of output. Such plans are clearly inapplicable to education for there is no way of measuring

output on a "piece work" basis. Incentive methods of compensation, moreover, are likely to be complicated and to require considerable management. It has been one of the basic findings of human relations research in industry during the past quarter-century that economic incentives have only limited utility in encouraging superior performance, and that they often create special problems of morale and of supervisory-employee relations.

In the opinion of the committee, the experience of industry does not indicate that merit rating as that term is generally understood could be successfully adapted to education. However, we feel that the schedule and policy we have designed fulfill the desirable feature of acknowledging superior professional service where it is demonstrated. We believe that inferior professional service can be treated as such under this schedule. Beyond these features we are not prepared to venture further in the merit field.[7]

Among other less obvious but highly significant features of this design is the spirit of professionalism that is implicit in the relationship between dollars and teachers' time. Teachers and administrators have long been harassed by the unprofessional implication of "piece work" attaching to odd bits of pay for odd bits of professional work by teachers beyond the customary working day. The committee took the position that teachers are professional people, that under the proposed design they would begin to realize, relatively speaking, professional salaries; that their hours should not be counted as those of piece workers. In its passages directed primarily toward teachers the report stated:

We expect the Winnetka faculty to participate actively and vigorously in finding ways for teachers to increase substantially their efficiency in working with children.... Teachers are a rare commodity.... We establish as a condition of the new schedule that the Board of Education and the teachers search for ways to [increase productivity through] higher performance, and, if necessary, longer hours and harder work by all concerned, consistent with the higher salaries prescribed....[8]

The reader may be startled by this admonition to teachers, as was our faculty. Recoiling at first, and then rallying through the Planning and Advisory Committee, the faculty accepted the challenge along with the marked salary improvements. It is only because of this acceptance that the tremendous volume of curricular revision, research, and the writing of instructional materials has been possible during these past few years. The faculty rose to the lay committee's challenge; hardly

---

[7] *Op. cit.,* pp. 16-18.
[8] *Op. cit.,* pp. 45-46.

an afternoon between four and six is without two or three professional committee meetings. Saturday mornings and vacation periods are not sacred. During each of the past three summers volunteer teachers numbering up to a third of our faculty at times have worked up to two weeks beyond the close of school.

Finalizing this condition, largely for the benefit of new teachers joining our staff, the Planning and Advisory Committee of the Faculty adopted the following statement on April 2, 1959, three months after the lay committee's report had been published:

> The "contract year" is defined as 176 teaching days, plus two or three days of teacher institutes, as set by law. The responsibilities of a Winnetka teacher, in addition to classroom teaching, may include, when need arises, a reasonable number of days beyond the conventional school year, at a time mutually convenient. It is further held that professional work to be performed should be distributed as justly as possible among those qualified to perform it.

It must be noted that this arrangement is not a device for "getting more work out of teachers without paying them." It is intended to give teachers an improved view of themselves as important professional people, with a feeling of freedom to contribute actively to their profession without appearing to be different or self-seeking. Professional work beyond the school day and school year is the standard, rather than the exception. Insofar as compensation is concerned, teachers are earning up to $4,000 more per year than they did under the earlier salary design—far more than they would ever earn in the "bits and pieces" of extra pay for extra duties. (Those teachers carrying out a major task beyond the classroom, such as writing a local textbook, often work beyond the "reasonable" expectation. In such cases the Board of Education pays a modest supplementary stipend.)

In addition to the dollars of the salary schedule, and the subtleties of increased professional dignity implicit in the foregoing expositions, the compensation design carried other benefits, including shared costs of health, major medical and life insurance. Further, the Board of Education pays full premiums for a supplemental annuity above and beyond the benefits of the teachers' retirement system.

The design, while essentially the creative product of a lay advisory committee working in close companionship with the administration, was shared constantly, step by step during its development with the Welfare Committee of the faculty. As its final dimensions began to take form, the Welfare Committee (normally, that militant body of teachers who periodically, according to the rules, must shed their teacher's mantle, in order to "negotiate," "demand," "bargain") declared that the pattern of compensation was far beyond anything that they would have recommended. Correspondingly, I am certain that if the Citizens' Advisory Committee or the Board of Education had been circumscribed in their deliberations by having to confront a Welfare Committee of negotiators across the table, nothing significant would have come of this study.

School-Home Relations

Without claiming uniqueness, and certainty acknowledging our own imperfect and evolving arrangements, I offer this subject particularly to the deeply interested school patron or the student of school administration who finds an interest in us as a case study. This topic might well be named *public relations, community relations, public understanding,* or some other similar term. In any case, we place the highest possible importance on this subject, knowing full well that, if at the moment we enjoy strong support and apparent high faith from the community, this condition could change suddenly through errors of judgment, accidents of timing, faulty or non-existent communication.

An expression of the community's feeling toward its schools was made concrete in early 1961 when the municipal government engaged the services of the Center for Metropolitan Studies at Northwestern University for a survey of community attitudes on many subjects. Given an opportunity to reveal their feelings toward the schools, 95% of the respondents indicated satisfaction, with 5% dissatisfied. Regretting sincerely the unhappy 5%, and struggling to win their regard, we find gratification in the 95%, acknowledging that schools and children are likely to be the object of far more volatile emotional concern and divisiveness than streets, sidewalks, police service, parks and utilities. In any case, we accept with very real humility, and no smugness whatsoever, the evidence that most of the people in town have a good feeling toward their schools. This section is intended to examine how this condition may be accounted for, and the means we employ for school-

home relations. Lawrence A. Cremins in his scholarly and vivid analysis
of education's recent history makes the point:

> The surprising thing about the assault [against progressive education] of
> the fifties is not that the [progressive] movement collapsed, but that it collapsed
> so readily. . . . Given the political realities of American education, no program
> can survive that ceases to assiduously cultivate lay support. . . . They [the progres-
> sives] committed a supreme blunder during the thirties when they allowed the
> movement itself to become professionalized.[9]

Whether or not this accusation is relevant to Winnetka during the
1930's or the 1940's, I cannot say. I do know that in 1956 when I proposed to the Board of Education and the faculty substantial lay involvement in the affairs of education, there were earnest exclamations of
surprise, and anxiety and expressions of "abdication of our responsibilities" and "invasion of academic freedom." The ensuing years have
brought a full understanding and appreciation of this process to the
Board and the faculty, with the result that lay participation has become
normal and expected.

But, starting at a much more basic and concrete level, the most important single instrument of our school-home relations is the parent-
teacher conference. Formally scheduled at all levels two or three times
a year, in lieu of report cards, the conference, lasting upwards of a half
hour, and preferably attended by both parents, is the central means of
communication. Face to face, sharply focused, and deeply motivated
toward mutual understanding of a very special and precious human
being, the parties to the conference establish, by and large, a communion of spirit translating our schools and our purposes as they relate
specifically to the needs and growth of the individual child under consideration. This calls for highly skilled teachers, a mutually respectful
setting, and unhurried time for studious preparation for the conference
by both parties. We encourage absolute candor in the exchange of information. We find this process, not only our key to public relations,
but also a far more relevant instrument for reporting pupil progress
than marks or grades. New teachers joining us, even though experienced
perhaps in the parent-teacher conference technique, undergo intensive
instruction in our processes, generally finding them more extensive and
systematic than those experienced elsewhere. An essential feature of

---

[9] Cremins, Lawrence A., *The Transformation of the School*, Alfred A. Knopf,
N.Y., 1961, pp. 347-350.

our conference is the *Conference Guide and Record,* a four-page form which is sent home in blank to the parent before the conference for study and preparation in the categories about which information and counsel are to be exchanged. The teacher spends up to three or four hours in preparation for a given conference. (*See* Appendix B, Parent Conference Guide and Record.)

There is little foot-dragging on the part of parents in their response to the conference calendar. While not all of our teachers excel in this sensitive role, the general quality of the conference has earned the genuine respect of parents. We still provide a narrative and check list report card, in addition to the conferences, above Grade III, twice a year. We count the conferences as the more rewarding of the two media.

The next step removed from the parent-teacher conference is the principal, in his role as communicator and interpreter of his school. Through the use of P.T.A. committees and the parent organization as a whole, the principal makes constant and effective use of lay counsel in the day-to-day decisions affecting his pupils and teachers. The limitations of the P.T.A., as relating to involvement in matters of school administration, are clearly defined in Board of Education policies, precluding the invasion of the principal's responsibilities in the affairs of his school. However, on the *principal's initiative,* issues are raised and resolved with the P.T.A.'s help, by and large resulting in wiser decisions than would be true without the lay involvement.

The role of the principal in the one-to-one relationship with parents is wholly as significant as that of the teacher. Quite often problems concerning an individual child reach dimensions beyond those with which the teacher can deal effectively. In such cases the principal, in conference with the parent, performs what is probably his most important single function, that of chief counselor in his school. Acknowledging that problems of sufficient gravity to warrant the principal's direct involvement are often fraught with hostility, emotion and defensiveness, the principal's execution of this task becomes all the more strategic in terms of school-home relations.

At the system-wide level there are numerous, though less individualized, instruments for communication. The superintendent meets monthly with the Central P.T.A. Board, bringing together some 35 officers and committee members as well as school principals from all the P.T.A.'s. This group becomes, for all practical purposes, a continuing lay-professional advisory body on broad policy matters. At times, subjects are aired confidentially before this group even before being considered by the Board of Education. At other times, new policies, possibly possessing the marks of controversy, while being deliberated by the Board of Education are put before this group for reactions and recommendations. There is a spirit of genuine shared responsibility in these sessions which the administration treats with the highest respect, and which the lay members appear to enjoy.

There are, of course, the usual expectations for the Superintendent of Schools, the central staff, and the faculty to be on call to any and all parts of the community, where we welcome invitations to explain the schools. The Superintendent of Schools assumes, as part of his normal duties, the involvement in church, civic, recreational and social groups, where, *without end*, questions concerning the schools abound. People may not always like my answers, but at least they know they can get at me to argue their points. Most of the argument is of a cordial tone, and offered in good faith.

Finally, under this topic, I would mention again the place of lay advisory committees. The term *advisory* is intentionally expressed, and is clarified with all concerned at the start of a period of work. An earlier section gave prominence to the function of the lay advisory committee on teacher salaries, which is a case in point. The Board of Education, upon inviting the committee to serve, and naming its chairman, reserves the right to accept or reject the committee's recommendations. If a committee does its work well, and if the Board of Education through one of its members and the Superintendent of Schools retains active liaison with the committee (which is absolutely essential), then the two groups will never find themselves very far apart. If the Board, having named a lay committee to an important task, and having received the committee's recommendations, fails broadly to concur in the recommendations, it does so at its peril. For future committees will be doubtful of their own importance, and will be less ready to make personal sacrifices for the task to be done. The function of the school administration as articulator, translator, communicator, guide and professional consultant to both the Board and the lay committee is paramount to the success of the proposition.

Early in my membership in Winnetka, it became clear that a substantial body of citizens were dissatisfied with some elements of our

Photo 5: Citizens' Advisory Committees, working with the faculty and the administration, have been active in Winnetka's educational evolution. Dr. Marland (center) counsels curriculum committee of citizens and teachers in the checks and balances inherent in roles of each.

school program. Probably the most important single act of community relations was undertaken in January of 1958, the middle of my second year. We announced a general meeting, at which the superintendent would speak upon his over-all appraisal of the school program and would provide the means for all concerned to express their views, their dissatisfactions, their complaints and their criticisms. The largest auditorium was packed, with many standing. At the conclusion of the address, prepared forms were distributed, on which those in attendance were encouraged to indicate the areas of their concern, *i.e.*, report card procedures, insufficient homework, pupil discipline, excessive social emphasis, etc. No speech-making from the floor was allowed. Those with concerns and criticisms were advised that in the weeks following the meeting, they would be invited to sit in quiet council with appropriate faculty members, and with other parents of like interests, to explore in detail the facts relating to their dissatisfactions.

I have yet to discover any useful purposes served by "remarks from the floor" in the audiences relating to educational controversy. Issues may be aired, it is true. But the airing of issues generally reveals a highly subjective and partially informed spokesman, who necessarily speaks in an emotion-charged environment. There is nothing wrong with this, except that such measures *do not lead to solutions.* They merely tend to put the faculty or the Board of Education or some other body of protagonists on the defensive, in which position neither an army nor a school system is likely to accomplish forward movement. Solutions derive from quiet discourse within small groups of individuals who are willing to take the trouble to become *informed in depth* before taking a position. In school matters, such groups should have the benefit of professional counsel *at all times.* Every school problem I know about is a subtle and complex problem, having no glib, black-and-white solutions. Solutions are discovered only after deliberation and study, in an atmosphere of honesty and reasonableness.

Following the meeting, the returns were tabulated, resulting in nine study groups, ranging in size from 10 to 35 members, each identified with a separate area of concern. A faculty chairman was named to lead each study group, and two or three teachers, chosen for their relevance to the subject, were asked to serve with the laymen. A few of the groups met two or three times that winter, completed their investigation, apparently satisfied their anxieties, and discharged themselves.

Others, confronting more complex issues, continued actively for six months or more, concluding their work with sober recommendations to the Board of Education suggesting constructive changes. In nearly all cases teachers and laymen reached a position of consensus, deriving from a study of the issues *in depth*, as distinguished from the superficial discourse often characterized as "cocktail conferences."In any case, the school administration and the Board of Education took the recommendations seriously and introduced a number of constructive changes. More important, by sending a letter to each of the 150 or more lay participants in the several study groups reporting the outcomes of the several studies, the administration gained a spirit of general warmth and affirmation in the community by making it clear that criticisms could receive sober attention, be they unfounded or of the kind that could lead to constructive change. The cocktail conferences took on a different color that winter; invalid as they are, superficial as they are, they are one of the weather vanes of public feeling in a suburban school system. We preferred to have them aiming in our direction.

As an example of the type of Board of Education action which initiates the lay advisory committee, the memorandum below is typical. First the Board of Education had selected the membership of the lay advisory committee, numbering eight couples, from a list of some 40 to 50 suggestions solicited from the P.T.A. leadership. Then each had been invited by the Board of Education chairman to serve. Following a receipt of acceptances, the following memorandum was reviewed and edited in a Board of Education meeting, then conveyed to the newly appointed committee, with information copies furnished to the members of the faculty committee who would be working with the laymen. This particular memorandum happens to be the most recent in point of time, but it follows the same scope and sequence of numerous similar "charges" that had been furnished by the Board to other lay advisory committees:

Memorandum to the
Lay Advisory Committee on
Teaching the Values of Freedom
in a Divided World

The Board of Education is grateful for your willingness to assist in the assessment of our social studies curriculum. Our Board has selected you from a list of names proposed by the several P.T.A.'s. This memorandum seeks to describe the lay committee's general role in relation to the Board of Education, and to offer specific guidance in the task at hand.

We believe that the practice of engaging the assistance of advisory committees of citizens to share in the development of educational policy in close partnership with the faculty serves the following purposes:

a. An advisory committee, named for a given task, is able to devote its energies *in depth* to a given assignment, serving as an informal extension of the Board of Education. While the Board of Education is occupied with numerous and varied tasks, the advisory committee, with active liaison membership from the Board of Education, can devote itself completely to the one task at hand.

b. The advisory committee, by its representative nature, brings to the Board of Education a wide spectrum of community judgment and insight, increasing the Board's basis for ultimate policy determination.

c. The members of the advisory committee serve as interpreters for increasing the communication between the schools and the community, drawing upon their knowledge of the faculty and the instructional program.

d. Specialized training, experience and competence can be enlisted for the confrontation of problems for which the Board of Education and the faculty may be less well equipped.

We invite your committee to address itself basically to the following questions: Is there a new mandate from our American society at large calling for education at large to apply itself more intensively to the cultivation of the values of freedom in the generations now in our schools? If such a mandate is emerging, in what ways shall the schools respond, without departing from the very processes of freedom which we seek to enhance? Has the increasing scope of international communism as a force in the lives of our people generated a need for a re-evaluation of elements of our present social studies curriculum? Can the affirmative values of freedom be more meaningfully and realistically learned by children, in the context of comparison and appraisal against the practices of international communism? Can the scope and objectives implied in the foregoing questions be made relevant to the child of the upper elementary grades without running the risk of instilling anxiety in the child, or detracting from the transcending goals of world brotherhood and understanding?

These are large questions, in which the faculty have been deeply concerned for the past two years. Starting in January 1960, a faculty retreat first explored these questions, giving rise to a continuing inquiry within the staff during the ensuing period. As a starting point, a small faculty committee has drafted a tentative revision to the social studies curriculum, for Grades V through VIII, including additional instructional material. The revision treats the reality of international communism as elements of history, economics, politics and geography along with the many other social studies learnings of the schools.

In cooperation with the faculty committee, the lay advisory committee is asked to study this design in the light of the questions raised above. It is expected that the draft may undergo substantial changes through your collaboration with the staff. Or indeed, following study, your committee may recommend no action in this direction at this time.

The Board of Education will designate one of its members to work closely with you, as will Dr. Marland, our superintendent. When you have completed your work, we will be grateful for your report and recommendations. The Board of Education will then apply itself to your suggestions, acknowledging and reserving the obligation to take full responsibility for the ultimate instructional program that may be designed.

Winnetka has little company at this time, as far as we know, in pursuing these profound questions. We have, historically, endeavored to press to the front of educational evolution, as we have been doing recently in other subject areas. Whatever we do here will be observed thoughtfully by educators beyond our community.

C. B. McDougal,
President, Board of Education

The involvement of lay committees does *not* threaten the teacher, *if the initiative and guidance is retained by the Board of Education and the school leadership.* The employment of lay committees *does not imply the abdication of the Board of Education.* On the contrary, if the Board is big enough to examine the immensity of its task, and to know that it could not, if it would, devote the time and energy necessary to study each important issue in depth, it will find that its decisions will be wiser, community acceptance more prompt, and its own task enriched and heightened by sharing large problems with other citizens serving as advisors. We have used lay advisory committees in many areas including, beyond the salary committee, each curriculum area, plant, school organization, civil defense, and other similar fields, each one of which calls for study in depth.

If we, at this time, are traveling with a favorable wind in school-home relations, we believe this condition derives first from devoted and skillful teachers, willing to spend the extra hours for person-to-person communication, and secondly from the total attitude of Board, faculty and administration which welcomes honest and responsible citizens into the study of education's affairs, reminding ourselves as responsible professionals that we are also the servants of society. We work hard at this task . . . we count it as something much larger than public relations.

Adventures in Learning

This is the name we have attached to our summer school. Starting in 1959, under the perceptive leadership of veteran Winnetka teacher Odeyne Gillett, our summer offering was transformed from what had

been a recreation-centered and remedial-centered offering to a demanding academic and creative offering with numerous experimental overtones. Wholly supported by tuition, and staffed by volunteer Winnetka
teachers who take their chances on how much the tuition kitty will
afford in salaries, the program occupies the morning hours for six weeks
after the close of school each June. The offerings range from typing and
journalism to chemistry; from modern mathematics to homemaking;
from drama to music composition and harmony. Children of kinder-
garten-primary level pursue a creative program surrounding a given
project for the term, with high emphasis on field trips and the library.
All other children, irrespective of age or grade, are grouped by "centers
of interest." Strange as it sounds, a fourth grader and a seventh grader,
sitting side by side, seem to flourish, according to their maturity, when
exploring the identical topic at hand—let us say, molecular construction.
Classes average about 12-15 children in number. Participation is wholly
voluntary. Most children enroll because they want to; a few because
their parents think it a good idea. The former profit more.

The Perceptually Handicapped Child

With a long history of concern and attention to the child with
physical or mental handicaps, the Winnetka Schools in 1959 were instrumental in organizing and systematizing a large regional school district, embracing some 23 communities for cooperative services to the
handicapped. As state laws, not only in Illinois but in the nation at
large, began to encourage attention to special education during the
1950's, the usual listings of exceptional categories included the educable
mentally handicapped, the trainable mentally handicapped, the ortho-
pedically handicapped, the deaf and hard-of-hearing, the visually handicapped and the speech handicapped. As we pursued the necessary surveys leading to the regional organization, we became more and more
aware of an exceptional child about whom very little is known, and
who is not ordinarily listed among the categories of special education—
the perceptually handicapped child. We found that in an enrollment
such as ours, in the neighborhood of 2,300 pupils, there were to be
expected, typically, eight or ten educable mentally handicapped, two
or three trainable, one or two orthopedic, the same in sight-saving and
deaf, perhaps 10 in hard-of-hearing. But to our great concern, as we

came to know more about the subject, the unlisted and undeclared category of "perceptually handicapped" produced 30 or 40 children. These children were enrolled in our regular classes.

Perhaps we were especially alert to this category for reason of the proximity of Cove School in nearby Evanston, one of the few private institutions concerned exclusively with the perceptually handicapped. We were convinced that many other communities, like ourselves, had significant numbers of these children enrolled, and had (as we had done) classified them simply as slow learners, emotionally disturbed, or both. Without attempting here a full and scientific definition of the perceptually handicapped, we describe him as a child with limitations in his learning function, resulting from brain damage, yet possessing normal intelligence. The symptoms are obscure and are not readily diagnosed. Yet we have begun to learn much about this handicap.

With the initial support of a local foundation, and under the direction of Newton Calhoun, our extremely able school psychologist, we have trained a teacher through a year's internship at Cove School, and at Syracuse University, and have begun a limited program for six of the 30 or more children now in our classes. The experiment is under the guidance of a staff of expert consultants who meet monthly with the administration to suggest procedures and evaluate progress. We are fortunate in having the Director of Cove School as a member of this committee. The teacher of the perceptually handicapped works for about an hour a day with each child, taking him from his regular classroom to a separate room for this specialized, patient, ever-so-labored instruction.

Perhaps in four or five years we will have some useful evidence for others. We establish as the hypothesis for this experiment that there are many more perceptually handicapped children than most schools realize, and that there are ways, *within the public school context,* to provide a successful learning experience for these children, in order that their intellectual potential may be fulfilled. They are not mentally handicapped. They simply do not learn the way other children learn.

The Gifted Child

The only significant contribution that we have to offer in the category of the gifted may be our method of identification and follow-up. We have, for inclusion in our cumulative folders, what we call the "blue flag sheet." Any teacher, at any time who perceives in a child the qualities which meet our definition of giftedness, initiates the "flag sheet," describes the circumstance validating the identification, and forwards the slip to the principal for posting in the child's file. The distinctive color tends to call attention to this child as other teachers refer to the folder. Gradually, other information accrues, with anecdotal notes from other teachers posted to the flag sheet. Clearly, the psychological test is one criterion for selection, but by no means is it exclusively so. Indeed, we may have a 150 I.Q. on record for a given child who has shown no signs of giftedness in his behavior, and for whom there will be no blue flag sheet. (This, however, would be exceptional.) As the child progresses through the grades, without ostentation or particular emphasis, his teachers expect more of him. Starting at Grade III he is from time to time scheduled singly or in a small group to work directly with the science consultant, or the mathematics consultant, or the librarian, or the creative activities teacher. All concerned place higher demands upon him than upon the less able. By Grade VII, there is limited homogeneous grouping which may place him in a swift-paced French class, or an advanced science or math class. We do not group homogeneously across the board at any level—only a few stepped-up classes in Grades VII and VIII. Most of the acceleration of content and expectancy can be wholly realized within the progression afforded by our curricular philosophy and the supporting goal record cards and self-instructional materials.

Elementary Foreign Language

Starting in the fall of 1960, following a six-month study by a joint faculty and lay advisory committee, we introduced conversational French for all children at Grades III, IV, and V. We had been offering French at Grade VIII as an elective (chosen by about half of the eighth graders) for some years. At this time we do not contemplate offering French at Grades VI and VII, resting on the hypothesis that the experience in the middle grades will provide an early ease of pronunciation and a good ear, as well as a positive feeling for *any* foreign language. We believe that this facility will carry over from Grade V to

Photo 6: Third-graders learn conversational French from a non-certificated "aide" who, as a native *Francaise,* visits the elementary grades daily for about 20 minutes. Each elementary school has its French Assistant, a qualified parent in the community.

Grade VIII, following which the broad array of language opportunities at high school and college will follow.

One unusual feature of our program is our staffing solution. Acknowledging that certificated teachers with superior pronunciation are hard to find for elementary classes (the professional linguists preferring high school and college teaching), we accepted the fact that bilingual excellence was our prime criterion, the certification matter less relevant, and the choice of *which* language still less relevant. Accordingly, we sought and found for each elementary school a superior bilingual person, wholly innocent of certification or other teaching formal qualifications, and as much at home in French as in English. We call them French assistants. They escape the certification barrier by serving as "aides" to the classroom teacher. They move from class to class, Grades III through V, for about 20 minutes of instruction a day.

After three years we are well satisfied with the program. It is early to predict the long-term effect upon children. The accents I hear in the classrooms are excellent. All of the instruction is in French—for 20 minutes. After a beginning vocabulary has been established, the French assistant endeavors to carry on *in French*, whatever the current theme of instruction is—mathematics, social studies, or art. This latter claim is more ambitious than reality yet allows. It is a hopeful part of our design.

The French assistants work mornings only, and receive a modest salary, separate from the conventional schedule. They are housewives of our community who were born or have lived in France.

The Learning Laboratory

Currently on our planning boards, but not yet realized, is an instrument of Junior High instruction that holds much excitement for us. Following is an extract of a study document drafted in 1960 which has served as a springboard for the faculty and the Board of Education to develop the notion further:

> A number of basic conditions, largely relevant to the Junior High School, prompt us to seek an educational design and facility which may greatly increase the effectiveness of the school. We suggest a major departure from the conventional organization for instruction through the development of a Learning Laboratory.

a. Self-motivation, self-reliance, curiosity, self-teaching and the ability to think critically are characteristics of the education program in these schools. We wish to enhance them.

b. We are increasingly distrustful of the validity of specific class sizes or specific periods of time for the most effective learning. We hold that varying sizes for instructional groups, and varying periods of time for different kinds of learning are defensible.

c. While we expect nearly all children to acquire the foundation learnings in all subjects prescribed by the curriculum, we believe that they will progress through these learnings at widely different rates . . . even more widely different from those of our present program, provided a more complete freedom for systematic, independent progress, and a more individualized relationship with teachers can be designed.

d. Beyond the foundation expectations, we believe that many children, say 60 percent or more, are capable of developing extraordinary scholarly interests and enthusiasms in one or more specific fields of inquiry at Grades VII and VIII. We further believe that such interests, exercised with considerable independence within a well-guided and well-equipped environment, will produce high intellectual motivation, work habits and satisfaction toward the continued broad academic expectations of high school and college. In other words, the child possessed of extraordinary knowledge of turtles . . . or Greek history, or the classic ballet . . . quite independent of the general curriculum goals, and given the freedom and resources to pursue this interest without limit, comes into possession not only of facts about turtles, Greece or the ballet, but, more important, acquires a zest and competency for learning, for critical thinking, for habits of independent intellectual pursuit that will carry over into other learnings and behavior. He will gain certain *internal satisfactions* that will provide enduring value as he proceeds to confront increasingly demanding intellectual tasks.

e. While the foregoing condition implies a freeing of children for independent intellectual pursuit, both in the foundation expectations of the curriculum, as well as in unstructured personal inquiry, we place a high emphasis upon the teacher-child relationship, on a one-to-one basis, and small-group basis, both in learning and in counseling.

f. Increasingly, as subject matter becomes more specialized, notably in the fields of science, mathematics, and foreign language, we are aware of the need for greatly increased efficiency in the deployment of a limited number of specialized teachers to gain maximum communication with children. As an element of this departure from conventional school organization, we contemplate, in addition to the increased *individual* work, increased large group work. Closed circuit television, systematically and carefully employed, gives high promise of a useful solution to this problem.

g. We are well aware that some of the implications of the foregoing items, relating to the increased autonomy of children in the school setting, are incompatible with some Junior High age children. Some will not be ready to respond successfully to the removal of the conventional checks and balances of periods, classrooms and ever-present teachers. We must allow for this.

PLANT IMPLICATIONS

In the light of the foregoing learning implications, we contemplate the following plant needs, subject to continued study by teachers and architects:

a. We suggest a space capable of accommodating perhaps 100 or more children, singly or in small groups, working at many different things. Carrels, conference cubicles, comfortable chairs, carpeting, easy access to the library, work tables characterize this space. It would be a place where children would go, desirous of learning, singly or in groups. It would be a respectful place, quiet, efficient, comfortable, attractive. It would permit easy flow from classrooms. It would probably have no bells or periods. Indeed, it should not even have a clock.

This space would be called a "library of tools" for individual learning. It would have a full range of film projection devices, facilities for listening to recorders, and for dictation. It would have appropriate self-instruction materials in such fields as spelling, mathematics, grammar, science, foreign language, vocabulary, where a child could accomplish many of the foundation expectations of the curriculum with or without the presence of the teacher. It would have a system of pupil accounting or record-keeping to simplify the arrangements for independent progression in prescribed content. Moreover, it would be a place for generous and suggestive access to un-prescribed content.

All of this space and activity would be under the supervision of a manager or director . . . a teacher of unusual diversity and competency.

b. Contemplating richly increased library resources, we will need more space for stacks, vertical files, periodical collection and music collection, all close by the Learning Laboratory—indeed a part of it.

c. There should be a space provided for teachers which might be called a media workroom. This space should be in close support of the Learning Laboratory. Here teachers would develop the materials and devices for large group or individual instruction in all types of media. There should be an ever-building collection of materials for individual self-instruction in the Learning Laboratory, developed by children and teachers.

In summary, we have a school of some 700 children, spread about equally among Grades VI, VII and VIII. Under the plan conceived above, many children at Grades VII and VIII would be gradually guided toward the processes of increasing academic independence. Initially, before actual construction takes place, there must be a period of trial to provide at least a limited experience with the reorganized pupil day. During this period, staff and architects should collaborate for the refinements of design which will respond to the general objectives cited herein.

For generations the schools have endeavored to equip children for adult living and vocation in the world as viewed by adults. This is no longer good enough. The curriculum of fixed or pre-conceived objectives is growing farther and farther apart from what will be the social, technological and academic environment of 1980 or 2000. Adults today cannot presume to declare what will be the necessary knowledges and skills and understandings of even a decade hence. Nor is it fruitful for us to attempt to predict what the world and its people will expect of the educated man.

Therefore, *adaptability to change* becomes a paramount objective of learning in itself. Since, beyond certain foundation expectations, we grow less and less certain of what man needs to know, we declare that first and foremost he needs to know how to learn independently. He needs to have the intellectual security and self-confidence that derive from having mastered the skills of independent inquiry. The world will change, but the nature of man will not. If we fit his nature, his behavior and his attitudes well for whatever the future discloses, he will be able to confront the unfolding truths of his lifetime with composure, wisdom and creativity.

In process for two years now, this project is beginning slowly to take form, as we put some of its parts to trial. Following a promising period of pilot study in a small "mock-up" of a Learning Laboratory, we are now in the process of constructing an addition to the Junior High School which will include the new Learning Laboratory. Larry Perkins, partner in Perkins and Will, architects, was the young creative giant who had most to do with the invention of Crow Island School 25 years ago. C.W.'s Chapter Twelve told this remarkable story. It was natural for us to call Larry back for the Learning Laboratory. He has worked intimately with the faculty and administration in the design of what may be an educational space of extraordinary significance, as we try to create facilities for the neo-education. Of one thing we are certain: teachers will be more important and will have an even larger task in the Learning Laboratory relationship than within the present conventional and historic arrangements.

* * *

There are too many "current events" in Winnetka to record with good order. I would speak of our Department of Educational Counsel (the psychologist and counselors) and the important work they are doing on the leading edge of education. Our Stanine Form (*see* Appendix C, the Stanine Form), developed by our psychologist, is too complex to describe briefly. It is, in my judgment, the single most effective tool in the field of reporting to parents. Our extraordinary attention to realistic citizenship and economic literacy in our Junior High School is another subject, deserving a full chapter in itself. I omit it, only because it is not truly a *current* innovation in Winnetka, going back to the days of Rae Logan, wise and creative Junior High principal, followed by Donald Cawelti (now assistant superintendent). Both of these men fostered, through elaborate and extensive pupil organizations, a setting for extraordinary learning beyond the conventional curriculum, including concrete, working institutions of pupils portraying the various types of American economic enterprises, and other institutions, such as cooperatives, publicly owned corporations, labor unions and an insurance company. These organizations are designed to portray *in fact* the responsibilities and obligations of literate economic citizenship.

There is much that could be said of our instrumental music program, under the tireless artistry of Milton Goldberg. Starting at Grade III, and culminating at Grade VIII, these young musicians after five years of study produce symphony and ensemble music that in recordings has been mistaken for adult performance. Many other distinctive features of our program must go unmentioned.

Values

I started this chapter with a cloudy and loosely conceived message concerning the evolution of our philosophy as it relates to the *structure* of *content*, and the corresponding relevance of appropriate learning *within* the structure for children much younger than convention now prescribes. I close the chapter with an equally illusive and intangible account of an equally pervasive and insistent issue that now commands our attention: *the teaching of values.*

As I was encouraged to describe our groping for *structure* by the forceful message of Bruner's Wood's Hole Report, so I am encouraged to speak of values, upon reading a recent issue of the Ohio State University *Newsletter,* in which Edgar Dale (whose essays I find to be among the most discerning and provocative in all current educational literature) speaks on the same subject:

> When we read of the fall and decline of a nation or a civilization, disturbing questions arise. During the critical years of decline did the leaders sense their lessened power and prestige, their increasing decadence. . . . Have we now in the United States shifted to the philosophy of the greatest goodies for the greatest number?
>
> . . . Now our great need is for uncommon schools designed to develop inventiveness, innovation, the imaginative pioneering spirit. The advances in research and innovation are geometrical; the development of our [people] is arithmetical. . . . A decadent society says, "What's your hurry? We have all the time in the world." A viable, dynamic society asks. "What are we waiting for?"
>
> But to act responsibly we must have a commitment to values.[10]

I am further encouraged to reveal our struggle to bring values into the curriculum upon reading the *Report of the President's Commission on National Goals.* In its concluding paragraphs this monumental admonition to our people says:

> Above all [note, *above all*, after declaring 15 major goals], Americans must demonstrate in every aspect of their lives the fallacy of a purely selfish attitude—the materialistic ethic. Indifference to poverty and disease is inexcusable in a society dedicated to the dignity of the individual; so also is indifference to values other than material comfort and material power. Our faith is that man lives not by bread alone, but by self-respect, by regard for other men, by convictions of right and wrong, by strong religious faith.[11]

A year before the President's Commission reported, and two years before Edgar Dale wrote his statement, 25 members of the Winnetka faculty spent a long winter weekend at a state park lodge in Illinois. We called this event the Starved Rock Retreat. Our purpose was to leave behind the clutter of the day, find isolation and uninterrupted discourse as we attempted to redefine the place of the schools in this time of history. One does not expect from such meetings an immediate and crystal-clear solution, nor indeed did we find one. But our total faculty (not only those in attendance) has not been the same since. We are moving to a new dimension of education, still to be defined.

Extracts of one of the prepared papers which characterized the Starved Rock Retreat are offered to illuminate this message:

> In the course of history there have been 25 great civilizations that have come to prominence, then withered to mediocrity or oblivion. We must ask our-

[10] Dale, Edgar; *The Newsletter*, November, 1961: Bureau of Educational Research, The Ohio State University, Columbus.

[11] *Goals for Americans, The Report of the President's Commission on National Goals*, by the American Assembly (Englewood Cliffs, N.J.: Prentice-Hall, Inc., 1960), p. 23.

selves whether it is not conceivable that this could happen to us if there is not some new central force, presumably education, that gives our people a transcending sense of purpose . . . beyond materialism.

A craving for peace and the removal of hostility is the foremost wish possessed by Americans, and I dare say that a craving for peace is the foremost wish possessed by human beings throughout the world. This becomes, then, a search for universal brotherhood, a transcending purpose for our time.

. . . We in the schools, kindergarten through high school, are the *only universal instrument* through which America may act with concert to affect the hearts and minds of men.

. . . Most of us in education have stood for a long time against anything that implied compulsion, that implied coercion, that implied indoctrination in learning. This has been a cornerstone of America's greatness, and the key to our diversity, ingenuity, and creativity as a people. This must not change. But technology has foreshortened time and space from vast and infinite distances to immediate and very present proximity. Can the same proximity of spirit be attained with that of body through education, without resorting to indoctrination? We must find ways to help children develop *their own* convictions about freedom consistent with the tempo of today's swift evolution; not leaving freedom's learnings to chance, nor risking the greater evil, coercion. Deep as the problem is, and lagging though our knowledge of man behind our knowledge of things, we contradict ourselves if we contemplate indoctrination for brotherhood. But, if we in the schools are society's only universal instrument for bringing about change and movement in what people believe, what is our job concerning brotherhood? We are the chief custodians of the hearts and minds of the men who confront the world of 2000 A.D. The kind of culture our children will create, the way they will vote (if they do), the nature of civilization in its upward or downward curve is being determined in our classrooms now. This is the realm of the spirit. Without the spirit, without emotion, without conviction, we are nothing as a nation or as a civilization.

The great, fundamental ethic of Western culture may be called love. Some call it brotherhood of man under God. In any human undertaking there must be a massive foundation principle upon which the day to day choices and decisions are made. It is clear that whatever the underlying principles or ethics of communism may be, they raise a glorious cosmic vision for the followers, controlling them in a disciplined grip that makes personal sacrifice joyful, that makes the human being erase himself with depraved eagerness and makes communism the ultimate good. If we are to compete successfully with totalitarianism in half the world, we must find an equally commanding and compelling truth which to Americans in the 1960's is as much a source of glorious cosmic vision as that possessed by and possessing the communist. Our truth has been and continues to be the brotherhood of man. To deny this or to accept a less worthy ethic is to stoop to our ideological adversary. It is in these terms, our own terms, not on totalitarianism's materialistic terms, that our future must be shaped. The schools, avoiding indoctrination, have a tremendous new dimension to fulfill in bringing about a deep commitment to these terms as distinguished from the cynical, passive, comfortable, complacent acceptance of things as they are and as they have been. We have the new task of equipping society to devote itself with great dedication to its foundation principles and to work creatively toward peace and goodwill, not as a fat, comfortable winner, but as a lean, hard runner competing for its very existence. That is the statement of the problem.

That meeting took place in January of 1960. Since that time a small committee of the faculty, with the warm and patient support of the Board of Education, have been wrestling with the challenge. Movement has already started, unstructured, intuitive and possessed of a good faculty unity. Here is a very small example of a concrete outcome:

One of the pupil organizations at junior high school, noted above, is called the International Relations Club. At the time of the emergence of Nigeria as an independent nation, Sally Massey, sixth grade teacher and sponsor of the club, suggested that some notice might be taken of this important event. The children wrote a warm letter of congratulations to Prime Minister Balewa, welcoming his country to the society of free peoples. They received the Prime Minister's reply, signed by him, a few days later. Immeasurable good things, free of indoctrination or compulsion, happened to those children who composed the letter and received the reply:

> Cabinet Office
> Lagos, Nigeria

Dear Miss Massey and students,

I thank you for your letter of 9th January in which the students of Skokie School congratulated me and my people on our orderly system of government.

We certainly need the prayers and good wishes of kind people like you and for my part, I shall continue to work for the peace of the world and for the betterment of humanity. It is my earnest hope that democracy as practised in Nigeria will be a model for other nations to follow.

I wish you all God's blessing and success in your studies.

> Yours sincerely,
> [Signed] *Abubaker Balewa*
> Prime Minister of the Federation
> of Nigeria

We shall continue to search for ways to teach values. We will avoid coercion and indoctrination, even in these unsteady times. Perhaps there is a good, non-coercive method, swifter and more sure than what we now know. But we feel deeply the unfulfilled opportunity in the schools to develop far more effectively the truths of the human spirit that distinguish freedom from slavery at home and abroad; between our Bill of Rights and the imperfect democracy we now know.

When these basic values have begun to find their places in the hearts and minds of children, other important but lesser values will follow.

The closing chapter will have a little more to offer on this subject as we look ahead.

Conclusions

Winnetka has, by no means, been alone in its struggle to intensify the academic learnings of children, and to search for a new order of education. Bruner's "widespread renewal of concern for the quality and intellectual aims of education" should not be viewed as an abandonment of the clear gains made by education in its devotion for 30 years to objectives concerned with social, emotional and physical growth as well as intellectual. There is strong evidence that our intellectual gains in recent decades have been substantial. Notwithstanding the fact that a higher and higher percentage of children are attending school (whereas the slower in years past would have been bypassed, especially at high school), the evidence produced by our test publishers reveal that, successively, standardized achievement tests have been made more demanding of scholarship at all levels in each periodic revision. The College Entrance Examining Board offers the same testimony. Presidents of universities note the successive upgrading of entrance standards over the past decade, giving large credit to the public schools for the change.

A further sign of the accelerated search for quality is the recent joining of forces between educators and scholars of the content disciplines. Examples of this promising union are being felt in our mathematics and language arts curricula, responding respectively to the School Mathematics Study Group and Project English. Correspondingly, the National Science Foundation's infusing of millions of dollars into the in-service education of teachers is a clear sign of the times.

But whether or not we are producing a better product now than we were a few years ago, society is saying that a still better product is expected. And the "better" part has to do with scholarship. One might more precisely describe it as the optimum intellectual fulfillment of each child.

This chapter has sought to reveal this evolution in our Winnetka Schools, but it has sought also to reveal the continued attention to corollary goals. Our research in the *academic underachiever* is essentially research in mental health; our investigation of a new role for the schools in *teaching about communism* is only partly intellectual and partly a philosophical inquiry.

We have sought here to identify other important investigations either recent or continuing in Winneka, which may bear fruit for others: Our work in teachers' salary design and related policies has been received with much interest nationally. We feel we have made some modest contribution in the *school-home communications* category, including the employment of *lay advisory* committees.

Noted for possible relevance to others who also search for better ways to teach and learn, we have reported on research on the *consultant's role,* the *summer program, the gifted child, foreign language in the elementary school,* and our exploration of a new notion, the *Learning Laboratory.*

These are some of the signs of ferment in the Winnetka faculty. We hope at least here and there the reader will find an idea he can capture, or, perhaps, take satisfaction in knowing that he is already ahead of us in our hunt for better ways.

CHAPTER TWENTY-THREE

Review

and Preview

The schools of America, if they are true to their purpose, are indeed the mirror of society, responding, even if slowly, to the changing needs of our civilization. This little village on Lake Michigan's shore, which the Indians had named Beautiful Place long before Marquette and Joliet paddled along its bluffs, seems to have had a destiny in educational ferment. It is a "good" ferment, as distinguished from the ferment of hostility and stridency. But it is not by any means a ferment lacking in honest controversy. For indeed, controversy is the trigger of change. And change is constant, if the schools are responsive to the changing society. We in Winnetka may be likened to the tiny pinpoint of a recording thermometer that has written, for good or bad, the profile of educational evolution for a half-century. Different from many school systems, we are small enough to present an observable anatomy which we have not taken pains to conceal; and we are large enough to have assumed the realistic dimensions of a public institution not always attainable in a conventional laboratory school.

Progressivism Inescapable

Carleton Washburne came upon Winnetka when progressivism, *writ large*, was inescapable, if Winnetka was to respond, as a laboratory, to society's needs. Cremins notes this period in our history with well-documented support: [1]

> To look back on the nineties is to sense an awakening of social conscience, a growing belief that this incredible suffering [of economically depressed people in America] was neither the fault nor the inevitable lot of the sufferers, that it could certainly be alleviated, and that the road to alleviation was neither charity nor revolution, but in the last analysis, education.

Washburne's creative leadership opened new doors to the process of learning for all children, both the quick and the slow, the favored and the unfavored. He led his community and faculty to an understanding of and a deep and abiding appreciation for the individual child, not only as an intellectual being, but a creature possessed of physical, emotional and social parts, quite as essential for development as the mind. He gave high prominence to the release of creativity in children, and to the processes of self-discipline and controlled self-government or citizenship. This was a freeing of the spirit, an illumination of human dignity that was intrinsic to the progressive school's "mirror" of our culture in the 1920's.

The Schools Still Serve Society

Perhaps the progressives made the mistake of too closely following George Count's persuasion that teachers should dare to contrive a new social order. Perhaps they should have listened more closely to Dewey than to his translators. For Dewey declared that the schools could

---

[1] Cremins, Lawrence A., *ibid*, p. 59.

never be the "main determinant of political, intellectual or moral change. . . . It would be revolution enough," said he, "were educators to begin to recognize the fact of social change and to act upon that recognition in the schools." [2]

As we view ourselves now in Winnetka, we are carrying forward the essential strands of the fabric Washburne wove. Indeed, there are few schools in the United States that do not, today, pursue the fundamental truths that were first championed by the progressives in Winnetka and elsewhere. But today's schools, spurning "isms," have swung with society's pendulum. This is not to say that teachers and school administrators blindly follow the vacillating commands of the transient citizen-spokesman. His is the voice of the flute or the bassoon or the cymbal in society's symphony. The teacher's ears must be tuned instead to the broad tones of the *full orchestration*, sometimes sharp and clear, sometimes cumbered in unrhythmic dissonance—but always there, sounding.

A Time of Re-examining Education by Teachers

Society began to demand a clearer picture of what education was and what it was not. It sought a more concrete system for intellectual fulfillment than the progressives had taken time to describe. Guilty or not, the schools were accused of anti-intellectualism in their preoccupation with the "other parts." Guilty or not, the schools were charged with complicity in the rising curve of crime, immorality, mental ill-health and intellectual torpor in America. Those who searched in the 1950's for scapegoats for whatever social irregularities were current found solace in pointing to the permissiveness of the schools of the 1930's and 1940's.

Writers of popular books on the schools, some honest, some not honest, fished profitably in the troubled waters of education during the 1940's and 1950's. Best sellers about the failure of the schools made their authors rich and their readers frightened. There had to have been a fundamental distrust of the schools on which scrupulous and unscrupulous writers could prey, or else their sometimes outrageous mes-

---

[2] Dewey, John, "Education for Changing Social Order," NEA, *Addresses and Proceedings,* 1934, pp. 744-752.

sages would have been their undoing. There was enough truth in their accusations, however, to cause sober teachers to re-examine education in the 1950's.

It was in this setting of high concern and ferment that my good fortune brought me to Winnetka in the mid-1950's. If there had been an imperishable Washburne, leading consistently from 1919 to the present, the evolution would have been no different in its color. His genius would have led more vigorously, more scientifically, and more productively, but the trend would have been the same. For the schools *are* society's servants, and Washburne would not only have tolerated this fact, but would have *willed* it, just as he willed his share of the explosion that was progressivism.

Enduring Characteristics in Winnetka Education

For all the changes and on-going objects of inquiry that now characterize the Winnetka Schools, as briefly cited in the foregoing chapters, much of Washburne's plan remains. It has been freshened, adapted, perhaps amputated here and there, and grafted to a new branch. But our extraordinary concern for the individual child, and the processes of instruction, staffing and record-keeping that implement that concern, are as real as they were in C.W.'s mid-1930's. The experiment that is called Winnetka, furthermore, could not have remotely succeeded without a faculty of exceptionally competent, dedicated, imaginative and proud teachers. In this respect, too, we are unchanged. While only a few of C.W.'s early colleagues are still on our faculty, the heritage of creativity, selflessness and zest for inquiry has been passed on to the younger successors.

There is another element that characterizes our way of life in Winnetka. I am sure Washburne knew it and nurtured it. And so have I. It is *love*. Overstreet tells us that "... love is an activity, not a passion ... the essence of love is to labor for something—to make something grow.... To love is to be related to [an individual] as representing mankind." I hesitate to verbalize this element of education in Winnetka, lest I profane it. Yet to conclude this message without noting its high prominence in our affairs would be to fail in my task. There is love in our schools. It flows from teachers to pupils, and it flows between the

schools and the community. Indeed, I hope it is found in the administration; I know it is found in the Board of Education. It was the essence
of the "new superintendent's" remarks upon his first appearance before
the full faculty when he talked of "exchange of faith." In all humility,
I declare that this force is essential to a good system of education. And
it is a force which, like marriage, must never be taken for granted, but
must be a constant object of joyful and sacrificial labor.

Washburne has often stated that his effectiveness in Winnetka was
attributable as much as anything else to the vision, wisdom and high
devotion of his Boards of Education. I can, with unhesitating conviction, claim the same advantage. The governmental process of the community has consistently sought out and attracted to the Board of
Education citizens of the highest competence, with declared commitment to superior education. Not always agreeing, but unswervingly
seeking the best possible education for children within the means at
hand, the Boards have remained non-partisan, completely selfless, and
inspiring to their executive officer.

The community continues to demand the impossible, and willingly
lends its strength in time or treasure when help is asked. We will never
wholly satisfy our patrons . . . we will, indeed never satisfy ourselves.

A Momentary Plateau

We are looking ahead now, in Winnetka, having come through a
time of major curricular, public relations, budgetary, organizational and
philosophical upheaval. There appears to be a good consensus surrounding our present position, not only in the faculty and the Board of
Education but in the community as well. It is, therefore, time to listen
closely to the subtle signals that will herald the next act as we try to
anticipate the demands that will be put upon education. It has been
rightly observed that the schools rarely discontinue any obligation.
There is an eternal accretion of new tasks and expectations, calling for
increased teacher competence, efficiency, and sense of balance. In our
present preoccupation with academic excellence, we are in no way re-
ducing or compromising our historic devotion to the social, emotional
and physical learnings. We accept our *increased* responsibility for an
increased degree of intellectual fulfillment, without subtracting other
components of the curriculum.

What Is Society's Next Charge to the Schools?

For over 300 years the American school has risen to the expectations of the changing culture. Starting with the church-oriented instruction of the colonies, and progressing through the tradesman period to the classical, the agricultural, the industrial, the socially oriented, the humanistic, and, lately the science-technology concerns and the preoccupations with world understandings and peace, the school has followed the course of social history, even as it has contributed to its shape. There now seems to be a distant and as yet unclear signal that emerges from the coming together of our science-technology and our moral and ethical responsibility in free world leadership. There is an increasing awareness in our people that man's knowledge of *things* has outstripped his knowledge of himself. There are increasing signs that our possession of goods or security has become more to be desired than freedom. The spirit of sacrifice for principle—the risking of "life, liberty and sacred honor" in the interests of greater good—has lost its passion.

A Return to Values

This is the concern underlying the *values* topic in the closing passages of this book. We are reminded of Thucydides of Athens who says for Pericles: "We are a free democracy, but we obey the laws, more especially those which protect the oppressed and *the unwritten laws the transgression of which brings shame.*" (The italics are mine.) The "unwritten laws" of the Western culture are the *values* of the Judeo-Christian, as well as the Greek democratic tradition, which have given us our dignity and freedom, and which, now that we no longer struggle for freedom, we think we no longer need. Plato, lecturing on freedom in the earliest and perhaps the purest of the democracies, told the men of Athens that the most excellent constitution, the best laws, were mere forms unless the people obeyed the voice of God within them. The first purpose of a government was to train its citizens in *right doing.* Drawing upon the teachings of Socrates, Plato told them that,[3]

---

[3] Hamilton, Edith, *The Echo of Greece*, W. W. Norton and Co., Inc., N.Y., 1957, pp. 20-45.

as a matter of self-preservation, the State should advance "the education in excellence from youth on, which makes men *passionately desire to become perfect citizens, knowing both how to rule and be ruled.*" (The italics, again, are mine.)

It seems to me that in this time of unprecedented material prosperity and unprecedented military anxiety we have forsaken to a degree our heroic American trait of putting first things first. We have taken for granted the spirit of sacrifice that made our nation great. We have, as evidenced by repeated tests, submitted to a physical and intellectual conformity in our colleges and secondary schools that belies the term *liberal education.* We have grown to tolerate dishonesty in government and law enforcement; we are calloused to breaches of integrity in business, large and small. We continue, a hundred years after Gettysburg, to heap indignity upon our dark-skinned brother and then wonder at his occasional thrusts against us at home and abroad. We preen ourselves in our moments of "sacrifice," making certain the benevolence can be easily spared, and carefully recording its dimensions for tax purposes; our largesse abroad for the reinforcement of underdeveloped peoples is grudgingly admitted to our national budget when its relevance to our own survival is noted, and we wonder at the ingratitude, forgetting that "the gift without the giver is bare."

Values are the principles by which men live, by which the day-to-day decisions, large and small, are made—individually, politically, and corporately. Values are what Thucydides called the "unwritten laws" and which Plato found far more important than those of the constitution. It is to our values as a people—perhaps as Western civilization—that I think the schools now must look for the next task. The schools and the curriculum have never been an end in themselves; the mathematics, the arts, the sciences, the compositions and literature are useless and futile exercises unless they equip man for the purposes of being civilized, as distinguished from being savage. The distinction lies in the spirit, in the exercise of will, in the discrimination between good and evil, in the acceptance of responsibility for others, in the pursuit of beauty and truth. These are the purposes of education, beyond the skills and tools.

Some will quarrel over whether these functions are properly the charge of the schools. Indeed, the school has no monopoly on them, as the home and church and other institutions exercise their larger

stake in the arena of moral and spiritual values. But indeed, the schools
are the *only universal instrument* through which our society can make
its needs known, and demand responsive attention. How the schools
will go about this task, I do not know. Teachers have, since the beginning of time, taught values, often by example, sometimes by precept,
generally by indirection and happenstance. Emulation by children of
respected adults seems to be the most ancient and most enduring curriculum of values. It is evident that the convictions possessed by the
early adolescent and the pre-adolescent are enduring—his values at age
14 are likely to be those of his adulthood.[4]

Communism's Competition May Serve as Motivation

I find in our present clash of ideology with international communism the greatest motivator toward good ends that we could possibly contrive. For the very values we would enhance are those that are
despised by our cold war enemy. We, as a people, glorify justice, and
we have watched the triumph of injustice in half a world. We, as a
people, glorify God, and we have watched the totalitarian pervert our
God into an insidious religion with its prophets, its bible, its martyrs
and saints, its sacrificial zeal and even its Moses and its Christ. We
glorify freedom, and we have seen freedom die; we glorify the immortal
dignity of civilized man, and we have seen immortality and dignity
derided. We glorify honor and integrity and our competitor knows no
honor but the perverted honor of unjust means justifying more unjust
ends. We espouse brotherhood in our fundamental creed; the totalitarian knows no brotherhood, even among the co-conspirators. We pit
our educational strength to the task of freeing and uplifting the hearts
and minds of men; his education subverts the hearts and minds of men
ever more surely to intellectual and cultural bondage.

If it were not for our competitor, I believe we would already have

---

[4] *Note:* Current research (1961-62) by Goldstein at the University of Iowa and
by Jackson at the University of Chicago offer unhappy evidence that little change
occurs at the high school or college in the values with which the student arrives at
the institution. These investigators give support to Herbert Zim's findings that convictions and commitment (in the field of science careers) are most often developed
in children before age 14. It may well follow that convictions in the arena of man's
humanity to man become rooted most effectively at the same age.

grown softer than we are. This clash, then, is not without its beneficial side, if we only turn the power of our concern to education's ends. In Plato's aging years, he anguished over Athens' decline, as her people became too sure of their freedom, too comfortable in their luxury. He had seen freedom's excesses in irresponsible Athens "... freedom without any counterbalancing weight of responsibility, and he wanted none of it. By that time Athens had reached the end of freedom and was never to have it again." [5]

Values are not self-evident, hereditary, attainable by purchase or memorization. They are internalized by induction and deduction, by emulation, by experience and by intelligent application. They have to do with the heart and mind. Truth needs witnesses, said Albert Camus. Teachers are the historic and eternal witnesses of truth. When truth is violated, when our values are corrupted, if we teachers do our job well, I would look for the people of the next generation to be capable of a greater wrath than ours. I would look for them to have a deeper and more certain passion for good; I would look for them to be capable of higher indignation at the transgression of "unwritten laws," and I would expect them to possess an inner peace better than ours, deriving from these clearer convictions, and their more disciplined application.

We speak again of war in our time, incomprehensible though it might be. We have known war and bloodshed, and if need be, God forbid, we shall know it again. But shedding blood or dying is one thing; losing one's soul is quite another. While we devote great intellect and treasure to our military ramparts, let us give equal devotion to the more important spiritual ramparts. For without will, without the passionate pride of free people, without the values that have given us 2000 years of civilization, there would be no point in warring ... or surviving.

Perhaps the teacher, in this time, will give reality to Toynbee's hope:

> This century could be the first age since the dawn of civilization in which people dared to think it practical to make the benefits of civilization available to the human race.

---

[5] Hamilton, Edith, *op. cit.*, p. 48.

I am deeply indebted to *Mrs. Geraldine Clader,* Board of Education member; *Miss Helen Danforth,* teacher; and *Miss Odeyne Gillette,* teacher, for their critical and constructive review of the manuscript of this book.

Appendices

Appendix A Goal Record Cards, Grades I-VIII
All Subjects

Appendix B The Parent Conference Guide and
Record—Primary and Intermediate

Appendix C The Stanine Form, with Explanation

Winnetka Public Schools
LANGUAGE ARTS GOAL RECORD CARD 2

Pupil_____ Teacher_____ Year_____

Indicate S (Satisfactory) or N (Needs Improvement) in the following areas.

READING

Tests Used _____ Score

Vocabulary Building
- Forms plurals, adding s or es ....
- Forms rhyming words ....

Comprehension
- Grasps general idea ....
- Picks out specific facts and details ....
- Understands sequence of events ....
- Predicts outcomes ....
- Reads and follows directions ....

Type of Reader
- Fluency: ____
- Independence: ____
- Attitude: ____

Phonetic, Structural Analysis
- Hears and identifies initial consonants ....
- Hears and identifies final consonants ....
- Hears and identifies initial consonant blends, (sh, wh, th, ch) ....
- Hears and identifies long vowel sounds ....
- Hears and identifies short vowel sounds ....
- Understands and applies final silent e ....

Group at end of year: ____

Instructional Materials

HANDWRITING
- Can form all letters ....
- Can write all letters from dictation ....
- Packing ....
- Spacing ....
- Rate of writing ....

SPELLING
Level at end of year: ____
List at end of year: ____

GRAMMAR AND USAGE — GROUP WORK AND PREVIEWS

GROUP WORK (to be completed when appropriate)

Punctuation

Capitals:
First word in sentence
Names of persons, nicknames
Days of week, months, holidays, special days
I as a word

Periods:
After declarative sentence

PREVIEWS OF THIRD GRADE WORK (any time of year)

Punctuation

Capitals:
Names of people, places, nationalities
Personal titles
First word each line of poetry
Heading, greeting, closing in letter

Periods:
After abbr. and initials

Question Marks:
After interrogative sentence

Exclamation Points:
After exclamatory sentence
After interjection

Commas:
Heading, greeting, closing in letter

Apostrophe:
Contractions
Possessives

Use of Dictionary:
Alphabetical order

Winnetka Public Schools
LANGUAGE ARTS GOAL RECORD CARD 1

Pupil_____ Teacher_____ Year_____

Indicate S (Satisfactory) or N (Needs Improvement) in the following areas.

READING
Sight Vocabulary

Test used ____
Number wrong ____

Comprehension
- Reads with understanding ....
- Selects important points ....
- Recalls materials read ....

Phonetic Skills
- Hears and identifies initial consonants ....
- Hears and identifies final consonants ....

Type of Reader
- Fluency: ____
- Independence: ____

WRITTEN COMMUNICATION
Handwriting
- Identifies and forms all letters ....
- Writes alphabet from dictation ....
- Packing ....
- Spacing ____ Page
- Rate ....

Group at end of year: ____

Book last used: ____

Instructional Materials

Practical Writing
- Writes first and last name ....
- Copies simple sentences ....
- Beginning to use sentence form ....
- Copies simple letters ....

Creative Writing
- Writes simple letters ....
- Writes stories independently ....

PREVIEWS (any time of year)

Capitals:
First word in sentence
Names of persons and nicknames
Days, months, holidays, special days
I as a word

Periods:
After abbreviations (months of year, days of week)
After declarative sentences

Question Mark:
After interrogative sentences

Exclamation Points:
After an interjection
After an exclamatory sentence

ORAL COMMUNICATION
Speaking
- Speaks correctly and distinctly ....
- Voice audible to group ....
- Vocabulary ....
- Dictates experiences ....
- Participates ....

Listening
- Listens with attention ....
- Listens with comprehension ....
- Follows oral directions ....

Figure 7

Appendix A: Goal Record Cards
Grades I-VIII

Winnetka Public Schools
LANGUAGE ARTS GOAL RECORD CARD 4

Pupil _____ Teacher _____ Year _____

READING

GRAMMAR AND USAGE	Date
First Review of Capitals	
Capitals for Titles	
Writing Sentences in Paragraphs	
Dictation I	
Capitals—Names of Particular Places	
Abbreviations	
Commas	
Dictation II	
Friendly Letters	
Thank-You	
Invitation	
Family	
Appreciation	
Exclamation Point	
Writing Poems	
Contractions	
Review of Sentences and Capitals	
Dictation III	
General Review	

Instructional Materials _____

HANDWRITING

Indicate satisfactory (S) or improvement needed (N) three times during year.

	1	2	3
Spacing			
Packing			
Letter Formation			
Rate			
General Appearance of all Written Work (Ink for 2 and 3)			

Language Projects:

SPELLING

Indicate level and list number at beginning, middle, and end of year.

LEVEL _____
LIST _____

GRAMMAR AND USAGE—GROUP WORK AND PREVIEWS

GROUP WORK
(to be used when appropriate)

Parts of Speech

Nouns: Recognition, number, gender, as subject

Verbs: Recognition, action and being, as predicate

Punctuation

Capital Letters: Abbreviation of proper nouns

Commas: Words in a series; Proper names in direct address

Apostrophe: Possessives

Hyphen: To divide words at end of line

Use of Dictionary
Alphabetical order
How to pronounce words
Syllables
Guide words
Definitions

PREVIEWS (any time of year)

Parts of Speech

Nouns: Proper, common, possessive

Adjectives: Recognition; Modifiers of nouns and pronouns

Pronoun: Recognition; Number and gender; As subject

Punctuation

Capital letters: First word in quoted sentence; First word in quoted documents, historical events; Outlining

Periods: Imperative sentences; Outlining

Commas: Yes and no in conversation; Proper names in direct address; Inside address of business letter

Colon: After salutation of business letter; Between hour and minute

Quotation marks: Exact words a person wrote or said

Winnetka Public Schools
LANGUAGE ARTS GOAL RECORD CARD 3

Pupil _____ Teacher _____ Year _____

READING

Group at end of year _____

Instructional Materials Used _____

GRAMMAR AND USAGE	Date
Sentences	
Questions	
Dictation I	
Sentence Sense	
Paragraphs	
Dictation II	
Capital Letters: Names of Persons	
Dictation III	
Capital Letters: Days, Holidays, Months	
Dictation IV	
Capital Letters: Particular Places	
Letter Writing	

HANDWRITING

Indicate satisfactory (S) or needs improvement (N) three times during year.

	1	2	3
Spacing			
Packing			
Letter Formation			
Rate			
General Appearance			

SPELLING

Indicate level and list at beginning, middle and end of year.

LEVEL _____
LIST _____

GRAMMAR AND USAGE—GROUP WORK AND PREVIEWS

GROUP WORK
(to be completed when appropriate)

Punctuation

Capital Letters: Particular places, persons, nationalities; Personal titles; Book, poem, story titles; First word each line poetry; Heading, greeting, closing in letter

Periods: After abbreviations and initials

Question Marks: Interrogative sentences

Exclamation point: Exclamatory sentence; Interjection

Commas: Heading, greeting, closing in letter

Apostrophe: Contractions

PREVIEWS OF FOURTH GRADE WORK (any time of year)

Parts of Speech

Nouns: Recognition; Number and gender; Use as subject

Verbs: Recognition; Action and being; Use as predicate

Punctuation

Capital Letters: Abbrev. of proper nouns

Commas: Words in series; Proper names in direct address

Apostrophe: Possessives

Hyphens: To divide words at end of line

Use of Dictionary
Alphabetical order

How to Pronounce Words
Syllables
Guide words
Definitions

Winnetka Public Schools
LANGUAGE ARTS GOAL RECORD CARD 5

Pupil_____ Teacher_____ Year_____

See CURRICULUM GUIDE for GROUP WORK and PREVIEWS to be done.

GRAMMAR AND USAGE — Date

- Capitals
- Abbreviations Review
- Commas
- Dictation Review I
- Friendly Letter Review
- Business Letter
- Dictation Review II
- Sentences
- Subject and Predicate
- Nouns
- Pronouns
- Verbs
- Possessives
- Dictation Review III

SPELLING

Indicate level and list three times during the year to correspond with reporting periods.   1   2   3

- Level
- List

HANDWRITING

Indicate S (Satisfactory) or N (Needs Improvement) three times during the year to correspond with reporting periods.   1   2   3

- Spacing
- Packing
- Letter Formation
- Rate
- General Appearance
- Ability to read clear types of cursive writing (2 and 3)

INDIVIDUAL PROJECTS — Date

USE OF DICTIONARY, DIRECTORY, INDEX

- Arranging Words Alphabetically
- Finding Words in the Dictionary
- Meanings of Words
- Vowels and Consonants
- Syllables and Hyphens
- How to Pronounce Words
- Indexes

LIBRARY LESSONS

- Library Worksheets

Winnetka Public Schools
LANGUAGE ARTS GOAL RECORD CARD 6

Pupil_____ Teacher_____ Year_____

See CURRICULUM GUIDE for GROUP WORK and PREVIEWS to be done.

GRAMMAR AND USAGE — Date

- Review I
- Dictation: Review I
- Review II — How To Pronounce Words
- Review III — Subject and Predicate
- Possessives, Singular and Plural
- Dictation: Possessives
- Review: Friendly Letters
- Kinds of Sentences
- Subjects and Predicates
- Review IV
- Dictation: Review IV
- Simple Quotations
- Review V
- Dictation: Review V
- Review: Business Letter
- Comma after Oh, Yes, No, Well
- Comma in Direct Address
- Dictation: Use of Commas
- Nouns, Common and Proper
- Review of Pronouns
- Adjectives
- Outlining
- Review VI
- Dictation: Review VI

SPELLING — Date

- Beginning:
  - Level_____ List_____
- First Report Period:
  - Level_____ List_____
- Second Report Period:
  - Level_____ List_____
- End of Year:
  - Level_____ List_____
- Auxiliary Spelling Lists:
- Individual Projects:

HANDWRITING SURVEY

LIBRARY SURVEY

READING SURVEY

Winnetka Public Schools
LANGUAGE ARTS GOAL RECORD CARD 8

Pupil _____ Teacher _____ Year _____

See CURRICULUM GUIDE for GROUP WORK to be done.

GRAMMAR AND USAGE	Date	Individual Projects:	Date
1. Review: Subject and Verb			
2. Review: Agreement of Verb with Subject.			
3. Review: Pronouns as Subjects and Objects			
4. Review: Pronouns as Predicate Nominative, Object of Preposition, Indirect Object			
5. Review: Principal Parts of Verbs		**SPELLING**	
6. Review: Conjugation of Verbs		Beginning:	
7. Review: Special Verbs		Level ____ List	
8. Review: Adjectives and Adverbs		First Report Period:	
9. Prepositional Phrases		Level ____ List	
10. Infinitive Phrases		Second Report Period:	
11. Gerund Phrases		Level ____ List	
12. Participial Phrases		End of Year:	
13. Coordinate Clauses		Level ____ List	
14. Adverbial Clauses		Auxiliary Spelling Lists:	Date
15. Adjective Clauses			
16. Noun Clauses			
17. Punctuation Review			
18. General Review			

Winnetka Public Schools
LANGUAGE ARTS GOAL RECORD CARD 7

Pupil _____ Teacher _____ Year _____

See CURRICULUM GUIDE for GROUP WORK and PREVIEWS to be done.

PART 1 — GENERAL LANGUAGE	Date	PART 2 — (CONTINUED)	Date
I. Punctuation Review I		II. Parts of Speech (Continued)	
II. Punctuation Review II		C. Verbs	
III. Comma in Apposition		1. Phrases with Auxiliaries	
IV. Divided Quotations		2. Tense	
V. Punctuation Review III		3. Agreement with Subject	
VI. Extracting an Outline		4. Conjugation	
VII. Developing an Outline		D. Adjectives	
Report Title:		1. Articles	
		2. Proper	
		3. Predicate	
		4. Comparison	
VIII. Minutes of Meeting		E. Adverbs	
IX. Punctuation Review IV		1. Recognition	
X. Library Lessons		2. Comparison	
PART 2 — GRAMMAR		F. Prepositions	
I. Sentence Structure		G. Conjunctions	
A. Simple		H. Interjections	
1. Subject			
2. Predicate			
B. Compound		Individual Projects:	
C. Diagraming			
II. Parts of Speech			
A. Nouns		**SPELLING**	
1. Subject		Beginning:	
2. Direct Object		Level ____ List	
3. Object of Preposition		First Report Period:	
4. Indirect Object		Level ____ List	
5. Predicate Nominative		Second Report Period:	
6. Types		Level ____ List	
a. Common		End of Year:	
b. Proper		Level ____ List	
c. Collective		Auxiliary Spelling Lists:	Date
d. Compound			
B. Pronouns			
1. Subject			
2. Direct Object			
3. Object of Preposition			
4. Indirect Object			
5. Predicate Nominative			
6. Possessives			

Winnetka Public Schools

Language Arts Goal Record of Writing for Grade _____
(For Use in Grades 3 to 8)

Pupil _____ Teacher _____ Year _____

At least one piece of written work each week is expected of pupils. Some will do more. The writing may be related to any subject field or take any worthy form. Titles of written work fulfilling this expectation should be entered below.

	Title	Date
1.		
2.		
3.		
4.		
5.		
6.		
7.		
8.		
9.		
10.		
11.		
12.		
13.		
14.		
15.		
16.		
17.		
18.		
19.		
20.		
21.		
22.		
23.		
24.		
25.		
26.		
27.		
28.		
29.		
30.		
31.		
32.		
33.		
34.		
35.		
36.		

Winnetka Public Schools

Language Arts Goal Record of Reading for Grade _____
(For Use in Grades 3 to 8)

Pupil _____ Teacher _____ Year _____

The number of books read during the year will vary with the grade level and type of book. Teachers in consultation with each other and with their groups will set standard as to the number of books pupils at a given grade level will be expected to read. Books read should be recorded below.

	Title	Author	Type of Book	Date
1.				
2.				
3.				
4.				
5.				
6.				
7.				
8.				
9.				
10.				
11.				
12.				
13.				
14.				
15.				
16.				
17.				
18.				
19.				
20.				
21.				
22.				
23.				
24.				
25.				
26.				
27.				
28.				
29.				
30.				
31.				
32.				
33.				
34.				
35.				
36.				

Winnetka Public Schools
MATHEMATICS GOAL RECORD CARD 1

Pupil _____ Teacher _____ Year _____

	Check
Can count 10 objects	
Can read and write numerals to 10	
Recognizes number groups up to 5	
Recognizes patterns of objects to 10	
Can read and write numerals to 20	
Can count objects to 100	
Recognizes numbers to 100	
Can read and write numerals to 50	
Recognizes addition and subtraction symbols	
*Understands meaning of the inequality signs	
Can count objects:	
by 2's to 20	
by 5's to 100	
by 10's to 100	
Recognizes geometric figures:	
triangle	
circle	
quadrilateral	
Recognizes coins (1c, 5c, 10c, 25c)	
Knows addition combinations 10 and under using objects	
Knows subtraction combinations 10 and under using objects	
Recognizes addition and subtraction vertically and horizontally	
*Can construct simple plane figures with straight edge and compass	
Shows understanding of numbers and number combinations (check one)	
1. Using concrete objects	
2. Beginning to visualize and abstract	
3. Makes automatic responses without concrete objects	
*Can tell time	
1. Hour	
2. Half hour	

*(Goals starred are not essential for all students)

Comments:

Winnetka Public Schools
MATHEMATICS GOAL RECORD CARD 2

Pupil _____ Teacher _____ Year _____

	Check
Addition combinations 10 and under (automatic response)	
Subtraction combinations 10 and under (automatic response)	
Can count to 200	
Can understand zero as a number	
Can understand place value to tens	
Can read and write numerals to 200	
Can read and write numeral words to 10	
Can read and write number words to 20	
Use facts in 2-digit column addition (no carrying)	
Roman numerals to XII	
Can tell time:	
Half hour	
Quarter hour	
Calendar (months, days of week, dates)	
Coins and their equivalent value to 25c	
Recognition of 50c coin and $1.00	
Recognize and use ½, ¼, ¾ of a whole	
Addition facts to 18 (aim for mastery)	
Subtraction facts to 18 (aim for mastery)	
*Can identify simple plane figures:	
Quadrilateral	
Pentagon	
Hexagon	
Octagon	
*Can use compass to bisect line segment, construct triangles, and construct perpendiculars	
Word problems: (check one)	
1. Can set the problem up	
2. Can understand process involved	
3. Can notate word problems	

*(Goals starred are not essential for all students)

Comments:

Winnetka Public Schools
MATHEMATICS GOAL RECORD CARD 3

Pupil _____ Teacher _____ Year _____ | Date

Roman Numerals to XX
Calendar (dates)
Clock — to minute
Multiplication facts (products to 20)
Addition — 2-digit numbers, no carrying
Subtraction — 2-digit numbers, no regrouping
Fractions — ½, ⅓, ¼, ¾, ⅙ (whole & group)
Addition — 2-digit numbers, with carrying
Division facts (to 20)
Review I
Roman numerals to L
Addition — 3-digit numbers, 3 addends
Subtraction — 2-digit numbers with regrouping
Money — making change to $1.00
Review II
Multiplication facts — 3's, 4's, 5's
Subtraction — 3-digit numbers
Addition and subtraction of money — 3-digit numbers
Simple multiplication
Review III
Division facts — 3's, 4's, 5's
Simple Division

Individual Projects:

Winnetka Public Schools
MATHEMATICS GOAL RECORD CARD 4

Pupil _____ Teacher _____ Year _____ | Date

Fall group work (2-4 weeks)
Meaning of numbers
Addition
  Addition facts speed review ( )
  Test
Subtraction
  Subtraction facts speed review ( )
  Test
Review test I
Linear measure (inches, feet, and yards)
Easy simple multiplication
  Easy multiplication facts speed review ( )
Story problems test
Easy short division
  Easy division facts speed review ( )
  Story problems test
  Easy short division speed base ( )
Review test II
Multiplication and division facts I
  Facts test
  Multiplication facts I speed base ( )
  Division facts I speed base ( )
Multiplication and division facts II
  Facts test
  Multiplication facts II speed base ( )
  Division facts II speed base ( )
Review test III
Multiplication and division facts III
Bar graphs
Multiplication and division facts III
  Facts test
  Multiplication facts III speed base ( )
  Division facts III speed base ( )
Multiplication and division facts IV
  Facts test
Multiplication and division facts complete
  Table and facts test
  Multiplication facts speed base ( )
  Division facts speed base ( )
Simple multiplication complete
Short division complete
Multiplication by ten
Meaning of fractions
Review test IV
Previews of 5th grade work
Meaning of decimals
Compound multiplication
Long division
Fractions complete
Graphs
Perimeters

Individual Projects:

Winnetka Public Schools
MATHEMATICS GOAL RECORD CARD 5

Pupil _____ Teacher _____ Year _____

                                       Date

Our number system through millions ....

Addition
    Basic addition facts speed review ( ) ....
    Column addition (5-digit numbers) ....

Subtraction
    Subtraction facts speed review ( ) ....
    Subtraction complete (5-digit numbers) ....

Making change ....

Roman Numerals through M ....

Multiplication
    Multiplication facts complete speed review ( ) ....
    Simple multiplication speed base ( ) ....
    Compound multiplication (4-digit number by 2-digit number) ....
    Properties of multiplication ....

Division
    Basic division facts speed review ( ) ....
    Short division speed review ( ) ....
    Long division (2-digit divisor and 2-digit quotient) ....

Liquid measure ....

Fractions
    Meaning of fractions ....
    Addition and subtraction of like fractions ....
    Addition and subtraction of unlike fractions ....

Decimals
    Meaning of decimals ....
    Addition and subtraction of tenths, hundredths ....

Ratio ....

Measurements
    Perimeter — triangles, rectangles, squares ....
    Area — triangles, rectangles, squares ....
    Weights — ounces, pounds, hundred-weights, tons ....

Informal geometry ....

Graphs ....

Individual Projects:

Winnetka Public Schools
MATHEMATICS GOAL RECORD CARD 6

Pupil _____ Teacher _____ Year _____

SPEED REVIEW (Number in 3 minutes)   Date

Addition Facts .... ( )
Subtraction Facts .... ( )
Multiplication Facts .... ( )
Division Facts .... ( )

	Date			
Column Addition	(	) Fall	(	) Spring
Subtraction Complete	(	) Fall	(	) Spring
Compound Multiplication	(	) Fall	(	) Spring
Short Division	(	) Fall	(	) Spring
Long Division	(	) Fall	(	) Spring

Units of Individual work (preceded by small group instruction)

Number system through billions ....

Roman numbers through M ....

Sets ....

Review:
    Addition of whole numbers ....
    Subtraction of whole numbers ....
    Multiplication of whole numbers ....
    Division of whole numbers ....

Factors and primes ....

Informal geometry ....

Linear measure ....

Area and perimeter ....

Review:
    Meaning of fractions ....
    Addition and subtraction of like fractions ....
    Addition of unlike fractions ....
    Subtraction of unlike fractions ....

Multiplication of fractions ....

Division of fractions ....

Addition and subtraction of decimals ....

Multiplication of decimals ....

Division of decimals ....

Simple graphs ....

Individual Projects:

Winnetka Public Schools
MATHEMATICS GOAL RECORD CARD 7

Pupil _____ Teacher _____ Year _____

SPEED REVIEW (Number in 3 minutes)

	Date
Addition Facts	
Subtraction Facts	
Multiplication Facts	
Division Facts	

	Date	
	( ) Fall	( ) Spring
Column Addition	( ) Fall	( ) Spring
Subtraction Complete	( ) Fall	( ) Spring
Compound Multiplication	( ) Fall	( ) Spring
Short Division	( ) Fall	( ) Spring
Long Division	( ) Fall	( ) Spring

Units of Individual work (preceded by small group instruction)

What is Mathematics?
Number symbols
Whole numbers
Non-metric geometry
Factoring and primes
Rational numbers and fractions
Non-metric geometry Unit 2
Rational numbers and the number line
Decimals
Ratio and percent

Individual Projects:

Winnetka Public Schools
MATHEMATICS GOAL RECORD CARD 8

Pupil _____ Teacher _____ Year _____

SPEED REVIEW (Number in 3 minutes)

	Date
Addition Facts	
Subtraction Facts	
Multiplication Facts	
Division Facts	

	Date	
	( ) Fall	( ) Spring
Column Addition	( ) Fall	( ) Spring
Subtraction Complete	( ) Fall	( ) Spring
Compound Multiplication	( ) Fall	( ) Spring
Short Division	( ) Fall	( ) Spring
Long Division	( ) Fall	( ) Spring

Units of individual work (preceded by small group instruction)

Measurement
Area and volume
Parallels, Polygons, and prisms
Circles
Statistics and graphs
Operations with rational numbers
Equations and inequalities
Coordinates in the plane and the Pythagorean property
Real numbers
Scientific notation, decimals, and the metric system

Individual Projects:

Winnetka Public Schools
SCIENCE GOAL RECORD CARD 3

Pupil _____ Teacher _____ Year _____

The four major third-grade science areas are listed in heavy, LARGE LETTERS; the principal science studies are listed in LIGHT CAPITALS; and the dates when these topics and studies are completed should be written on the solid date lines.

Subhead goals and optional activities are in small type; when completed, they should be described and dated on the dotted lines.

Science texts and other resources are described in the Winnetka Science Curriculum Guide.

I. LIVING THINGS   Date

NATURE OF LIVING THINGS ....
(15+ Concepts)

Group Activities ....
....
....

Individual Projects ....
....
....

TEST ....

II. MAGNETISM

NATURE OF MAGNETISM ....
(10+ Concepts)

Experiments ....
....

Other Activities ....
....
....

TEST ....

III. AIR   Date

NATURE OF AIR AND
ATMOSPHERE ....

Experiments ....
....
....

Other Activities ....
....
....

TEST ....

**IV. PHYSICS AND CHEMISTRY OF
CANDLES**

EXPERIMENTS ....
....
....

Fire Safety ....

Other Activities ....
....

TEST ....

**SCIENCE-SOCIAL STUDIES
PROJECTS** ....

Pioneer Science ....
....

TEST ....

Winnetka Public Schools
SCIENCE GOAL RECORD CARD 1 AND 2

Pupil _____ Teacher _____ Year _____

	Reading, Telling Check	Classroom Experiences Check	Projects Check
SEASONS			
*Weather			
*Thermometers			
ANIMALS			
*PLANTS			
FOODS			
EARTH-UNIVERSE			
Day-Night			
Sun			
Air			
Water			
Land About Us			
Moon, Planets, Stars			
Outer Space			
ENERGY, FORCES			
Gravity			
*Magnets			
*Sound			
Electricity			
Light			
Heat			
Other forms of energy			
*Simple Machines			
Friction			
HEALTH & SAFETY			
Sleep			
Personal Cleanliness			
Dental Care			

OTHER ACTIVITIES, EXPERIENCES, OBSERVATIONS, TRIPS:

_____

_____

*Winnetka Science Curriculum Guidebook contains specific concepts and suggested treatment for the various primary grades.

Winnetka Public Schools
SCIENCE GOAL RECORD CARD 4

Pupil_____ Teacher_____ Year_____

The six major fourth-grade areas are printed in heavy, LARGE TYPE. The essential science topics are printed in light CAPITALS; and the dates when these topics are completed should be written on the solid date lines.
The subhead goals are written in small type; they should be described and dated on the dotted lines when completed.
Science texts and other resources are described in the Winnetka Science Curriculum Guide.

I. MATTER, ENERGY AND CHANGE
SELECTED PROPERTIES OF MATTER
EXPERIMENTS
PROPERTIES OF WATER
EXPERIMENTS (solutions, etc.)
CRYSTALS
WEATHER FACTORS
TEST

II. OUR CHANGING EARTH
MINERALS
GEOLOGICAL PROCESSES (Rock Formation)
Other Processes
IDENTIFY ROCKS & MINERALS
CROW ISLAND MUSEUM (4 or more tests)
Other Activities
TEST
History and Sequence of Earth Changes

III. ANCIENT PLANTS & ANIMALS: THEIR EVOLUTION
Nature of Ancient Reptiles (Dinosaurs, etc.)
Fossils
Other Activities
TEST

IV. HEALTH & SAFETY
TEETH (Structure, Growth, Care)
TEST

V. ANIMALS OF THE SEASHORE
Activities

VI. SOLAR SYSTEM
SUN, PLANETS, SATELLITES
CONSTELLATIONS
Other
TEST

CHEMICAL CHANGE
Physical vs Chemical Changes (2+ Concepts)
Elements, Compounds, and Mixtures (4 Concepts)
Basic Chemistry Concepts

Qualitative Identification (2+ Concepts)
Atomic Structure and Chemical Change (3+ Concepts)
Enrichment Projects: Atomic, Physical, Chemistry

TEST

VERTEBRATE BODY AND HUMAN GROWTH
(Study of Baby From After Birth to Adolescence)
PRETEST and Review of Skeletal and Muscular Systems:
(Sight, Hearing, Digestion)
Nervous System and Brain (10+ Concepts)
Respiratory System (4+ Concepts)
Circulatory System & Heart (8+ Concepts)
Dissection of Veal Heart; Use of Model; Making Diagram
Life-Size Human Anatomy Model

TEST

ENDOCRINE SYSTEM AND HUMAN REPRODUCTION
Nature of Endocrine Glands (4+ Concepts)
Human Reproduction (10+ Concepts)
Evaluation of Individual Goals
Written Quiz on Factual Phases
Infant Growth

BACTERIAL DISEASES AND RESISTANCE
Nature of Bacteria and Viruses (10 major concepts)
Experiments with Petri-Culture Growth (3+ Concepts)
Health Text Concepts

SCIENCE NOTEBOOKS
FINAL TEST

Date

Winnetka Public Schools
SCIENCE GOAL RECORD CARD 6

Pupil _____ Teacher _____ Year _____

	Date			Date
I. FOOD: CHEMISTRY AND HEALTH		**III. ELECTRICITY** (cont.)		
Purposes of Foods		Magnetism (Review from Grade 3)		
Chemical Food Types		Electric Generators; Cells;		
Experiments		Conductors; Circuits		
		Electrical Safety		
Concepts-Balanced Diet		Other		
Nutrition Project				
Other		TEST		
		IV. ASTRONOMY		
TEST		PRETEST		
		Review (Hynek, Ch. 1)		
II. LIGHT		Observatories (Hynek, Ch. 2)		
PRETEST		Galaxies (Hynek, Ch. 9, 10)		
Reading, study exercises,		Advanced Concepts (Hynek,		
and experiments on Nature		Ch. 11-17)		
of Light; Path and Speed;		Other		
Reflection and Refraction;				
Color; Human Eye and				
Optics		**V. WATER AND WATER SUPPLY**		
Other		Nature of water (review, Gr. 4)		
		Water Impurities		
		Water Supply Systems		
TEST		Model Water Plant		
III. ELECTRICITY &		Other		
ELECTROMAGNETISM				
PRETEST		TEST		
Static Electricity		**VI. LOCAL OUTDOOR LIFE**		
		MAJOR CONSERVATION		
		CONCEPTS		
		FIELD TRIP (Nature Center)		
		TEST		

Winnetka Public Schools
SCIENCE GOAL RECORD CARD 5

Pupil _____ Teacher _____ Year _____

The five major fifth-grade science areas are printed in heavy, **LARGE TYPE**. The essential science topics are printed in light CAPITALS; and the dates when these topics are completed should be written on the solid lines.

The subhead goals are in small type; they should be dated on the dotted lines, if and when each sub-topic is completed.

Science texts and other resources are described in the Winnetka Science Curriculum Guide.

	Date			Date
I. CHARACTERISTICS OF MAMMALS		**IV. HUMAN GROWTH AND**		
MAJOR CONCEPTS (See Guide)		**HUMAN REPRODUCTION**		
Observations		Winnetka Outline of Major		
Care: Experiments		Concepts		
		Resource Reading & Discussions		
Other				
		Final (Individual, Group)		
TEST		Evaluation		
II. NEWTONIAN PHYSICS OF		**V. PHYSICS OF SOUND**		
MACHINES		MAJOR CONCEPTS (See Guide)		
MAJOR CONCEPTS		EXPERIMENTS		
EXPERIMENTS				
		Other		
Other Activities				
		TEST		
TEST				
III. HUMAN BODY: SELECTED				
SYSTEMS				
SKELETAL AND				
MUSCULAR SYSTEMS		TEST		
Experiments				
Related health topics				
Other Activities				
TEST				

Winnetka Public Schools

SCIENCE GOAL RECORD CARD 7

Pupil_____Teacher_____Year_____

	Date
THE SCIENTIFIC METHOD:	
How Scientists Think and Work (6 Concepts)	
THE CELL: UNIT OF LIFE	
Types and Properties of Living Cells (8 Concepts)	
Characteristics of Simplest Animals: Protozoa (7 Concepts)	
Microscope Projects_____	
TEST	
CLASSIFICATION OF LIVING THINGS	
Animal Classification (5 major Concepts)	
Plant Classification (3 major Concepts)	
Enrichment Studies_____	
TEST	
PROPERTIES OF MATTER AND KINETIC MOLECULAR LAW	
Matter and Energy (4 Concepts)	
Properties of Solutions (2 Concepts)	
Kinetic Molecular Law (2 Concepts)	
Our Ocean of Air	
Enrichment Studies_____	
TEST	
HEAT ENERGY AND ITS EFFECTS ON MATTER	
Change of State (5 Concepts)	
Individual and Small Group Studies_____	
TEST	

Winnetka Public Schools
SOCIAL STUDIES GOAL RECORD CARD 2

Pupil _____ Teacher _____ Year _____

PROJECT AREA (Check specific topics studied)

	Check		Check
THE FARM IS A BUSINESS		**SPECIAL HOLIDAYS PATRIOTIC DAYS**	
Kinds of Farms			
Foods			
Soil			
Stock			
COMMUNITY SERVICES		**OTHER PROJECTS**	
Helpers			
Stores and Services			
Village Government and Buildings			
Recreational Facilities			
THE AMERICAN INDIAN		**FIELD TRIPS**	
Many Tribes of Indians			
Southwest Indians		**CURRENT EVENTS**	
		CITIZENSHIP RESPONSIBILITIES	

Winnetka Public Schools
SOCIAL STUDIES GOAL RECORD CARD 1

Pupil _____ Teacher _____ Year _____

PROJECT AREA (Check specific topics studied)

	Check		Check
HOME		**OTHER PROJECTS**	
Family Members		How the Farm Helps Us (suggested)	
Houses		Holidays (suggested)	
Food			
Clothing			
Recreation			
SCHOOL		**FIELD TRIPS**	
Classroom			
School Plant			
Personnel		**CURRENT EVENTS**	
Facilities			
Responsibilities as Members		**CITIZENSHIP RESPONSIBILITIES**	
COMMUNITY			
Community Helpers (Policeman, Fireman)			
Stores			
Post Office			
Transportation (Car, Bus, Train, etc.)			

Winnetka Public Schools

SOCIAL STUDIES GOAL RECORD CARD 4

Pupil _____ Teacher _____ Year _____

A study of the earth and its changing climatic and physical conditions will help you to understand how man's way of living is determined by where he lives.

AREA OF STUDY

OUR EARTH AND WAYS OF LIFE Date

Climates

MAP STUDIES

Map Booklet — Grade 4

EARLY PEOPLES OF THE WORLD

Early Man

Early Discoveries and Inventions

An Early Culture (   )

OTHER PROJECTS Date

Dramatization

FIELD TRIPS

Crow Island Museum

CURRENT EVENTS (List publications)

CITIZENSHIP RESPONSIBILITIES

Winnetka Public Schools

SOCIAL STUDIES GOAL RECORD CARD 3

Pupil _____ Teacher _____ Year _____

AREA OF STUDY

Date

INDIANS OF AMERICA

PILGRIMS AND COLONISTS

COLONIAL LIVING

WESTWARD EXPANSION

PIONEER LIFE AND CULTURE

LOCAL AND NATIONAL HISTORY Date

FIELD TRIPS

Pioneer Room

OTHER PROJECTS

CURRENT EVENTS (List publications)

CITIZENSHIP RESPONSIBILITIES

Winnetka Public Schools
SOCIAL STUDIES GOAL RECORD CARD 6

Pupil _____ Teacher _____ Year _____

Early cultures and customs and the events of the past have made great contributions to present-day civilization.

AREA OF STUDY

MAP STUDY	Date		Date	THE MIDDLE AGES	Date
Local (School, Village, State)					
Hemisphere					
Global Areas				MEDIEVAL TRADE AND COMMERCE	
EARLY CIVILIZATIONS				RENAISSANCE AND REFORMATION	
Egyptians, Babylonians, Phoenicians, Hebrews					
India and China					
BEGINNINGS OF WESTERN CIVILIZATION IN GREECE				OTHER PROJECTS	
SPREAD OF WESTERN CIVILIZATION BY ROME				CURRENT EVENTS (List publications)	
WORLD RELIGIONS				FIELD TRIPS	

Winnetka Public Schools
SOCIAL STUDIES GOAL RECORD CARD 5

Pupil _____ Teacher _____ Year _____

Our country has been a land of opportunity for many people from before the coming of the white man up to the present day. The brave, adventurous men and women who settled in this land and the people who migrated in later years from many places of the world have contributed to the development of the United States.

AREA OF STUDY

OUR COUNTRY BEGINS	Date	CHICAGO	Date
Before the White Man		Early Chicago	
Period of Exploration		A City Grows	
Colonization		Chicago Today	
Expansion and Settlement			
		OTHER PROJECTS	
LIVING IN THE U.S. TODAY			
The People			
Regional Studies		FIELD TRIPS	
Interdependence of People			
		CURRENT EVENTS (List publications)	
		CITIZENSHIP RESPONSIBILITIES	

Winnetka Public Schools

SOCIAL STUDIES GOAL RECORD CARD 7

Pupil_____ Teacher_____ Year_____

Objective: An understanding and appreciation of the interrelatedness of countries of the world.

AREA OF STUDY

GEOGRAPHIC TERMS & CONCEPTS	Date

EASTERN HEMISPHERE	Date

Australia

Africa

Asia
Near East: Iran, Iraq, Turkey, Arabia, Israel

Middle East: India, Pakistan

Far East: Japan, China, Korea, Mongolia, Laos

U.S.S.R.

Europe

WESTERN HEMISPHERE

Mexico

Central America

Caribbean Area

South America

Canada

CURRENT EVENTS (List publications)

OTHER PROJECTS

FIELD TRIPS

Winnetka Public Schools

SOCIAL STUDIES GOAL RECORD CARD 8

Pupil_____ Teacher_____ Year_____

Objective: An understanding and appreciation of the struggle to establish and maintain our democratic way of life.

AREA OF STUDY

	Date
EXPLORATION & DISCOVERY	
COLONIZATION	
AMERICAN REVOLUTION	
U.S. CONSTITUTION	
HAMILTON, JEFFERSON, ADAMS	
FRONTIER EXPANSION	
JACKSON ERA	
CIVIL WAR & RECONSTRUCTION	
EARLY WEST	
INDUSTRIALIZATION	
HUMAN RELATIONS	

	Date
OVERSEAS EXPANSION	
GAY NINETIES	
THEODORE ROOSEVELT	
WORLD WAR I	
ROARING TWENTIES	
DEPRESSION AND NEW DEAL	
SOCIALISM, COMMUNISM, FASCISM, DEMOCRACY	
RISE OF DICTATORS	
WORLD WAR II	
UNITED NATIONS	

CURRENT EVENTS (List publications)

OTHER PROJECTS

FIELD TRIPS

Date ______ School ______

Parent's Name ______

Child's Name ______

Teacher ______ Grade ______

PLEASE BRING THIS FORM TO YOUR SCHEDULED CONFERENCE. IT WILL BE YOUR RECORD.

WINNETKA PUBLIC SCHOOLS

CONFERENCE GUIDE AND RECORD FOR PARENTS AND TEACHERS

Grades I and II

We are sending this combination guide and record as a convenience for you in looking forward to our conference. We urg you to go over the following pages carefully to see how you can contribute to our conference and to be informed concernin areas of progress your child's teacher will be evaluating.

This form has been made inclusive to cover items of concern in the total school program. Some of the topics will be mor relevant to your child than others. If some thought is given before the conference to those that relate to your child, we ca move along more expeditiously when we get together.

Your conference is scheduled for ______ at ______ o'cloc

in ______.

Sincerely yours,

COOPERATIVE ACTION AGREED UPON IN OUR CONFERENCE

______ to continue present program unchanged

______ to pursue the following plan: (date each agreement separately as developed during the year)

Figure 8

Appendix **B**: The Parent Conference Guide and Record
Primary and Intermediate

— 2 —

You are invited to select from the following topics those that seem important to you for helping us to understand your child better. A space is provided for you to record essential information for use during the conference and for subsequent reference immediately after the conference.

TOPICS	PARENTS' NOTES Before and after conference
1. How does your child enjoy going to school? What does he say about school, his teacher, other children? Does he tell about what he does in school?	
2. How does he get along with family members; with playmates?	
3. Does he accept routines easily? (bedtime, mealtime, stopping play, putting away toys, etc.)	
4. How does he accept new situations? (with ease, easily upset)	
5. Does he have some regular responsibilities at home?	
6. Is he developing self-discipline? (accepts controls easily, cooperates willingly). What kinds of controls do you use?	
7. Is he developing good health habits, getting regular and sufficient sleep, eating wisely and adequately, learning personal grooming? Does he have some physical difficulty we should be aware of?	
8. Does he have any special interests? What does he like to do at home?	
9. Are there other things about your child we should know? Are new developments occurring that should be brought to our attention? Do you have any suggestions to help us in guiding your child?	

Name _____ Teacher _____ Date _____

As your child's teacher, I am preparing to discuss the following aspects of his growth in school with you.

ACADEMIC PROGRESS	
SUBJECTS	**NOTES** Before and After Conference
WORK HABITS: Does he listen attentively? Does he follow directions? Does he work carefully and accurately without disturbing others? Does he complete work in a reasonable amount of time? Does he make constructive use of free time?	
READING AND LANGUAGE:	
ARITHMETIC:	
SOCIAL STUDIES:	
HANDWRITING:	
SCIENCE:	

— 4 —

GROWTH AS AN INDIVIDUAL:

Does he assume responsibility? Use good judgment? Show initiative? Does he respect rules, authority, personal and public property?

Does he show a questioning mind?

Is his work self-motivated?

Is he adjustable to change?

Does he feel responsible for putting forth his best efforts?

GROWTH AS GROUP MEMBER:

Does he participate in group activities?
Does he cooperate and get along well with others?
Respect the rights of others?

Does he contribute to group discussions?

Does he show willingness to serve both as a leader and as a follower?

Is he learning the obligations and practices of citizenship in a democracy?

Note: Pages 1-4 to be used for initial conference annually. For subsequent conferences, pages 3 and 4 will be furnished in blank to the parent, and will be completed for the cumulative file by the teacher.

Date _____ School _____	**PLEASE BRING THIS FORM TO YOUR SCHEDULED CONFERENCE. IT WILL BE YOUR RECORD.**

Date _____ School _____

Parent's Name _____

Child's Name _____

Teacher _____ _____ Grade _____

PLEASE BRING THIS FORM TO YOUR SCHEDULED CONFERENCE. IT WILL BE YOUR RECORD.

WINNETKA PUBLIC SCHOOLS
CONFERENCE GUIDE AND RECORD FOR PARENTS AND TEACHERS
Grades III to VIII

We are sending this combination guide and record as a convenience for you in looking forward to our conference. We urge you to go over the following pages carefully to see how you can contribute to our conference and to be informed concerning areas of progress your child's teacher will be evaluating.

This form has been made inclusive to cover items of concern in the total school program. Some of the topics will be more relevant to your child than others. If some thought is given before the conference to those that relate to your child, we can move along more expeditiously when we get together.

Your conference is scheduled for _____ _____ at _____ o'clock

in _____.

Sincerely yours,

COOPERATIVE ACTION AGREED UPON IN OUR CONFERENCE

_____ to continue present program unchanged

_____ to pursue the following plan : (date each agreement separately as developed during the year)

You are invited to select from the following topics those that seem important to you in helping us to understand your child better. A space is provided for you to record essential information for use during the conference and for subsequent reference immediately after the conference.

TOPICS	PARENTS' NOTES Before and after conference
1. What is your child's reaction to school?	
2. What are his out-of-school activities?	
3. What are his special interests?	
4. Does he have some regular responsibilities at home?	
5. How does he react to authority and control? Is he developing self-discipline?	
6. Is he developing good health habits?	
7. Does he have some physical difficulty we should know about?	
8. Are there other things we should know about your child?	

— 3 —

Name _____ Teacher _____ Date _____

As your child's teacher, I am preparing to discuss the following aspects of his growth in school with you.

ACADEMIC PROGRESS: In the following subject areas, we will evaluate his achievement in relation to his capacity and in relation to his total grade group.	
SUBJECT	**NOTES** Before and after conference
LANGUAGE ARTS:	
SOCIAL STUDIES:	
ARITHMETIC:	
SCIENCE:	
OTHER AREAS OR COMMENTS:	

— 4 —

WORK HABITS:

Does he listen attentively?

Does he work steadily, carefully and independently?

Is his work neat and orderly?

Does he get it done on time?

GROWTH AS AN INDIVIDUAL:

Does he assume responsibility?

Does he use good judgment?

Does he show initiative?

Does he respect laws, authority, and personal and public property?

Is he showing evidence of developing a sense of values?

Does he make good choices in moral judgments?

Does he show a questioning mind?

Is his work self-motivated?

Is he adjustable to change?

GROWTH AS GROUP MEMBER:

Does he cooperate and get along well with others?

Does he respect the rights of others?

Does he show a willingness to serve?

Is he gaining experience both as a leader and as a follower?

Is he learning the obligations and practices of citizenship in a democracy?

PARTICIPATION:

What contributions has he made to school and class enterprises?

Note: Pages 1-4 to be used for initial conference annually. For subsequent conferences, pages 3 and 4 will be furnished in blank to the parent, and will be completed for the cumulative file by the teacher.

STANINE ACHIEVEMENT AND ABILITY PROFILE CHART

Winnetka Public Schools, Winnetka, Illinois

Name: ______________ (Last) ______________ (First)

Grade	Adviser	Core Teacher
VI		
VII		
VIII		

ACHIEVEMENT:	Grade:	STANINE SCORES 1	2	3	4	5	6	7	8	9
Reading Comprehension	III									
	IV									
	V									
	VI									
	VII									
	VIII									
Reading Vocabulary	III									
	IV									
	V									
	VI									
	VII									
	VIII									
Language Usage	III									
	IV									
	V									
	VI									
	VII									
	VIII									
Spelling	III									
	IV									
	V									
	VI									
	VII									
	VIII									
Arithmetic Reasoning	III									
	IV									
	V									
	VI									
	VII									
	VIII									
Arithmetic Fundamentals	III									
	IV									
	V									
	VI									
	VII									
	VIII									
ABILITY:		1	2	3	4	5	6	7	8	9
Group Test	Kdg									
	III									
	V									
Individual Test	______									
	______									
RELATIVE AGE IN GRADE:										

Figure 9

Appendix **C**: The Stanine Form with Explanation

STANINE ACHIEVEMENT AND ABILITY PROFILE CHART

Winnetka Public Schools — Winnetka, Illinois

This profile chart was developed by the Winnetka staff over a seven-year period from 1952 to 1959, in response to an expressed need for better communication of certain information from teachers to parents. The information comes from standardized tests and only results from these tests are used to prepare the profile.

In Winnetka a child's relative potential for doing schoolwork is measured by intelligence tests. His learning from year to year is evaluated by achievement tests. All these scores are converted into comparable units, or standard scores, on a nine-point scale. The term stanine was applied to such a scale when it was first used during World War II by the Air Force.

It is the purpose of the stanine chart to convey the following broad appraisals of a child: (1) his potential or ability in relation to other Winnetka children, (2) his performance on standardized achievement tests in relation to his ability, (3) his performance on standardized achievement tests in relation to other Winnetka children, (4) an approximation of the child's ability and performance in terms of the national population.

On this scale, stanine 1 is low and 9 is high. Stanine 5 is average for Winnetka children. On most tests the national average appears at stanine 3 when Winnetka norms are used. The printed blue area, three stanines wide, represents a child's band of expectancy, or the average of the intelligence tests which are shown toward the bottom of the chart. The red crosses represent scores on achievement tests from year to year. The lines which join the crosses in each subject area show the relationship of achievement scores one to another and to the range of expectancy. A child's position in intelligence and achievement within the Winnetka population is thus shown graphically. His standing in relation to the national norms may be judged by interpolating the national average at roughly stanine 3.

Since chronological age is also important in predicting what a child may be expected to achieve, his relative age in his grade is plotted at the bottom of the chart. A very young child with stanine 1 for relative age in grade would not have had as many months of experience, regardless of his I. Q., as others in his grade. If his achievement scores were found to lie below his blue range, i. e., nearer his chronological age stanine, the condition may be explained by his relative age.

While the stanine intervals are equal, the number of children scoring at each stanine varies widely from 20% at stanine 5 to 4% at stanines 1 and 9. This is just another way of saying that many more children are average than extreme. The percentages of distribution among stanines are as follows:

$$
\begin{array}{ll}
\text{1 and 9:} & 4\% \\
\text{2 and 8:} & 7\% \\
\text{3 and 7:} & 12\% \\
\text{4 and 6:} & 17\% \\
\text{5} \quad : & 20\%
\end{array}
$$

During conferences each year a child's stanine chart is discussed by his teacher or adviser with his parents. The stanine profile chart is only a part of the reporting process. Of equal or greater importance are the parent-teacher conferences which deal with the less measurable and tangible conditions surrounding a child's aptitudes and accomplishments. At best, our present level of confidence in intelligence and achievement testing prompts us to include these measurements as only one part of our appraisal of a child. It is for this reason that the stanine device limits itself to broad interpretations, rather than attempting an artificial exactness that would be unjustified by the evidence available.

Subject Index

393

Name Index